Blue

sustainable
development

3

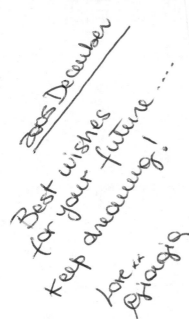
David PEARCE
R. Kerry TURNER
Timothy O'RIORDAN
Neil ADGER
Giles ATKINSON
Inger BRISSON
Katrina BROWN
Richard DUBOURG
Samuel FANKHAUSER
Andrew JORDAN
David MADDISON
Dominic MORAN
Jane POWELL

CENTRE FOR SOCIAL AND ECONOMIC RESEARCH ON THE GLOBAL ENVIRONMENT

C|S|E|R|G|E

EARTHSCAN

Earthscan Publications Ltd, London

First published in the UK in 1993 by
Earthscan Publications Limited
120 Pentonville Road, London N1 9JN

Web site: http://www.earthscan.co.UK
Email: earthinfo @earthscan.co.UK

Reprinted 1994, 1996

A catalogue record for this book is available from the British Library.

ISBN: 1 85383 183 2

Typeset by DP Photosetting, Aylesbury, Bucks
Printed and bound by Clays Ltd, St Ives plc.

Earthscan Publications Limited is an editorially independent subsidiary of
Kogan Page Limited and publishes in asociation with the International
Institute for Environment and Development and the World Wide Fund for
Nature.

Contents

Part I Sustainable development

Part II Sustainability and the state of the UK environment

List of illustrations

FIGURES

TABLES

BOXES

Notes on the authors

David Pearce is Professor of Economics at University College London and Director of CSERGE.

R. Kerry Turner is Professor of Environmental Economics at the University of East Anglia and Executive Director of CSERGE.

Timothy O'Riordan is Professor of Environmental Sciences at the University of East Anglia and Associate Director of CSERGE.

Neil Adger is Senior Research Associate in CSERGE at the University of East Anglia.

Giles Atkinson is Overseas Development Administration Fellow in CSERGE at University College London.

Inger Brisson is SØM Fellow in CSERGE at University College London.

Katrina Brown is Senior Research Associate in CSERGE at the University of East Anglia.

Richard Dubourg is National Rivers Authority Fellow in CSERGE at University College London.

Samuel Fankhauser is Research Associate in CSERGE at University College London.

Andrew Jordan is Research Associate in CSERGE at the University of East Anglia.

David Maddison is Research Associate in CSERGE at University College London.

Dominic Moran is Research Associate in CSERGE at University College London.

Jane Powell is Research Fellow in CSERGE at the University of East Anglia.

The main author responsibility for the Chapters in *Blueprint 3* is as follows:

Chapter 1 – Pearce and Turner; Chapter 2 – Pearce, Turner, Dubourg and Atkinson; Chapter 3 – Atkinson and Pearce; Chapter 4 – Fankhauser and Pearce; Chapter 5 – Dubourg; Chapter 6 – Turner, Powell and Brisson; Chapter 7 – Brown; Chapter 8 – Adger; Chapter 9 – Moran; Chapter 10 – Maddison and Pearce; Chapter 11 – Maddison and Brown; Chapter 12 – Jordan and O'Riordan.

Preface

This is the third volume in the *Blueprint* series. *Blueprint for a Green Economy*, or 'Blue 1' as we call it, was published in September 1989 and became a best seller, at least by the standards of serious books about the environment. It has been translated into several languages and reprinted many times. The story it had to tell was essentially that solving environmental problems necessarily requires solving economic problems first, especially by removing those distortions that arise from the failure to place an economic value on environmental assets and their services, and the failure to reflect those economic values in the workings of the market-place. Such distortions tilt the 'playing field' between conservation and unconstrained economic development unfairly and against conservation. Policies to correct the distortions include the repricing of goods and services through pollution taxes and other 'economic instruments'; revising the way we appraise major investments, for example in road construction; and revising the way we record economic progress through the various measures of national economic activity (gross national product, GNP, for example).

Blue 1 was intended as a text for the UK economy. In the event, it secured much wider adoption and achieved considerable attention in other countries where the issues are similar and the solutions the same. In *Blueprint 2: Greening the World Economy*, published in 1991, we extended the ideas of *Blue 1* to international and global issues – global warming, ozone layer depletion, tropical forests, the population problem and so on. *Blue 3* now returns to the UK again and looks more closely at the empirical evidence on the state of the UK environment, the UK's contribution to global problems, and the issue of how to measure sustainable development. It is therefore a mixture of 'state of the environment' reporting and an update on the theory and measurement of sustainable development. *Blue 1* introduced the concept and ideas of sustainability. Since then a substantial literature has arisen on the meaning and measurement of sustainability. We try to capture the spirit of that literature and show how the concept is not only definable but measurable too.

Some of the issues taken up in *Blue 1* and *Blue 2* merited more specialised development. To this end the separate volume by David

Pearce, *Economic Values and the Natural World*, (Earthscan, London, 1993) should be seen as part of the Blueprint series, as should the volume by David Pearce, Edward Barbier and Anil Markandya, *Sustainable Development: Economics and Environment in the Third World* (Earthscan, London, 1990). The developing country dimension is also treated at length in David Pearce and Jeremy Warford, *World Without End: Economics, Environment and Sustainable Development*, (Oxford University Press, Oxford, 1992). Finally, as a result of *Blue 1* we received a great many requests for references to introductory texts on environmental economics. As there wasn't one, we wrote it – see R. Kerry Turner, David Pearce and Ian Bateman, *Environmental Economics: an Elementary Introduction*, (Harvester-Wheatsheaf, London, 1993).

Sustainable development is more fashionable in 1993 than it was in 1989. There is, for example, a United Nations Commission on Sustainable Development (located in New York); countless institutes for sustainable development; and the World Bank has a Vice President for Environmentally Sustainable Development. In truth, 'sustainability' has got carried too far – it is far from clear, for example, that researching the idea of a 'sustainable city' is anything other than climbing on a bandwagon. Some economists object to the whole notion of sustainable development and prefer to think in terms of 'optimal' growth of human well-being. As we show in the early chapters of this volume, however, what is optimal may not be sustainable (as the economics literature showed in the 1970s), and what is sustainable may be simply awful. It follows that sustainability cannot be an over-riding, single dimension objective for society, and we doubt if anyone has ever suggested it should be. Like all ideas, while it is being thought through it tends to grab the headlines and the uninitiated may get the wrong impression that it is the only objective of relevance. But it does not follow that sustainability is redundant in the face of a search for better, or even 'optimal' futures. Sustainability reminds us that there are future generations, that they are with us now through the very fact that generations overlap each other, and that we can very easily shift unacceptable burdens on to them. Sustainable development, as opposed to sustainability, reminds us of other social objectives, most notably the plight of the poorest in the world community. Those who feel that sustainable development is too 'future oriented' have perhaps confused the wider philosophy of sustainable development with the narrower focus of sustainability. We address these issues in the early chapters.

For the authors of this volume, then, sustainable development remains an important multi-faceted objective that has already captured the imagination of the world community. We hope *Blue 3* contributes further to the design of practical measures to achieve, or at least move towards, sustainable development.

Blue 3 differs from *Blues 1* and *2* in its affiliation. *Blues 1* and *2* emanated from the partnership of University College London (UCL) and the International Institute for Environment and Development (IIED) through their joint venture, the London Environmental Economics Centre (LEEC). LEEC continues to exist but is now a wholly IIED venture. UCL established a new institute with the University of East Anglia and it is this centre, the Centre for Social and Economic Research on the Global Environment (CSERGE), which has produced *Blue 3*. All the *Blue 3* authors are members of CSERGE, which has published widely on environmental issues and also plans a *Blue 4* and many other publications.

DWP
August 1993

Acknowledgements

Blue 3 is the product of the Centre for Social and Economic Research on the Global Environment (CSERGE). CSERGE emerged from a competition launched by the UK Economic and Social Research Council (ESRC) when it decided to develop a programme of environmental research. Two of the last three in the competition, UCL and UEA, decided to narrow the odds by merging forces. That merger actually cemented research relationships that had gone back many years. We owe a debt of thanks to Howard Newby, Chairman of ESRC, for believing in us.

CSERGE started life in 1991 with a dual base in London and Norwich. It is an interdisciplinary centre with a focus on environmental economics and management. In addition to our core staff of economists, ecologists and political scientists, we have an extensive network of international lawyers, international relations experts, epidemiologists and others. We wish to thank all our colleagues, including those who have not contributed to the current volume, for the discussions that have led up to *Blue 3*.

Jonathan Sinclair-Wilson of Earthscan has once again advised, cajoled and supported us throughout and we owe him a special debt of thanks.

Claire Moore grappled valiantly and excellently with the final manuscript. We are truly grateful.

Finally, Sue Pearce and Merryl Turner have tolerated much during the writing of this book and our other CSERGE activities.

We dedicate *Blue 3* to the memory of Ann O'Riordan.

DWP, RKT, TO'R

PART I
Sustainable development

Chapter 1

Defining Sustainable Development

SUSTAINABLE DEVELOPMENT AND SUSTAINABILITY

The idea of organising an economic system so that it produces an enduring flow of output is not at all new. Foresters and fisherpeople have long been concerned with *sustainable yields*, ie harvesting trees and fish at a rate less than or equal to the growth rate of the biomass. Assuming there is fairly good knowledge of the dynamic behaviour of the resource in question – ie how it grows over time – it is possible to plan for sustainability. Notice that what is being sustained is both the output and the resource in this instance, simply because they are the same thing (timber and trees, for example). Failure to plan for sustainability results in disappearance of the resource in question, perhaps for some period while stocks are given a chance to regrow, or perhaps permanently if that chance is not given. The fact of various moratoria on fishing certain stocks of fish testifies to the failure to plan for sustainability, and the entire disappearance of some species and habitats is one extreme result of that failure. Arguably, extinction may not matter much if there is some other resource to which one can turn. Trees can always be grown somewhere else. Sometimes there are alternative fish stocks to be exploited; often there are not.

The extension from fish and trees to whole economies is fairly logical. If there is a concern for future generations' well-being it seems wise to ensure that the economy is itself sustainable so that future generations can be as well off as we are now. What would it mean for an economy to be managed 'sustainably'? As with the fishery and forestry example, it is both the output of the economy that needs to be sustained, *and* the underlying resource base that gives rise to that output.

Economies do not rely on renewable resources, like fish and trees, alone, although many come very close to it. So the first link in the comparison between sustainable yield and a sustainable economy appears to break down. If non-renewable resources, such as coal and oil, are available, why not use them? Non-renewable resources should be used to generate human well-being, but the requirement for sustainability would suggest that they be used in such a way that their substitution by renewable resources (solar, wind and wave energy, for example) is encouraged at the same time. Moreover, they should be used in such a way that their environmental effects are fully accounted for. So, sustainability means making sure that substitute resources are made available as non-renewable resources become physically scarce, and it means ensuring that the environmental impacts of using those resources are kept within the Earth's carrying capacity to assimilate those impacts.

For some people, this idea of maintaining some overall equilibrium between resource use and resource availability is the essence of 'sustainable development'. At one extreme, some would argue that non-renewable resources are 'running out' and that the switch to renewable resources cannot, in any event, compensate for their scarcity. The issue is one of 'lifestyle'. We have to cut back on the demands we make for resources. The call for lifestyle changes usually confuses two things: the growth of an economy, and the growth of the resources used to sustain that economic growth. It is possible to have economic growth (more gross national product – GNP) *and* to use up fewer resources. There are very good reasons as to why we should prefer this solution to the problem to one in which 'lifestyle change' means reducing GNP per capita. The first is that GNP and human well-being are inextricably linked for the vast majority of the world's population. Failure to keep GNP high shows up in the misery of unemployment and in poverty. Anti-growth advocates are embarrassingly silent or unrealistic on how they would solve problems of poverty and unemployment. Fanciful ideas abound, including one that suggests that economic growth in the 'North' should be sacrificed for the benefit of the 'South', as if not demanding goods and services in the rich countries would somehow release them for poor countries. The actual outcome, of course, is that they would not be produced at all, and everyone loses. Economic growth matters and the philosophy of sustainable development embraced in this volume acknowledges that.

Advocates of lifestyle change involving wholesale rejection of economic growth have been losing ground for some considerable time. Fashionable in the early 1970s, it is not heard so much in the 1990s, a part reflection of its non-credibility. But if lifestyle change means reducing materials and energy consumption and avoiding biodiversity loss, then it is to be encouraged strongly. And that is quite different to reducing economic growth, as *Blueprint 1* made very clear. Sustainability on this analysis involves sustaining the overall stock of natural resources so that they are available for the future, as well as for the present. That means driving the ratio of resource use to GNP downwards, and encouraging the transition to renewable resources. Both activities involve technological change. The first means making a given unit of a non-renewable resource do 'more work', ie produce more GNP. The second means developing renewable energy technologies and closed systems of materials use (recycling). Here again we may note a difference in emphasis between advocates of sustainability and some modern day environmentalists. The former must believe in technological advance, whilst not being so simple minded as to regard all technological change as 'benign' (we know it isn't – think of CFCs). The latter also tend to be 'anti-technology'.

A free market economist would argue that we do not need to 'encourage' sustainability. It will happen naturally. As non-renewable resources get scarce, so their prices will rise and substitutes will be encouraged. If there are no alternative non-renewables, the renewable technologies will be phased in 'naturally'. The problem with this solution is that the resources that are most threatened are those without markets: the receiving capacities of the oceans, atmosphere and stratosphere for example, and the greater part of the world's biological diversity. Free markets are not environmentally benign even when they exist. No-one can argue that they can be expected to resolve environmental problems 'naturally' if they do not exist at all.

Clearly, worrying about sustainability because of a concern for future generations' well-being is not very relevant if resources are so large that they can be utilised for human well-being a very long way into the future. Not surprisingly, then, those who object to a preoccupation with sustainability also tend to be 'resource optimists': they believe we are not running out of resources. Resource optimists tend to point to evidence of expanding resource discoveries and to declining trends in resource prices (see Box 1.1). But this evidence relates to resources that are marketed, and these are not the focus of concern. So while it *may* be comforting (only may be, since the evidence is not conclusive) to observe no scarcity in some resources, it is hardly reassuring.

The observation that what is being sustained is both output and input also helps with understanding of the link between sustainability and sustainable development. The two are not necessarily the same. A sustainable future may well be awful. But a sustainable future in which both outputs and inputs are sustained ought not to be in that category. Sustainable *development* broadens the concern with output so that it embraces social goals other than GNP. It also broadens the concern with inputs from natural resources alone to all capital assets. Failure to

---

Box 1.1
ARE WE RUNNING OUT OF RESOURCES?

A useful indicator of scarcity is the 'reserves to production ratio', ie the total reserves of a resource divided by the annual production of that resource. This gives the number of years over which the reserves would last at current rates of production. For oil the ratio was fairly steady at around 30 from 1966 to 1986 and rose to 43 in 1992. For natural gas the ratio has risen steadily from 40 in 1966 to 65 in 1992.

Economists like to use prices as an indicator of scarcity, although there are technical disputes about the suitability of the indicator. The main problem with these indicators is that they do not relate to environmental resources thought to be of the most concern. Ozdemiroglu (1993) found the following relationships:

- petroleum, natural gas, aluminium, gold, silver, zinc – no statistically significant relationship – ie no price trend could be detected;
- thermal coal, copper, zinc, coconut oil and jute – prices followed a statistically significant time trend in the form of an inverted 'U', ie prices rose at first and then fell, indicating no economic scarcity;
- timber exhibited no trend other than a possible rising scarcity for Philippines logs.

These findings suggest that marketed natural resources do not show evidence of any scarcity.

Various attempts have been made to estimate rates of species extinction. All are open to question because of the limited information available and the fairly primitive procedures used to derive the estimates. One recent estimate suggests that perhaps 1–5% of species will be lost each decade (Reid, 1992). If this is correct, then biological diversity is being reduced.

Sources: oil and gas numbers from British Petroleum, *BP Statistical Review of World Energy*, BP, London, June 1993; natural resource prices from E. Ozdemiroglu, *Measuring Natural Resource Scarcity: a Study of the Price Indicator*, CSERGE Working Paper GEC 93-14, University of East Anglia, 1993; and species loss rates from W. Reid, 'How Many Species Will There Be?', in T. Whitmore and J. Sayer (eds), *Tropical Deforestation and Species Extinction*, Chapman and Hall, London, 1992

---

appreciate this is perhaps at the heart of the confusion in some minds over the focus of sustainable development. They have come to believe that it is about biodiversity and fashionable environmental issues, not about improving the environments and well-being of the poor. But that is simply a misreading of the situation, as the next section shows.

THE BRUNDTLAND COMMISSION

The World Commission on Environment and Development (1987)

(the 'Brundtland Commission') defined sustainable development as: '... development that meets the needs of the present without compromising the ability of future generations to meet their own needs.' (WCED, 1987: 43). This definition is consistent with that provided in *Blueprint 1*. Any society setting itself the goal of sustainable development should therefore develop economically and socially in such a way that it minimises those activities the costs of which are borne by future generations, and, where such activities are unavoidable, due allowance is made for compensating future generations for those costs.

The Brundtland Commission also emphasised the overriding priority of attending to the needs of the poor within any society, and in the world as a whole:

[sustainable development] contains within it two key concepts:
- the concept of 'needs', in particular the essential needs of the world's poor, to which overriding priority should be given; and
- the idea of limitations imposed by the state of technology and social organization on the environment's ability to meet present and future needs.

(WCED, 1987: 43)

The whole rationale for sustainable development therefore is to raise the standard of living – and especially the standard of living of the least advantaged in society – while at the same time avoiding uncompensated future costs.

How does the environment fit this requirement? Deteriorating environments and loss of natural resources represent one of the main ways in which today's generation is creating uncompensated future costs. Hence the conservation of natural resources and the environment is crucial to achieving sustainable development. This theme is developed more fully in Chapter 2.

While it is a popular pastime to collect different and incompatible definitions of sustainable development, inspection of the words and of their origins suggests that defining sustainable development is really not a difficult issue. The difficult issue is in determining what has to be done to achieve it.

What is being referred to is sustainable *economic* development. The term 'sustainable' is not open to much dispute: it means 'enduring' and 'lasting' and 'to keep in being'. So, sustainable development is economic development that lasts. Economic development could be narrowly defined in traditional terms as real Gross National Product (GNP) per capita, or real consumption per capita. Alternatively, it could be broadened to include other indicators of development such as education, health and some measure of the 'quality of life', including human freedom. One such exercise is to be found in the United Nations Development Programme's 'Human Development Index' (HDI) (UNDP, 1992). This combines measures of sub-goals – literacy, life expectancy and GDP – to provide an index of relative achievement, ie a score which is defined in terms of a country's position relative to other countries. Since the index is then an average of the relative achievements in each of the three main sub-goals, there is an implicit assumption of substitutability between the different components. More education might be at the expense of GNP for example.

Sustainable economic development now becomes fairly simply defined. It is continuously rising, or at least non-declining, consumption per capita, or GNP, or whatever the agreed indicator of development is. And this is how sustainable development has come to be interpreted by most economists addressing the issue (see for example Mäler, 1990; Pezzey, 1992; Pearce *et al*, 1990). Notice that defining sustainable development is not the same thing as searching for the necessary and sufficient conditions for achieving it – this issue is addressed in Chapter 2.

SUSTAINABLE DEVELOPMENT OR OPTIMAL DEVELOPMENT?

Some economists object to the notion of sustainable development, preferring the more traditional notion of 'optimal' development. Optimal, of course, simply means 'best'. Optimal development is defined as that path of economic development over time which makes potential human well-being as large as possible. Additionally, optimal development paths usually reflect the idea that $1 of well-being in the future is less valuable than $1 of well-being today. The idea here is that future generations will be better off than today's generation anyway, so that the extra $1 is worth less to them than an extra $1 is worth to us today. The way this judgement is built into the analysis of optimal development is through the process of 'discounting'. Discounting essentially lowers the weight given to gains in the future compared to gains today (Pearce *et al*, 1989). So, an optimal development path is one that gives rise to the maximum amount of (discounted) well-being over some defined time horizon.

The use of the term 'optimal' is something of a sleight of hand in this context. For if something is optimal, nothing else can be superior to it. The best is simply the best. But really what is happening is that 'optimal' is being defined in a particular way and what is optimal depends very much on what the purpose of development actually is. This is most clearly seen by contrasting optimality with sustainability. A development path can be optimal (maximising the discounted value of future well-being) but unsustainable (well-being eventually falls), as Figure 1.1 illustrates. Or it can be optimal and sustainable. Now, what is optimal and sustainable may well involve current generations in less well-being than they would have if the aim was optimality alone, as Figure 1.1 illustrates. But future generations might be better off.

How do we choose which is better? Clearly, if we ask for individual votes now we may be told that optimality is best, and future generations can look after themselves. Since they cannot vote, the procedure is somewhat biased. But if we are asked to vote on our own behalf and on behalf of future generations, the answer might be different. As Pezzey (1992) notes, much depends on how people vote – as individuals or as citizens. Like all normative philosophies, sustainable development has a moral undertone. It has attracted the attention it has precisely because many people feel that the present generation is being 'unfair' to future generations by depleting major sources of future well-being. If one either doesn't care about future generations, or if one judges that there are no significant problems being passed on to future generations, then there is little point in pursuing sustainable

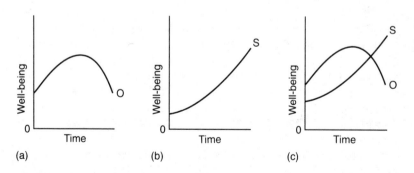

Note: Figure (a) shows a development path that is 'optimal' but not sustainable. Figure (b) shows one that is sustainable but which would not be optimal. Figure (c) compares the two paths and shows a situation in which the sustainable path makes future generations better off but current generations worse off

Figure 1.1 *Optimal and sustainable development*

development in so far as it addresses the concern about equity between generations. That leaves the focus on poverty now. While it is possible to be concerned about poverty now and not about future generations, especially if one believes that concern for the future actually impedes development for the poor now, it isn't very clear how the two concerns can be separated.

The absence of concern for the well-being of future generations could have stronger foundation if we could be sure they will be better off than this generation. But not only is there no certainty that this will be the case, the very problem of sustainable development arises precisely because it is believed that actions now are making future generations potentially worse off, not better off.

As defined in the previous section, sustainable development involves (a) making the present generation better off without making future generations worse off, and (b) focusing current development on the most disadvantaged. The two objectives may conflict. If the best way to help the poor is to industrialise rapidly using 'dirty' technology then that objective may conflict with the concern to improve the global atmospheric environment for future generations. Does the notion of 'optimal development' overcome this likely trade-off? The answer is that it does not for it maximises the *sum* of individual well-being. It does not carry with it any implication that the poor will not get poorer. The only way to ensure that is to rephrase the objective as maximising well-being subject to the requirement that the poor now are not made any poorer. And if that is the requirement, it is only a small step to rephrasing it a little further and saying that the poor in the next generation should not be any poorer than they otherwise would have been, and so on.

There are no very compelling reasons for preferring so-called 'optimal' development over 'sustainable' development. It is a conflict of value judgements, reinforced perhaps by differences in belief about just how serious the threats are to future well-being from actions by today's generation. Box 1.2 sums up the differences of view.

THE UK AND SUSTAINABLE DEVELOPMENT

Translated into realisable political action, sustainable development is more about changes of emphasis than a wholesale restructuring of decision-making. At best, it is likely to involve a further movement of environmental concerns up the political agenda. That simply reflects the fact that political change in democratic societies is a gradual affair, not a dramatic one. In the early 1990s it also reflects the existence of economic recession and the politicians' consequent reluctance to

---

Box 1.2
FOR AND AGAINST SUSTAINABLE DEVELOPMENT

Sustainability requires two assumptions:

1 FACT:
   current generations are adversely and significantly affecting future generations' well-being

2 VALUE JUDGEMENT:
   we ought not to be unfair to future generations.

(The fact could be correct, but if we do not care about future generations the fact doesn't matter).

Opponents of sustainability require one of the following statements:

3 current generations are not harming future generations (in which case the moral issue does not arise);

4 the well-being of future generations is not a moral concern (in which case item 1 can be true but irrelevant); or

5 the well-being of future generations is a moral concern but it is less important than the wellbeing of the poor now, and the two conflict.

---

embrace anything that might add to industrial costs and hence to a loss of 'competitiveness'. This *perceived* link between environmental regulation as an integral part of sustainable development and competitiveness is fundamental since it has a strong hold on government. It is also played upon by industrial lobbies who incessantly warn that less, not more, regulation is needed if we are to come out of recession and stay out of it. Yet very little evidence exists to suggest any marked relationship between environmental regulation and economic performance. Pearce (1993) reviews the evidence of the economic models that do simulate environmental regulation impacts on the economy and finds only a few studies where the linkage is thought to be significant. Most find either no relationship, a very slight deterioration in macroeconomic performance, or even an improvement. This is not altogether surprising when one realises that what environmental regulations tend to do is to boost one sector of industry (environmental abatement) and raise costs in another sector. Politicians' fears that the overall performance of the economy will be damaged are almost certainly unfounded. One element of the perceived link between regulation and macroeconomic performance is not therefore real.

But what does happen is that some gain and some lose, and any context in which this happens means that the gainers lobby for more regulation and the losers lobby for less. The industrial lobby against the European Community-proposed carbon tax was (and is) extremely forceful. Politicians tend to respond to the strongest lobby and there is no question that the pollution abatement industry is not a strong lobby in Europe generally, at least relative to those industries likely to be on the receiving end of new regulations. Since the losers from *not* having environmental regulation are necessarily less powerful (since they tend to represent non-market constituencies), the political lobby field is biased against environmental regulation.

How can environmentalists overcome this perception of the economic damage from environmental improvement? There are several strands to a political platform:

- Make sure that the environmental regulations in question are cost-effective: nothing is gained by imposing unnecessarily costly measures on industry when cheaper ones can serve the same end. This is the political argument for the use of market-based instruments advocated in *Blueprint 1*. Environmentalists ignore this argument at their peril. The 'high moral ground' stance combined with an irrational preference for regulations rather than market based approaches simply builds up the opposition; it does not defeat it.

- Encourage the industries that profit from regulation. It is small wonder that countries like Germany embrace strict environment standards when their industry stands to profit from them, domestically and through export sales.

- Get the message across that what is called 'economic' loss from regulation has a counterpart in the economic benefit from regulation. Improved health and quality of life are economic benefits. Despite the economists' long standing explanations about economic gains being the same as gains in human well-being, the idea persists that 'economic' means 'commercial' or 'financial'. It is in this context that altering the way we measure economic progress (Chapter 3) needs to be changed. In itself it is unlikely to have much effect. Its importance lies in changing the perception of 'economic' from meaning 'associated with a cash flow' to meaning 'achieving human well-being'.

- Learn to package regulatory proposals. The European Community made great strides in proposing a carbon tax which would be 'fiscally neutral': ie a tax that would not generate gains to government revenues. Very simply, revenues would be paid out again, in part in the form of reducing other taxes in the economy, especially taxes on effort and enterprise. In this fiscal neutrality concept lies a great advantage to industry: most would be far better off with a fiscally neutral environmental tax and lower profits taxes than they would with environmental regulation alone. Even the recession could benefit if tax revenues were recycled to lower the costs of employing labour, both benefiting industry and inducing increased labour demand and hence lowering unemployment. The reality is that many business leaders recognise these arguments but they have a final doubt – governments will not play fair. A neutral tax this year becomes a revenue raiser when budget deficits rise. But there are even ways round this problem, for example by recycling revenues as capital grants to industry. In that case their profit gains are 'up front' and cannot be reneged on by government.

If a real gesture is to be made on sustainable development it is this kind of approach that will be required. Perpetual haranguing of government and industry about the need for more regulations will be counter-productive, and indeed has been.

There are few signs in the United Kingdom that these kinds of reforms are likely. The government consultation document on sustainable development (Department of the Environment, 1993c), a precursor to its Sustainable Development Strategy Report to the UN Commission on Sustainable Development, offers a wholly unimaginative response to the issues by, amongst other things:

- claiming that it had already embraced sustainable development in a 1989 White Paper on environmental policy (DoE 1993c, para 1.6, referring to DoE 1989). The 1989 White Paper offered cosmetic changes to existing environmental regulations and relegated a discussion of market-based approaches to an annex, and barely discussed sustainable development as a concept. The more extraordinary claim is that 'the principle of sustainability (is) ... already an integral part of much of current policy and practice'. Chapter 3 and Part II of this volume show this is untrue;
- embracing economic instruments (again) without having introduced a single measure that could be identified as an economic instrument;
- indicating clearly that the UK will not be able to contain CO_2 emissions at their 1990 level beyond the year 2000. Most disingenuously, it is stated that 'There will remain the question of whether targets should be established beyond the year 2000 and, if so, how they should be achieved' (DoE, 1993c, para 2.11). Even to raise the question is to deny that the Rio Climate Change Convention has any meaning, but, as a scientific fact, stabilisation

by the year 2000 followed by emissions growth would have virtually no effect on rates of global warming.

Above all, the Consultation Document says little or nothing to indicate that the existing way of doing things will change. If anything, it promises retrogression. And it promises this only because of the fear that embracing sustainable development means upsetting the established order. There is an underlying political reality in that fear. Environmentalists have not succeeded in showing that they speak for ordinary people, perhaps because they often do not. That alone makes it important to present the case for sustainable development in the most constructive way.

2

The conditions for sustainable development

KEEPING CAPITAL RESOURCES INTACT

Sustainable development is about ensuring that some measure of human well-being is sustained over time. Fundamental to this approach to economic development is the requirement that any actions now which are likely significantly to impair the well-being of the future must be associated with actual compensation of the future. Otherwise, the future is worse off compared to the present. How can the future be compensated? The literature on sustainable development is generally agreed that the mechanism whereby current generations can compensate the future is through the transfer of capital bequests. What this means is that this generation makes sure that it leaves the next generation a stock of capital no less than this generation has now. Capital provides the capability to generate well-being through the creation of the goods and services upon which human well-being depends (Pearce *et al*, 1989, 1990).

What is capital? Capital comprises the stock of man-made capital – machines and infrastructure such as housing and roads – together with the stock of knowledge and skills, or human capital. But it also comprises the stock of natural capital including natural resources (oil, gas, coal), biological diversity, habitat, clean air and water and so on. Together, these capital stocks comprise the aggregate capital stock of a nation.

Weak sustainability

Unless there are special reasons for singling out one form of capital, the requirement for sustainable development then becomes one of passing on to the next generation an aggregate capital stock no less than the one that exists now (Hartwick, 1978; Solow, 1986). This 'constant capital rule' is known as weak sustainability in the sustainable development literature. Weak sustainability means that we are indifferent to the form in which we pass on the capital stock. We can pass on less environment so long as we offset this loss by increasing the stock of roads and machinery or other man-made capital. Alternatively, we can have fewer roads so long as we compensate by having more wetlands or meadows or more education. Weak sustainability therefore assumes that the forms of capital are completely substitutable for each other. As *Blueprint 1* put it, the bequest to the next generation:

> comprises a 'mix' of man-made and 'natural' capital. It is the aggregate quantity that matters and there is considerable scope for substituting man-made wealth for natural environmental assets.
>
> (Pearce *et al*, 1989: 48)

On the weak sustainability interpretation of sustainable development there is no special place for the environment. The environment is simply another form of capital.

This said, there is a crucial requirement for even weak sustainability to be achieved. This is that depletion of natural resources that are in fixed supply – non-renewable resources – should be accompanied by investment in substitute resources. In the energy context this means investing in renewable energy.

Strong sustainability

Are all forms of capital substitutable for each other? It seems fair to say that this is an assumption of the weak sustainability literature rather than a statement of fact. Ecologists would point to the limited nature of substitution between ecological assets and man-made assets. There are two reasons for this. First, some ecological assets would seem to be essential to human well-being even if they are not essential to human survival – the experience of space and amenity for example. Second, since natural capital has to be interpreted widely, many assets are essential to human survival, at least in the longer run: the basic biogeochemical cycles for example.

We might therefore designate those ecological assets which are essential in either sense as being *critical natural capital*. They are critical either to well-being or to survival. Some would argue that the ozone layer is an example of critical capital due to the profound ecological consequences that would arise from further significant ozone layer depletion. Others might cite the carbon cycle as critical capital, and hence global warming as a major threat. Loss of biological diversity is perhaps the most important loss of natural capital. The reason for this is that such losses may threaten the primary life support functions of ecological systems. Ecologists speak of the primary values of ecological systems as opposed to the secondary values which relate to the uses that humankind makes of ecological systems. Secondary values – uses such as food exploitation, timber supply, recreation etc. – are contingent upon primary values. By and large, then, primary values relate to critical natural capital.

If the forms of capital stock are not easily substituted for each other, then the strong sustainability rule requires that we protect critical natural capital at least. A broader interpretation is that the overall stock of natural capital should not be allowed to decline. There are therefore two variants of the natural capital rule. The first speaks generally of conserving natural capital. The second highlights the role of critical natural capital and focuses on its conservation, with or without some overall rule for conserving overall natural capital (Turner, 1992; Pearce, 1993).

Measuring sustainable development thus depends on the view taken about what is necessary to achieve it. On the weak sustainability rule we need to look at the overall stock of capital. On the strong sustainability rule we need to look at the overall stock of capital *and* pay special attention to the environment. Recall that environmental degradation was highlighted as the main way in which this generation threatens the well-being of the next generation. This gives added support for adopting the strong sustainability view.

There are other reasons for adopting this view:

● There is extensive *uncertainty* about the way in which natural capital stocks work. We do not understand the full workings of ecological systems. Uncertainty is always a reason for being cautious, unless society can be deemed to be indifferent to risk or positively to welcome it ('risk neutrality' and 'risk-loving'). Indeed, this uncertainty lies at the foundation of the precautionary principle whereby decision-makers do not wait for full scientific certainty before making decisions. The precautionary approach is especially important if the scale of damage from natural capital loss is likely to be large.

● When natural capital assets are lost it may not be possible to recreate them. This is the problem of *irreversibility*. Once lost, such assets are lost for ever. By contrast, man-made capital can be run down and then recreated, as can human capital (although the conservation of indigenous knowledge and crafts, for example, is important).

For these and other reasons, conserving natural capital is especially important to sustainable development.

Table 2.1 The sustainability spectrum

	TECHNOCENTRIC		ECOCENTRIC	
	Cornucopian	Accommodating	Communalist	Deep ecology
Green labels	Resource exploitative, growth-orientated position	Resource conservationist and 'managerial' position	Resource preservationist position	Extreme preservationist position
Type of economy	Anti-green economy, unfettered free markets	Green economy, green markets guided by economic incentive instruments [EIs] (eg pollution charges etc)	Deep green economy, steady-state economy regulated by macro-environmental standards and supplemented by EIs	Very deep green economy, heavily regulated to minimise 'resource-take'
Management strategies	Primary economic policy objective, maximise economic growth (Gross National Product [GNP])	Modified economic growth (adjusted green accounting to measure GNP)	Zero economic growth; zero population growth	Reduced scale of economy and population

	Very weak sustainability	Weak sustainability	Strong sustainability	Very strong sustainability
	Taken as axiomatic that unfettered free markets in conjunction with technical progress will ensure infinite substitution possibilities capable of mitigating all 'scarcity/limits' constraints (environmental sources and sinks)	Decoupling important but infinite substitution rejected. Sustainability rules: constant capital rule	Decoupling plus no increase in scale. 'Systems' perspective – 'health' of whole ecosystems very important; Gaia hypothesis and implications	Scale reduction imperative; at the extreme for some there is a literal interpretation of Gaia as a personalised agent to which moral obligations are owed
Ethics	Support for traditional ethical reasoning; rights and interests of contemporary individual humans; instrumental value (i.e. of recognised value to humans) in nature	Extension of ethical reasoning: 'caring for others' motive – intragenerational and intergenerational equity (ie contemporary poor and future people); instrumental value in nature	Further extension of ethical reasoning: interests of the collective take precedence over those of the individual; primary value of ecosystems and secondary value of component functions and services	Acceptance of bioethics (ie moral rights/ interests conferred on all non-human species and even the abiotic parts of the environment); intrinsic value in nature (ie valuable in its own right regardless of human experience)
Sustainability labels	Very weak sustainability	Weak sustainability	Strong sustainability	Very strong sustainability

Blueprint view

SUSTAINABILITY AND ENVIRONMENTAL IDEOLOGY

What the sustainability debate has, among other things, exposed is the insight that sustainability approaches differ because they are linked to alternative environmental ideologies. The classification system set out in Table 2.1 describes the full spectrum of sustainability perspectives, from 'very weak' to 'very strong' sustainability.

'Cornucopists' place a great deal of faith in the assumed extensive substitutability of the various forms of capital – man-made, human and natural. Acknowledged environmental problems would be dealt with by environmental taxes or some other regulation, but otherwise there is a prevailing belief that these problems are not significant, or that the costs of their control outweigh the benefits of their control. The 'accommodating' approach believes in the extensive scope for the decoupling of economic activity and environmental impact. Society's use of resources is therefore made more and more efficient over time. While total decoupling is not possible (economic activity will always use some resources) as long as the amount of resources used per unit of Gross National Product (GNP) goes down faster than GNP goes up, the impact on the environment can be reduced each year. This is even true of the demand for land space. While it is arguable that rising incomes lead to rising demand for land through, for example, a rising demand for food and hence agricultural land, most of the competition for land area comes from rising population growth. Exceptions to the decoupling argument include cumulative pollutants: pollutants that build up over time because the assimilative processes present in the environment cannot break them down into harmless substances, or 'lock' them away in sediment sinks in the deep oceans. Both cornucopists and accommodationists (most of the authors of this volume are the second grouping) put faith in technical change, although the latter warn against assuming that all technical change is benign and certainly warn against the *assumption* that technical change will solve problems.

Those of a deeper shade of green are 'ecocentrist'. Ecocentrists believe in more direct regulation and planning: neither free nor adjusted markets can solve the problem. Unlike the technocentrists, ecocentrists believe the scale of economic activity must be reduced. In so far as scale refers to materials and energy throughput, they share this view with the accommodationists. But they diverge markedly in believing that these materials and energy scale changes can only be brought about by changes in the scale of GNP, ie in economic growth itself. The darkest shade of green is the deep ecologist option in which society is closely regulated to achieve supreme environmental ends, or, if the prospect of extensive regulation is too reminiscent of failed central planning, it is achieved through a spiritual revolution in which the majority at least voluntarily change behaviour to accord with the overall objectives.

To sum up so far, sustainable development is economic development that endures over the long run. It must be undertaken in such a way as to minimise the effects of economic activity on the environment, whenever the cost impacts fall on future generations. Should such cost burdens be unavoidably imposed on the future, full compensation must be paid. The notion of capital bequests and the constant natural capital rule are consistent with the intergenerational equity (compensation) principle. Economic development can be narrowly measured in terms of GNP per capita, or real consumption of goods and services per capita. In later sections we will argue that in fact the traditional GNP measure needs to be modified and extended if it is to measure sustainable development. But for the moment sustainable development is defined as at least non-declining consumption, GNP, or some other agreed welfare (well-being) indicators such as education, health etc.

HOW HAS THE CAPITAL STOCK CHANGED IN THE UK?

Measuring changes in the overall stock of capital is complex, especially so when the issue is one of natural capital. This sub-section looks at indicators of man-made and human capital stock for the UK, leaving the assessment of natural capital to Chapter 3 and Part II.

Man-made capital

Historical estimates of man-made capital exist for the United Kingdom. Total man-made capital assets for a nation can be defined as domestic capital plus overseas assets. Table 2.2 shows estimates for the UK for the period 1856 to 1973. It has fairly systematically increased over time, although both World Wars had the effect of destroying capital, as the data show. The man-made capital stock data show that, on this count, the UK has, so far, met one of the conditions for sustainable development.

Human capital

The 'stock of knowledge' is obviously impossible to measure directly, but one indicator is investment in education. Table 2.3 shows two such indicators: (a) the ratio of teaching staff to pupils and students,

Table 2.2 *Gross man-made capital in Great Britain, 1856–1973*

Year	Gross domestic fixed assets £bn 1938 prices	Inventories	Net overseas assets	Total
1856	4.2	0.6	0.5	5.3
1873	5.9	0.7	1.5	8.2
1913	12.9	1.3	7.3	21.5
1924	13.8	1.4	4.9	20.1
1937	17.5	1.7	4.1	23.3
1951	20.4	2.4	−0.3	22.4
1973	41.4	3.9	1.5	46.8

Source: Matthews *et al* (1982)

and (b) expenditure on education expressed in per capita terms. Both show systematic increases over time apart from a rise in the pupil–teacher ratio for secondary school students in the first two decades of this century. We may safely conclude that the stock of knowledge in the UK has been increasing systematically.

POPULATION AND TECHNOLOGICAL CHANGE

Maintaining a stock of capital will not be sufficient for sustainable development if population is growing rapidly. For then the capital stock per head will decline. Offsetting this is technological progress which basically makes capital achieve more for any given amount of capital. For example, the amount of energy used in the United

Table 2.3 *Two indicators of human capital: a) Ratio of pupils to teachers in the UK, 1854–1979*

Year	Primary E & W	Primary Scotland	Secondary E & W	Secondary Scotland
1854	164	na	na	na
1891	49	56	na	na
1909	na	na	16	19
1921	31	35	19	27
1938	27	28	19	22
1979	23	23	16	15

Source: current expenditures, consumer price indices and population from Liesner (1989)

Table 2.3b *Real education expenditures per capita in the UK*

Year	Expenditure at 1980 prices (£ million)	Expenditure per capita (£ 1980)
1920	898	20.5
1930	1,662	36.2
1938	2,044	43.0
1950	2,960	58.5
1960	4,946	94.4
1970	9,133	164.0
1980	12,750	226.0
1987	13,947	245.0

Source: Data from Mitchell (1988)

Kingdom now is about the same as it was in 1973, twenty years earlier. Yet economic activity, as measured by GNP, has grown by 33% since that date. The same amount of energy has achieved more output due to its greater efficiency of use. In a country like the United Kingdom this balance between population growth and technological change tends to favour sustainable development because population growth is so low, at around 0.3% per annum since 1900. But in countries with population growth rates of 3% and 4% per annum, ten times that of the United Kingdom, the sustainable development imperative is far more important and can be achieved only with strong growth of capital stocks, technological change and a slowing of population growth. Rapid population growth is a formidable threat to sustainable development.

SUSTAINABLE DEVELOPMENT: THE INTERNATIONAL DIMENSION

The process of industrialisation has created an international economic system out of which the developed countries (the North) have gained the lion's share of the economic benefits. The gap between the rich countries and the poorer developing countries (the South), excluding a small number of 'newly industrialising states' such as Taiwan, South Korea and Singapore, has not been closing over time. It is the view of some commentators that poor countries are growing poorer because they are 'exploited' by the global trading system (United Nations Development Programme, 1992, ch 4).

The scale of this global economic activity now means that some of its impacts can be classified as global environmental change effects – eg acid rain, ozone layer depletion, global warming, and deforestation. *Blueprint 2* examined the causes and consequences of global environmental change (Pearce, 1991). There is a sense in which it is in the richer countries' own interest to undertake 'reform' of the international economic system, since both rich and poor have a common interest in the continued health of the global environment ('global interdependency thesis'; Turner, 1993). All countries therefore, to a greater or lesser extent, have an international ecological 'footprint' which must be taken into account in any analysis of sustainable development strategies. The UK economy has many impacts upon other countries. It contributes to other countries' income but also places demands on their natural resources (eg importation of natural resources such as forest products etc, and tourism). The UK also contributes to the pressures on global resources – climate system, ozone layer, waste assimilation capacities and biodiversity stock. In turn, other countries place demands on the UK's natural resources. Chapter 3 investigates ways in which this 'footprint' issue can be built into an analysis of sustainable development.

It is perfectly possible for a single nation to secure a sustainable development path, but at the cost of non-sustainability in another country. Thus many countries, including the UK, rely on imports of natural resources from developing countries. It is a distinctive feature of their international 'footprint'. This latter group frequently contains countries which do not have any other ('value added', semi-processed or fully-processed manufactured goods) alternative products to sell in international markets. The danger is that these 'primary commodity' exporting countries will maximise, over the short run, the revenue available from the exploitation of forests or other natural resources. In doing so they run the risk of reducing the stock available in the future – unsustainable development. The widespread concern in Europe about the use of imported tropical hardwoods is a good example of possible 'imported sustainability' at the expense of non-sustainability in other nations. Some analysts have also expressed concern that trade policy could be used as a mechanism to import sustainability by setting high environmental standards at home and importing cheap products from 'pollution havens' abroad (Young, 1992).

Barriers to international trade such as selective tariff arrangements are not conducive to sustainable development on a global basis. At the international level negotiations have been going on for many years to reduce tariff barriers and liberalise trade – the GATT (General Agreement on Tariffs and Trade) negotiations. So far progress has been slow, but sustainable development requires the phasing out of selective tariff barriers and/or their replacement with low but relatively uniform ones. One positive aspect of such a move would be the improvement in the prospects for developing countries to export value-added resource products. But the international economic system contains more than just trading interrelationships. Financial resource flows (official, private and direct investment) between the UK and the rest of the world affect the ability of other countries to pursue sustainable development policies. The UK directs a considerable amount of financial and other types of aid towards developing (especially Commonwealth Members) countries – this is discussed more fully in Chapter 3. Foreign aid could be targeted towards the goal of sustainable development. Such aid would represent a recognition of the argument that the wealthier countries of the world 'import sustainability' from the poorer countries of the world. While non-sustainability in the exporting countries must be partly a matter of policy choice, there is a case for returning sustainability to the exporting nations through environmentally sensitive aid. Such aid would focus on securing sustainable resource management in the export nations (Pearce *et al*, 1991, ch 9).

How far are existing international aid policies 'environmentally sensitive'? Most aid, whether direct from the UK or through the large multilateral agencies such as the World Bank, is linked to a system known as structural adjustment. During the 1980s structural adjustment aimed at the restructuring of developing country economies to cope better with the vicissitudes of the international trading economy. Structural adjustment became the lending vehicle by which the official financial institutions gained access to policy makers and, through 'conditionality', tried to induce profound changes in developing country economic policy and its enabling economic structures (Reed, 1992). Conditionality basically reduces to lending on condition that structural change is brought about (see Box 2.1).

Currently, there is a deep debate about the success or otherwise of structural adjustment lending. Did it actually lead to the stabilisation of distressed economies and did it create favourable conditions for longer-term (sustainable) economic growth? The evidence is mixed, but one shortcoming that is generally accepted (to a greater or lesser extent) is that up to the late 1980s, structural adjustment failed *directly* to address environmental deterioration problems. Such degradation of the natural resource base, combined with population growth, posed a significant threat to any improved economic performance generated by the restructuring process.

A limited amount of case-study analysis indicates that structural adjustment *per se* has not led to increased environmental degradation. Rather, the continued existence of a wide range of micro-economic

---

Box 2.1

STRUCTURAL ADJUSTMENT AND THE ENVIRONMENT

High interest rates, declining commodity prices and internal and external imbalances in the industrialised economies during the 1980s rebounded on to the international economic system causing a general recession. These conditions constrained the exporting potential of developing countries and increased their debt servicing problems. A significant number of developing countries became bankrupt in the sense that they could not pay the interest due on loans they had taken out. During the 1980s a trend developed that led to an annual net flow of capital from developing to industrial countries. In 1988, for example, US$32.5 million moved from developing to industrial countries; in 1980 there had been a reverse flow of US$40 billion. But in addition, developing countries were afflicted by deep set 'internal' problems – economic distortions and inefficiencies that were pervasive in their economies. It was this combination of structural economic weaknesses that structural adjustment lending aimed to alleviate.

Between 1980 and 1990 structural adjustment lending amounted to more than $28 billion, it flowed to 64 countries through 198 separate lending operations. Regional development banks and bilateral aid agencies, following World Bank priorities and policies, shifted their lending policy into line with structural adjustment objectives.

Structural adjustment lending up to the late 1980s was not intended to address environmental problems directly, although it does have environmental implications. Such implications cannot, however, be separated from the economic and social impacts of policy-based lending.

Donor organisations operated for many years without a project approval process that encompassed environmental impact assessment (CE). Since the late 1980s this situation is however changing. CE of aid projects are becoming more common and 'environmental conditionality', ie loan conditions that provide an incentive for sustainable investment and resource use, is beginning to emerge.

Sources: Reed (1992); Young (1992)

---

market failures, eg inappropriate resource pricing and government subsidies, played a prominent role in the resource degradation process (Pearce, 1993). Frequently, structural adjustment requires that these 'failures' be corrected, not for environmental reasons, but because of their deleterious effects on the economy, and hence on the prospects for economic growth. Ironically, then, if sustainable development is about protecting the environment, and structural adjustment assists with that protection through the better pricing of natural resources, then structural adjustment has the potential to *improve* sustainable development. This does not mean that actual policies have been successful. A clearer targeting of the environmental objectives is required. It does means that, contrary to much popular opinion, structural adjustment is often a precursor to sustainable development. Nor is that conclusion confined to the developing world. The rich world similarly subsidises energy, water and agriculture. International sustainable development requires a concerted international effort to liberalise trade and the domestic economy – a message that runs almost diametrically opposite to that being advanced by some environmental organisations. Structural adjustment, suitably reformed to include environmental conditionality could make a significant contribution to putting developing countries on a sustainable development path. And the same philosophy applies to the need for rich countries to put their own houses in order.

CONCLUSIONS

The achievement of sustainable development requires 'constant capital stocks' where 'constant' must be construed to mean constant or increasing. Weak sustainability demands that the overall stock of capital be 'constant', with no special regard being paid to environmental capital. Strong sustainability requires that both the overall stock and the natural stock be 'constant'. All forms of sustainable development are encouraged by technological change, and strong sustainability calls especially for said change that lowers the materials, land and energy content of economic activity. Sustainable development is most threatened by rapid population growth.

Any one country can achieve sustainability at the expense of others. Hence there is a need to identify and measure the 'international ecological footprint' of any one country's activity. Chapter 3 looks at this issue again.

Sustainable development requires structural change. While some environmentalists argue against structural change and against freer trade, both are more likely to improve the environment, and both are certainly needed if there is to be any hope for the world's poor. Protection and subsidies distort economic incentives all too often against the environment – as with subsidies to wasteful energy use, subsidies for excessive use of irrigation water and even drinking water, and subsidies for environmentally destructive land uses such as forest clearance. We cannot jump from these observations to say that free trade is always good or that structural adjustment is always desirable. It has to be environmentally sensitive and for that it is necessary that resources, goods and services are priced properly to reflect their full environmental costs, just as we argued in *Blueprint 1*.

Measures of economic progress

HAS THE UNITED KINGDOM ACHIEVED SUSTAINABLE DEVELOPMENT? INCOME AND EQUITY

If the United Kingdom has so far achieved sustainable development, it should show up partially in the quantitative record on the 'standard of living'. We take the standard of living to incorporate the usual indicators of real income or consumption per capita, but also some measure of the degree of inequality in society, and the services supplied by non-market assets such as the environment. The measures of interest, therefore, are income, equity, and environmental services.

Income per head

Figure 3.1 assembles some information on the UK long term record of Gross National Product per capita. Such indicators are subject to error due to (a) limited collection of statistics in the earlier periods, and (b) the use of single year prices for some 160 years of growth (1830–1991). But they suggest that income per head grew fairly systematically from the middle of the nineteenth century to the present day. To date, then, the UK has been 'sustainable' in the sense of rising real incomes.

The diagram shows the trend of real income and real income per capita in the UK from 1830 to 1991. 'Real' income is income with changes in price levels netted out so it refers to the real command over resources. Apart from the fall between 1913 and 1920, part of which is accounted for by the omission of Ireland at this date, real incomes rose consistently over time suggesting that income growth as defined here has been 'sustainable'.

GNP is measured at factor cost, ie excluding indirect taxes and including subsidies.

Inequality in the UK

If economic development was aimed at the most disadvantaged groups in society, then one might expect the distribution of income to improve

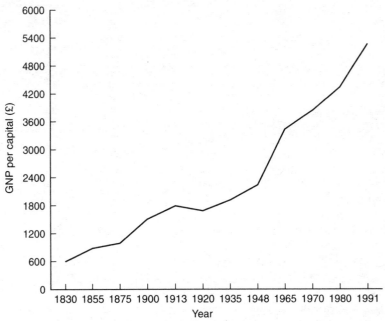

Sources: Historical GNP data and population from Mitchell (1988) and more recent GNP data from Central Statistical Office (1992)

Figure 3.1   *Real incomes in the United Kingdom, 1830–1991*

over time. That is, the incomes of the poorest groups should rise faster than the incomes of the richer group: it is not sufficient simply for the average real incomes of the poorest group to rise. Data for income distribution in the UK are shown in Table 3.1. The long run data in the table relate to male wage earnings, 1886 to 1990. They are to be interpreted as follows. In 1886 the median (average) wage was £1.21 per week. The lowest decile of earners (the lowest 10%) earned 68.6% of the median wage. The highest decile earned 143.1% of the median wage. In 1990 the median wage was £221.30 per week but the lowest decile earned 63.7% of the median. The highest decile earned 159.1%. Some idea of the degree of inequality can be obtained by dividing the highest decile number by the lowest decile – as shown in column 4 of Table 3.1. If this ratio rises, inequality gets worse. If it falls, inequality is lessened. From 1886 to 1976 the ratio fluctuates, but not wildly. Inequality was fairly constant over this period of 90 years. From 1976 to 1990 inequality worsens markedly. Wage inequality is actually worse in 1990 than it was 100 years previously.

Table 3.1 *Distribution of male earnings, 1886–1990*

Year	Lowest decile/ median wage (ratio)	Median wage £/week	Highest decile/ median wage (ratio)	Ratio of high to low
1886	0.686	1.21	1.431	2.09
1906	0.665	1.47	1.568	2.36
1938	0.677	3.40	1.399	2.07
1970	0.673	25.60	1.475	2.19
1976	0.702	62.10	1.449	2.06
1979	0.683	88.20	1.485	2.17
1982	0.683	125.20	1.526	2.23
1988	0.643	188.00	1.565	2.43
1990	0.637	221.30	1.591	2.50

Source: Gregg and Machin (1993)

Table 3.2 confirms the change in the 1980s. The lowest 20% of households earned 10% of all earnings in 1979 but only a little under 9% in 1987. The top 20% of households earned 34% of all earnings in 1979, but their share rose to 39% in 1987.

While the indicators show that the poorest groups in society improved their lot in absolute terms, their relative position worsened in a very short period of time – basically the decade of the 1980s – after some 90 years of relative stability.

Well-being of the disadvantaged in other countries

The United Kingdom's concern for the poorer countries can be measured by the flow of resources from the UK to the developing

Table 3.2 *Distribution of household income in the UK, 1979–1987*

	1979 % of net income	1979 cumulative %	1987 % of net income	1987 cumulative %
Bottom 20%	10.1	10.1	8.9	8.9
Next 5th	14.4	24.5	12.9	21.8
Middle 5th	18.2	42.7	16.9	38.7
Next 5th	23.0	65.7	22.2	60.9
Top 5th	34.3	100.0	39.1	100.0

Source: Central Statistical Office (1992, Table 5.16)

world. Table 3.3 shows UK overseas development assistance from 1974 to 1991. The figures show that UK overseas development assistance fell in real terms in the 1980s. As a proportion of GNP it fell from 0.52% in 1979 to 0.31% in 1989. In the mid-1970s, however, aid was fractionally above current levels as a proportion of GNP. In this sense of sustainable development, then, the UK has not met the general requirement indicated in the Brundtland Report.

How does the UK compare to other countries? In terms of percentage of GNP spent on overseas aid, Norway spent 1.1%; Denmark nearly 1% and Sweden and the Netherlands about 0.9%. Finland spent some 0.8%, France 0.6%, Canada 0.45%, Belgium and Germany 0.4%, all above the proportion spent by the UK. The USA spent only 0.2% (OECD, 1992).

ACHIEVING SUSTAINABLE DEVELOPMENT: 'GREEN' MEASURES OF ECONOMIC PROGRESS

Chapters 1 and 2 developed the idea that sustainable development means generating human well-being now without impairing the well-being of future generations. We can encapsulate this idea by talking of

Table 3.3 *UK overseas official development assistance, 1974–1991*

Year	£m current prices	£1985m constant prices	% GNP
1974	307	1089	0.37
1975	389	1083	0.38
1976	462	1187	0.38
1977	524	1113	0.37
1978	632/763	1206/1456	0.39/0.46
1979	1016	1693	0.52
1980	797	1112	0.35
1981	1080	1353	0.43
1982	1024	1192	0.37
1983	na	na	na
1984	1070	1131	0.33
1985	1184	1184	0.33
1986	1185	1154	0.31
1987	1160	1075	0.28
1988	1485	1332	0.32
1989	1584 (net)	1282	0.31
1990	1503 (net)	1137	0.27
1991	1814 (net)	1307 (est)	0.32

Source: British Aid Statistics (1992) Overseas Development Administration, London

sustainable income as that level of income that a nation can afford to consume without running down its overall capital stock. The components of this capital stock in question are man-made capital, human capital (including knowledge) and natural capital. The further consideration of this latter component of the overall capital stock can be integrated into an overall measure of sustainability to provide a 'greener' measure of economic development. In this way, measures of economic activity give a truer reflection of sustainable income and a wider interpretation of a nation's wealth in order to assess economic progress. This can further be extended to consider issues related to international trade in natural capital – ie measuring a nation's ecological footprint.

Economic progress has typically been interpreted as growth in human economic well-being. The association of growth with progress implies that we always wish to 'push on' from the level of progress we have thus far achieved. In order to give some meaning to the concept of progress, we need to have an idea of what is, or at least what approximates, 'well-being'. At the level of the national economy this has frequently been approximated by the magnitude of, and changes in, aggregate measures of economic activity – usually Gross National Product (GNP) or Gross Domestic Product (GDP). These current measures of economic activity are derived from the System of National Accounts (SNA) which, briefly, is set out as follows. Balance sheets set out the opening stock of assets at the beginning of the accounting period and the closing stocks of these assets at the end of the accounting period. The flow accounts measure production and the intervening changes in these assets during the accounting period and the resulting economic activity. The extent of this framework will be determined by the questions that society wishes to ask and the policy concerns which it wishes to address. Any framework should, in principle, be amenable to adaptation in the light of changes in these questions. 'Green' national accounts as they are also known have received a fair amount of discussion in both academic and policy-making forums. Although it is perhaps too easy to overplay the ultimate status of 'green accounts', their strength lies in providing an established framework within which heterogeneous information concerning the state of the environment can be arranged.

The increasing emphasis on issues relating to sustainable development provides one such rationale for adjustments to national accounts. The natural world can be viewed as natural capital capable of providing a flow of goods and services over time which in turn provides human well-being. If these stocks are currently being used up (ie run down) in pursuit of these ends, this is at the expense of the creation of future well-being. Ideally, we would like to record such a process within statistics such as national accounts. Yet, the current SNA fails, in almost all cases, to treat natural assets in this way. These short-comings are seen as detrimental to decision-making at the national level and the information that is recorded is biased in favour of current generations. Because of this, major efforts are under way to adjust the System of National Accounts (SNA) although these efforts are still in the process of development and are complementary to the existing accounts (see, for example, Bartelmus *et al*, 1991).

What form should the adjustments take? Some attention has been given to physical accounts, ie accounting for the volume of stocks and flows of natural resources. Indeed, Norway has experimented with accounts of this type with some success. A natural resource considered to be of strategic importance is measured in physical units (ie weight or volume) and its development over time can then be examined. Although this avoids valuation difficulties, policy-makers must use their own judgement as to whether an economy is on or off a sustainable development path (Bojo *et al*, 1990). Some physical indicators may rise and some may fall, necessitating a fair degree of overall subjective judgement in the absence of any consensus on the appropriate ranking of indicators.

A set of monetary accounts provides a basis for comparison with the more conventional measures, GNP or GDP. The SNAs already contain a parallel concept to those 'gross' measures of product, namely Net National Product (NNP) and Net Domestic Product (NDP). The production of output will involve some using up of man-made capital through the physical deterioration of machinery. This loss of assets is recorded as a 'capital consumption allowance' (CCA). This is deducted from GNP (or GDP) to obtain NNP (or NDP). The natural corollary to this is the amount of natural capital also used up, either directly or indirectly, in production processes and how can we adjust the current SNA and in particular NNP (and NDP), to account for these losses?

The value of depreciation of natural capital can take two forms: resource depletion and environmental degradation. In the former, it is the monetary value of the change in the *quantity* of the stock which is of interest. For the latter, it is the monetary value of the change in the *quality* of the stock that is of interest. It can be shown that the value of resource depletion is equivalent to depreciation (Hartwick and Hageman, 1993). Similar reasoning can be used when trying to express changes in environmental degradation in terms of deprecia-tion. The basic identity for NNP as it is usually measured (in money values) is written:

$$NNP = C + S - Detr.K_M$$

where:
NNP = Net National Product
C = consumption
S = gross national savings
$Detr.K_M$ = deterioration of man-made capital

Whereas NNP identifies only depreciation as it applies to man-made capital, 'green' NNP also recognises that the two sources of depreciation of natural capital should be deducted from sustainable income. Thus, our new identity is,

$$gNNP = C + S - Detr.K_M - Dep.K_N - Deg.K_N$$

where:
gNNP = 'green' Net National Product
$Dep.K_N$ = depletion of natural capital
$Deg.K_N$ = degradation of natural capital

Where natural capital is being used up then NNP is greater than gNNP. The new identity states that gNNP is equal to consumption plus the value of saving (although we could have used investment here) minus the sum of depreciation on the overall capital stock. gNNP can be interpreted as sustainable income after Hicks (1946). We will have more to say concerning the level of sustainable and actual consumption later. Our problem now is to derive appropriate monetary values for $Dep.K_N$ and $Deg.K_N$.

Resource depletion

The extraction of a non-renewable resource illustrates this concept of the value of resource depletion ($Dep.K_N$) in more detail. In the latter half of the 1970s the UK began exploiting its stocks of North Sea oil and so this resource can serve as an example suitable to the UK context (it could also be natural gas).

Our first question involves asking what are the determinants of the price of a unit of oil. For our purposes, this price consists of two components. The first is the marginal cost of extraction. This is the cost of extracting an additional unit of the resource. If the resource was available in infinite supply over time this might be the end of the story. However, by definition the resource is finite and we wish to consider a possible second component of price which reflects this scarcity – ie the fact that it can be and is likely to be exhausted. This second component is known as the rent. It is important to interpret this second component as a payment to future generations for using a finite resource now – it is the so-called 'price of scarcity' (Faber and Proops, 1993). For obvious reasons, the calculation of this rent is usually referred to as the 'net price' method – ie deduct the marginal cost of extraction from the market price of a unit of oil and the residual should be the rent (net price).

In order to arrive at a monetary measure for the depreciation we have to consider the total rent. This is simply the rent multiplied by the physical units of oil extracted during the accounting period. In practice, needless to say, valuation is less precise. In particular, marginal cost (MC) information is largely unavailable, so that empirical studies typically have used data on average costs (AC), which will be consistent only where MC is equal to AC. It is usually envisaged that MC will be greater than AC, where it becomes successively more difficult and hence costly to extract additional units of oil. Where total rents have been estimated using price net of average costs, depreciation is overstated and sustainable income (gNNP) is understated (Hartwick and Hageman, 1993).

Bryant and Cook (1992) have calculated estimates of total rent for the UK oil and natural gas sector using the 'net price' method. These results are presented in Table 3.4 both in terms of the absolute value (in 1985 prices) and as a percentage of GNP.

Relatively large total rents have accrued in a relatively short period in the early 1980s but fell significantly following the sharp drop in oil prices in 1986. These gains would have accrued to the extracting firms but much will go to government in the form of taxation. The question as to how to distribute these gains between generations falls directly

Table 3.4 *Estimates of total rent in the UK oil and natural gas sector*

Year	Total rents (£million, 1985 prices)	% total value of extraction	% of GDP
1980	9,200	75.9	2.8
1981	11,800	79.7	3.7
1982	12,500	77.5	3.8
1983	13,800	76.5	4.1
1984	16,300	78.6	4.7
1985	14,200	74.3	4.0
1986	4,400	50.0	1.2
1987	4,700	50.0	1.3
1988	1,700	26.7	0.4
1989	1,500	24.7	0.3
1990	1,900	28.6	0.5

Source: adapted from Bryant and Cook (1992)

upon the government. A frequent criticism has been that the UK government used these gains to increase current consumption rather than to build up new industry or technology through investment (Forsyth, 1986; Solow, 1993).

Will sustainable income be affected by a discovery? We might expect discoveries to increase sustainable income or adjusted NNP. The resource has become less scarce and hence the discovery enhances wealth. The important question is how much this affects current (sustainable) income (gNNP). It has been suggested that the total value of the discovery should be reflected in the current period sustainable income – ie rent multiplied by units discovered (Repetto, 1989; Hartwick, 1990). We could easily imagine situations where in any accounting period, the value of discoveries, calculated in this way, has exceeded the value of depletion – ie rent multiplied by units depleted. Indeed this has quite often been the case so that it is then possible to find that adjusted NNP is larger than both conventional NNP and GNP. This implies that we could consume more than our conventional accounts indicate sustainably, an implication which has caused some to question the development of 'green' national accounts (Young, 1993). Perhaps a more appropriate response to this scepticism is to find a more sensible treatment by which to reflect the effect of discoveries on sustainable income, one which does result in grossly (over-stated) counter-intuitive magnitudes. Hamilton (1993) suggests that discoveries should be valued at the marginal cost of the discovery of an additional unit of oil. This, he states, is a more defendable estimate of the price of investment in discovery effort which we would expect to be less than the rental value (described above). This is then, as before, multiplied by the units of oil discovered and its value can be used to offset the total rent from depletion accordingly.

The 'net price' method can also be applied to the depletion of renewable resources. The method is very similar to that of non-renewables but depreciation occurs only where overuse of this resource occurs – ie a rate of harvest over the rate of growth, so that the resource is being used unsustainably. Hence, the method is applicable to, for example, the forestry sector where stocks and flows are usually valued as a stock and flow of harvestable timber using market prices.

Environmental degradation

'Green' national accounting concepts can also be extended to examine changes in environmental quality such as in the case of air pollution, water pollution and soil erosion. We wish to arrive at a measure of the monetary value of environmental degradation (Deg.K_N). As with resource depletion, it is possible to treat these values as depreciation. By attempting to measure the change in a stock of, say, clean air, gNNP can be adjusted accordingly (Hartwick, 1990; Mäler, 1991). Again, this can be done by valuing the flows in the accounting period rather than the change in the value of the stock itself – eg the physical indication of which is the decrease or increase in environmental quality during the accounting period. However, as there is usually no market price for this degradation the 'net price' method cannot be used as in the case of depletion. Yet, some progress is possible and as Hartwick (1990) shows, there are two main effects we need to bear in mind when assessing possible values.

Firstly, decreases in environmental quality will have implications for productive potential and therefore future output and an allowance must be made for this asset erosion. Bartelmus *et al* (1991) value environmental degradation by the potential costs of restoration or abatement – ie the cost of returning the asset to its qualitative state at the beginning of the accounting period. Hartwick (1990) has shown that this is adequate if we use the marginal costs of abatement or restoration. An alternative requirement often proposed is to value the cost of returning the asset to an acceptable level of quality such as that set by a standard. Here, any unrestored degradation at the end of the accounting period will be 'carried over' and revalued in addition to degradation in the next accounting period.

Secondly, negative changes in environmental quality will also directly affect the well-being of individuals through loss of amenity. This is an additional loss which explicitly recognises the direct use and consumption of the services provided by natural capital – ie not used as input to the production of goods and services that individuals ultimately consume. Again, there is no market price for us to infer the value of an additional unit of pollution damage to individuals (and to add a further complication this should reflect the future loss entailed as well) (Mäler, 1991). This price might be inferred from direct valuation methods as in, for example, the setting up of experimental or surrogate markets – stated preference techniques such as contingent valuation methods. Work undertaken on valuation in this area has concluded that this research is often more fruitful than many might believe, but large problem areas remain (Pearce, Bann and Georgiou, 1992). However, while the implication of these valuation techniques for use in 'green' national accounts is limited, an illustration of a possible application is given in the next section.

One final aspect of the current debate is whether defensive expenditures can be considered part of sustainable income. Defensive expenditures consist of actual expenditures made to offset negative changes in well-being of some description. The most commonly stated argument is that as the expenditure is not undertaken in order to enhance well-being, it must not be included in sustainable income. An exact delineation of defensive and non-defensive expenditures is arbitrary. In fact, an often stated criticism is that in its logical extreme all expenditures are defensive, in that they are purchased in order to fulfil a need or want, however frivolous we might consider this to be. On this basis, sustainable income is zero. However, the debate usually restricts attention to the portion of expenditure that is devoted to mitigating adverse *environmental* change. Although, as Hamilton (1992) points out, the same logic applies as the expenditure does indeed contribute to well-being albeit in the face of pollution which has negative effects on well-being. We have argued in favour of valuing environmental degradation itself, so there is no need to also deduct the value of defensive expenditures (Mäler, 1991) for to do so implies double-counting. In fact, stated this way, environmental defensive expenditure designed to maintain or enhance stocks of natural capital such as pollution abatement might be treated as actual investment in natural capital.

An advantage of defensive expenditures is that they are observable and data can be found on these purchases. It is tempting therefore to use estimates of defensive expenditure as a proxy for Deg.K_N. This approximation may not be satisfactory but might provide some useful insights, in the absence of any more suitable value. ECOTEC (1993) estimated environmental defensive expenditures in the UK at £14 billion in 1990. This corresponds to about 2.5% of GNP in that year. Over half of this (£7.3 billion) is accounted for by pollution abatement. This result can be placed in the context of estimates of environmental damage for the USA, Japan, Germany (pre-unification) and Finland. The results are presented in Table 3.5, although strictly speaking they

Table 3.5 *Estimates of environmental degradation*

Country	Nature of damage	Year	Damage (% GNP)
Finland	Air pollution	1989	1.6
Germany	Air and water pollution	1990/1	4.4
Japan	Air and water pollution, waste disposal	1985	2.4
UK	Air and water pollution, waste disposal	1990	2.5
USA	Air and water pollution	1981	3.6

Sources: Finland, Offerstrom (1992); Germany, Pearce (1991); Japan, Uno (1991); UK, ECOTEC (1993); USA, Freeman (1990)

are not comparable, for each employs a different valuation technique for different aspects of damage for different years. Tentatively, Table 3.5 does indicate some order of magnitude of this 'damage' in the region of 1.6 to 4.4% of GNP.

We have argued that the degradation of environmental quality (Deg.K_N) decreases sustainable income in the same way as Detr.K_M and Dep.K_N. It therefore forms our last deduction to obtain gNNP. What has not been emphasised is that while Detr.K_M and Dep.K_N are deducted from GNP in order to obtain gNNP, Deg.K_N is an imputation that is 'dropped' into the identity for gNNP. It is not part of GNP as currently measured because, in the main, GNP measures marketed transactions. Harrison (1989) suggests that this depreciation should logically be included in an (adjusted) GNP (eg gGNP), which (perhaps ironically) implies increasing GNP by the value of Deg.K_N and then subtracting this value out to obtain gNNP along with our other depreciation terms. Harrison (1993) suggests that this is a logical step and not so perverse as it at first sounds, because it is the relative size (year-to-year changes or country comparisons) of these magnitudes that is usually emphasised rather than absolute values. GNP and NNP will also be understated by the value of non-marketed environmental services which could also be included in an expanded measure of welfare such as gGNP and gNNP (Peskin, 1989). The following section provides an example of this in the UK.

GREEN NET NATIONAL PRODUCT IN THE UK AGRICULTURAL SECTOR

Adger and Whitby (1993) impute values for some of the non-marketed services provided by natural capital within the UK agricultural and forestry sector and show how these relate to an adjusted sectoral account. These services would not be recorded in the standard accounts. Environmental services are non-marketed outputs supplied by natural capital while environmental damage (or degradation) is depreciation from the using up of an asset. Box 3.1 illustrates the results.

The services that are measured include the net value of carbon fixing which is positive – ie net of sectoral emissions. Other services include the recreational and amenity values of conservation areas which are valued using price data obtained from contingent valuation studies. Similar valuation techniques are used to value depreciation of natural capital – ie water quality deterioration. Government defensive expenditures are deducted on the basis that they do not add to welfare but, given the comments in the previous section, we might reasonably

Box 3.1
UK AGRICULTURAL AND FORESTRY ACCOUNTS

	Sustainable net product	£ million 1988
	GNP	5498
minus	Depreciation on man-made capital	1470
equals	**NNP**	4028
minus	Degradation of natural capital: (water pollution −11)	−11
minus	Defensive expenditures: (government expenditure to maintain landscape and conserved areas and to clean up pollution)	−58
equals	**ENVIRONMENTAL DAMAGE**	77
plus	Net carbon fixing	146
plus	Biodiversity	94
plus	Amenity: (of which: green belt +642 national parks +152)	794
equals	**ENVIRONMENTAL SERVICES**	1034
equals	gNNP	4993

Source: Adger and Whitby (1993)

question this deduction. Yet, we might wish to view the imputation as an approximation of (unmeasured) depreciation of natural capital. Overall the measured value of damage is less than the measured value of services. Therefore an adjusted sustainable NNP is greater than conventional NNP for this sector. The difference is substantial – in the region of 25 per cent. We should conclude that the results are partial and that many losses are excluded: slurry incidents and amenity and biodiversity loss through the loss of hedgerows are two such examples.

BALANCE SHEETS: ACCOUNTING FOR STOCKS OF NATURAL CAPITAL

In presenting a procedure for estimating sustainable income (gNNP) we have avoided the need to value stocks of natural capital directly. Sustainable development is a dynamic concept tied to concerns of the well-being of future generations (in addition to ensuring current well-being). While the concept of sustainable income is a useful tool for evaluating these issues, we must not lose sight of the complementary need for accounting for national wealth. This will entail the valuing of stocks and assets which can be presented in balance sheets. National wealth reflects the future production potential of an economy. Put this way, it is not surprising that conditions for sustainable development have been couched in terms of maintaining stocks of capital or in the case of strong sustainability, stocks of natural capital (see Chapter 2). Scott (1956) emphasised that knowledge of the path and extent of the underlying capital stock of a nation could inform the analysis of economic development. A narrow view of wealth can distort our perceptions of the wealth of a nation, especially in countries that are resource-rich (Hamilton, 1989). In particular, Scott stressed the now widely held view, that defining an increase in wealth narrowly in terms of increases in man-made capital does not necessarily indicate an overall increase in the wealth of a nation where natural capital is being run down to facilitate these increases.

National accounts record wealth in balance sheets. National wealth is made up of three components (Hamilton *et al*, 1993). Net financial assets and human-made tangible assets are respectively the net claim on foreign assets and the components of human-made capital. Where possible, natural capital stocks should be recorded in this way. Two problems arise in attempting to fulfil this requirement. The first is finding a correct measure of extent of the resource (volume or weight that makes up the physical account). The second problem is applying an appropriate value to these units of extent (monetary account). Hence, for obvious reasons, measurement will for the most part concern tangible privately owned natural assets such as mineral assets. Measurement difficulties are certainly not eliminated under these conditions (such as finding the extent of economically extractable oil) but are certainly more amenable to treatment, than for intangible, publicly owned assets such as the stock of clean air for which the problems become intractable. In the area in between, some natural assets are tangible yet are publicly owned so that no markets exist to derive the price of the services provided. If it is possible to impute values for these non-marketed services then it is also possible to derive some sort of stock value – ie the present value of the flow of non-marketed services over the lifetime of the natural asset. In fact, in this way the various different – mutually exclusive – uses of natural capital can be compared (Hartwick, 1993).

The examination of trends in total wealth can provide a useful complement to measurement of sustainable development based on the analysis of flows such as sustainable income. However, it is primarily the latter which we emphasise in the next section.

SUSTAINABLE DEVELOPMENT IN THE UK: A TEST

Earlier chapters discussed the conditions for sustainable development. Here, we have examined the implications of 'green' national accounts. The use value of these modifications is stressed as a measure of sustainable income – ie the maximum income that can be consumed forever and so leave each generation with the same level of well-being. If we equate gNNP with sustainable income, an indicator of sustainability is whether gNNP is non-decreasing over time (Bojo *et al*, 1990). Declining gNNP would indicate past trends of consumption in excess of the sustainable level. It would also be desirable to know how much of sustainable income that we actually consumed now (Proops, 1991). An approach that allows us to ask whether or not our present consumption exceeds sustainable consumption requires a focus on the relationship between non-declining well-being and constant capital in terms of a 'savings rule' (Hartwick, 1978; Solow, 1986). A rule that emerges from this reasoning states that an economy must save at least as much as the sum of the depreciation on the value of depreciation of human-made and natural capital ie ($S \geq Detr.K_M - Dep.K_N - Deg.K_N$). This can be reinterpreted as an index of sustainability by which countries could be ranked if we had some uniform criteria for measuring the depreciation of natural capital (Pearce and Atkinson, 1993).

Table 3.6 calculates this rule for the UK during the period 1980–1990 using estimates of gross national savings (S), depreciation on man-made capital (Detr.K_M) and the data from Bryant and Cook (1992) concerning total rents in the oil and natural gas sector (Dep.K_N). All are expressed as a percentage of GNP. This last figure is augmented by an approximation of the value of environmental degradation (Deg.K_N) which is assumed to be a constant proportion of GNP (2.5%) in each period (based on ECOTEC's findings for 1990 cited above). The figure in the last column gives an estimate of adjusted net savings ie ($S - Detr.K_M - Dep.K_N - Deg.K_N$) as a percentage of GNP.

Table 3.6 *A sustainable development test for the UK*

Year	S	Detr.K_M	Dep.K_N + Deg.K_N	Adjusted net savings sustainability index
1980	19.0	12.1	5.3	1.6
1981	18.1	12.4	6.2	−0.5
1982	17.6	12.0	6.3	−0.7
1983	17.8	11.8	6.6	−0.6
1984	17.6	11.8	7.2	−1.4
1985	18.4	11.7	6.5	0.2
1986	16.7	11.6	3.7	1.4
1987	16.7	11.3	3.8	1.6
1988	16.5	11.2	2.9	2.4
1989	16.5	10.9	2.8	3.7
1990	17.0	11.0	3.0	3.0

Sources: Bryant and Cook (1992), World Bank (1991), Central Statistical Office (1992)

Table 3.6 shows that this ratio was negative through much of the early 1980s. This indicates that the UK was not on a sustainable growth path for at least some of the period looked at. Figure 3.2 depicts this information in the form of a graph and compares it with the paths of gross savings (S) and net savings (S − Detr.K_M). Net savings in contrast to adjusted net savings (our sustainability) remain positive over the period. In fact, the latter only begins to climb above 1% after a fall in the value of natural capital depreciation which stems from a large drop in the total rents from the depletion of North Sea oil. Given the constancy of deterioration of man-made capital, the assumed constancy of degradation and the slight fall in gross savings it seems that the failure to remain on a sustainable path might be attributed to a dissipation of the total rents from oil and natural gas in current consumption as earlier implied. The average adjusted net savings ratio over the period is below 1%.

The test described above is for 'weak' sustainability. As such, it takes the form of a savings rule which states that the value of depreciation on natural capital did not matter in so far as this value was reinvested in other forms of income-generating assets as a form of actual compensation to future generations. These savings are usually assumed to be channelled into investments in man-made capital but can easily be envisaged to be in knowledge, pollution abatement, renewable natural capital – anything that enhances the productive potential of an econ-

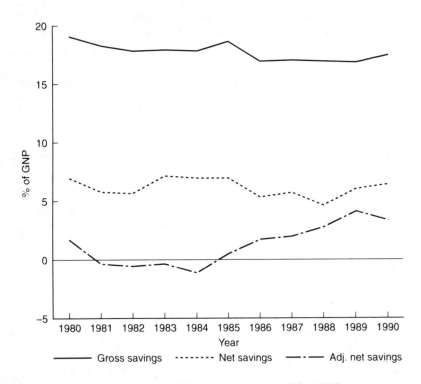

Figure 3.2 *United Kingdom savings ratios, 1980–1990*

omy. The assumption of substitutability is seen as a disadvantage of weak sustainability. In addition the test ignores factors such as technological change and population growth that will also influence the well-being of future generations. However, the test is able to provide at least some indications of sustainability at the macro-level in the UK by showing how an adjusted net savings measure causes us to revise the provisions actually made for future generations through capital bequests (made during the period 1980–1990).

If investment in alternative forms of wealth cannot be a substitute for the 'running down' of natural capital then compensation in the form of a strong sustainability rule might seem the appropriate constraint (see Chapter 2). How might we measure this constraint using the concepts introduced in this chapter? First of all, we have to decide what it is we wish to keep constant for, as Chapter 2 showed, the term 'constant natural capital' can take different meanings although three main variants stand out: maintain the total natural capital stock allowing for changes in the components of this stock (ie deplete non-renewables but build up renewables etc.); maintain 'critical' natural capital but allow for the possible use of the remainder of the natural capital stock according to a weak sustainability rule; treat all components of natural capital as 'critical' and maintain each individual component intact (ie each performs a unique 'critical' function). This last condition seems too stringent so we deal with the former two.

If it is the value of natural capital that we wish to maintain constant (rather than some physical quantity) then the concept of depreciation of natural capital can be of some use. Just as capital consumption allowance (CCA) provides an aggregate estimate of the Detr.K_M (in theory the sum of all individual Detr.K_M within the economy) then a similar estimation might be attempted for depreciation of natural capital (taking into account the sums of all significant individual changes in the quantity and quality of the various components). Given that we wish to maintain the stock of natural capital then a savings rule would need to identify the uses of savings to make sure that any overall depreciation is offset by investments in natural capital. If, however, certain components of natural capital provide 'critical' functions then measurement of sustainability would entail examining the path of these stocks over time separately. Any depreciation of 'critical' capital could be taken as a sign of unsustainability. A savings rule would not suffice because due to factors such as irreversibility – ie 'critical' natural capital cannot simply be run-down and then built-up – once it is gone it is lost forever.

Where natural capital is essential for human well-being in this way total economic value would be high, indicating that the depreciation from running down the stock would be large, indicating the loss entailed. It is therefore doubtful that alternative investments could generate the same return.

INTERNATIONAL TRADE AND 'ECOLOGICAL FOOTPRINTS'

So far we have considered the estimation of sustainable income for an economy in isolation. Similarly, the savings rule discussed in the previous section also implicitly assumed a closed economy – ie one without international trade, or assumes that this makes no difference to our conclusions. However, many resources are traded internationally and while the effects of environmental degradation are felt in a particular country the causes often may originate elsewhere. With this in mind it becomes possible to import or export sustainability which may change the nature of compensation for future generations suggested above. This potential was discussed in *Blueprint 1*.

Proops and Atkinson (1993) show how the results for the type of weak sustainability test described above would change if we consider international trade in natural resources. Firstly, we have to distinguish between resources used by an economy (ie imports and domestic use) and resources used for an economy (ie exports) in terms of final use or demand. In the closed economy rule a country would be required to save at least as much as the value of total rents from its resource-extracting activities without distinguishing between domestic use and exports. Now, the country is only required to save the total rents from the resource that is used domestically (ie net price times units of resource for domestic use). However, if the country imports the resource then it must save at least as much as the total rents in the value of the imported resource. On these terms, a country that currently uses little of its own resources but imports resources from another country might be unsustainable even though on our first (closed economy) rule it would look sustainable. Conversely we might find the opposite result for the resource exporter. The results for the open economy case might be interpreted as the compensation from the importer to the exporter for final use of the resource.

CONCLUSIONS

Measurements of 'sustainable income', achieved through modifications of the national accounts, can be used to give a first approximation of the sustainability or otherwise of an economy. In this respect, 'green' national accounts in the form of gNNP can be interpreted as an attempt to reflect the logic of the 'natural capital' school at the national level, where important decisions regarding the achievement of a sustainable development path are appropriately dealt with. A weak sustainability test can be achieved by examining the path of savings taking into consideration the need to compensate for the depreciation of capital – man-made and natural. The resulting net savings measure can be re-interpreted as an index of sustainability. This chapter suggests that such an index was negative for the United Kingdom for at least part of the period 1980–1990, although took an average value of just below 1. This was in part due to (a) the need to make good pollution damage, and (b) the running down of natural resources not made good by compensatory investment. We might conclude that the extent of this modified framework is to be determined by practical issues of strategic importance to sustainable development, rather than the wholesale application of national accounting concepts as applied to all natural resources within a particular economy. A reappraisal in the light of the desire to measure strong sustainability involves a more detailed examination of the natural capital stock and in particular the 'criticality' of the functions that the components of the total stock provide. The framework provided by national accounts offers a way to organise this analysis, although it remains useful to see these activities as a complement to, rather than a substitute for, other environmental data.

PART II

Sustainability and the state of the UK environment

——— ◆ ———

Chapter 4

Air quality

AIR QUALITY IN THE UK

Air pollution problems range from the potentially hazardous emission of gases like carbon monoxide to the fairly innocuous nuisance of odours from agricultural practices. Polluting effects can either occur directly or are due to secondary pollutants, which form as a result of chemical reactions of the original emissions with other substances in the atmosphere. Damage depends on the concentration level of a pollutant as well as on the duration of exposure of the affected population or environment. In some cases damage will not occur until a certain threshold level is exceeded, in others the impacts will be felt immediately. Air pollution impacts may occur locally, regionally or globally. The present chapter deals with the 'classic' local and regional air pollution problems associated with sulphur dioxide (SO_2), nitrogen oxides (NO_x), suspended particulates ('smoke') and tropospheric ozone (O_3). Global environmental problems of climatic change and the depletion of the (stratospheric) ozone layer will be the subject of Chapter 11. Transport related emissions will be discussed in the context of Chapter 10 on transport.

Current exposure levels with respect to major pollutants are summarised in Table 4.1. Over the last two decades SO_2 concentrations in the UK have steadily decreased from about 250 μg/m^3 in 1976/77 to about 110 g/m^3 in 1991/92 (DoE, 1992c; unweighted average of reported sites). This positive trend is due to a variety of reasons, including the imposition of stricter environmental regulations, but is probably chiefly the result of a general switch from sulphur-rich coal to other, less polluting fuels. Sulphur dioxide, together with black smoke, can cause temporary breathing problems and may increase the risk of respiratory diseases particularly for vulnerable groups like the elderly, children and persons with asthma. Its main impact however is as a precursor to acid rain.

The other major component of acid rain is emissions of nitrogen oxides. Through reaction with volatile organic compounds (VOCs), NO_x are also the main source for the formation of ground level ozone. Less notably, nitrogen oxides are pollutants in their own right,

Table 4.1 *Air pollution and pollutants in the UK*

Pollutant	Concentration/ exposure (1991/92)[a,b]	Threshold level[a,c]	Emission sources (1991)
Sulphur dioxide (SO_2)	110 µg/m^3	350/250 µg/m^3 [d]	Power stations (71%) Industry (16%) Domestic (4%)
Nitrogen oxides (NO_x)	67 ppb	104.6 ppb	Road transport (51%) Power stations (26%) Industry (8%)
Black smoke	81 µg/m^3	250 µg/m^3	Road transport (42%) Domestic (35%) Industry (15%)
Volatile organic compounds (VOC)	Various, depending on compound	various, depending on compound	Processes and solvents (44%) Road transport (36%) Offshore oil and gas (10%)
Tropospheric ozone	2 days with VOCs, 1 hour mean > 90 ppb	–	Reaction between NO_x and O_3 in the presence of sunlight
Acid rain	Various, depending on region	Depending on soil characteristics[e]	Chemical reaction involving SO_2, NO_x and Cl^-

Notes:
[a] 98th percentile daily concentration – ie the level exceeded by the highest 2% of daily mean values measured during the year
[b] Unweighed averages of the sites reported in DoE (1992a, b). Peak values may considerably exceed national average
[c] EC directives, unless otherwise stated
[d] 350 µg/m^3 for smoke concentrations below 150 µg/m^3, 250 µg/m^3 otherwise
[e] Eg critical loads calculated on behalf of UNECE (see section 4.5)

Source: Department of the Environment (1992a, b)

affecting crops and reducing plant growth. The health impacts of NO_x are however ambiguous, and epidemiological studies have so far failed to find significant morbidity impacts. The average concentration of nitrogen oxides has strongly increased over the last years, in the case of NO_2 by as much as 35% between 1986 and 1991. This is mainly due to a similar expansion in road traffic – the main source of NO_x emissions. Exposure is highest in urban areas and along busy roadside locations, where air quality frequently has to be classified as 'poor' or 'very poor', in some locations as often as once or twice a month on average (see DoE, 1992a).

The term 'acid rain' describes the deposition of SO_2, NO_x and chloride (Cl⁻) molecules in their respective acidic form, either dry through absorption by plants, trees or soils, or as wet deposits in rain, snow, hail or mist. Acid rain can cause a variety of damages to lakes, forests and buildings, as well as triggering the release of further harmful substances such as aluminium. Strongly acidic rainfall in Britain is recorded eg in Yorkshire and Humberside, while the west coast is generally less affected. Overall exposure also depends on the amount of rainfall, and the highest acidic loads in Britain are found in Northern Scotland, Cumbria, Wales and the Pennines, where a high acidity is coupled with high precipitation rates. Not all soils are equally resistant to acid depositions. Land with high concentrations in calcium and magnesium is better able to absorb acids and is thus generally less vulnerable to acid rain than areas with low concentrations of these substances. Particularly vulnerable soils are found in Northern Ireland, Wales and the Scottish Highlands. Given the above exposure patterns, these are also the regions most severely affected by acid rain.

Ground level ozone is formed through a series of chemical reactions between nitrogen oxides and VOCs, with sunlight being a necessary catalyst. Ozone concentrations are therefore highest in summer, as temperatures rise above 20°C. Exposure follows a clear geographical pattern with highest concentrations in the south and south-east, and lower levels in the north. Ozone can cause considerable crop damage, as well as having significant health effects. Long term exposure to high ozone levels may lead to chronic lung diseases and lung cancer.

THE INTERNATIONAL DIMENSION

The previous section highlighted four major areas of air pollution: SO_2 and NO_x emissions, acid deposition and ground level ozone. The latter two are secondary pollutants which are formed through chemical reactions of SO_2 and NO_x in the case of acid rain, and NO_x and VOCs in the case of tropospheric ozone. Improvements in air quality will therefore mainly depend on reductions in the emission levels of SO_2, NO_x, and VOCs. However, achieving these is not entirely a unilateral problem. Carried by air currents, pollutants can be transported over long distances, and emissions affecting the UK need therefore not necessarily have their origin in the UK. Conversely, British emissions do not affect only the UK but may be exported to the countries on the continent.

The dispersion pattern of most air pollutants is now quite well understood. Since 1978 the movements of SO_2 and more recently NOx emissions are monitored by the European Monitoring and Evaluation Programme (EMEP). Although dispersion may vary from day to day depending on weather conditions, an average picture can be drawn on the basis of average weather patterns observed over a longer period of time. An aggregated version of the 1991 EMEP transportation matrix for sulphur is reproduced in Table 4.2. It has to be read as follows. Rows tell us how much pollution from abroad a particular country was exposed to, while the corresponding column describes the spread of the country's own emissions. Thus in 1991 the UK received eg 38,000 tonnes of SO_2 from Germany and 52,000 tSO_2 from the rest of Western Europe. The table shows that in the case of the UK by far the largest part, 1 million tSO_2 or 85% of total depositions, were 'home made' and originated from sources within the country itself, one of the highest shares of domestic depositions observed. The major external source of depositions was Germany, accounting for a mere 5% of the total. In turn the UK exported 95,000 tSO_2 of its own emissions to Germany. UK depositions were particularly important for Scandinavia, where they accounted for more than 11% of total depositions (20% in Norway). On the whole, the UK was exporting almost ten times as much SO_2 as it received.

Because air pollution is transmitted across national borders, international agreements have emerged to deal with the problem. In 1979 the Convention on Long Range Transboundary Air Pollution was signed in Geneva. It came into force in March 1983 and was ratified by the UK in 1982. This was the first major attempt to secure concerted action on acid rain. Conventions are implemented through Protocols, and the first Protocol under the 1979 agreement related to sulphur dioxide and was adopted in July 1985 in Helsinki. It called for a 30 per cent reduction in emissions by each signatory country by 1993 on a base year of 1980. This was the '30 per cent Club'. The UK did not sign and neither did the USA, but the USA was already beginning the process of designing its own legislation to deal with cross-border pollution with Canada.

In 1988 a nitrogen dioxide Protocol was agreed in Sofia, entering into force early in 1991. This committed signatories to a freeze on emissions at 1987 levels by 1994. Twelve countries additionally committed themselves to a reduction of 30 per cent in NO_x emissions. The UK ratified this Protocol in 1990. Why did the UK sign one agreement but not the other? Reducing sulphur emissions means addressing energy production generally through conservation and fuel switching, as well as through add-on technologies such as flue gas desulphurisation (FGD). The issue of cost was therefore of paramount

Table 4.2 Origins of sulphur depositions in Europe, 1991 *(1000t SO₂)*

Receivers	UK	GER	SCA	Emitters WEU	FSU	EEU	O/U	Total
United Kingdom (UK)	1052	38	2	52	3	15	69	1232
Germany (GER)	95	1951	14	205	8	304	122	2699
Scandinavia (SCA)	134	173	251	39	140	137	277	1151
Other Western Europe (WEU)	218	429	7	2477	30	476	533	4171
Former Soviet Union (FSU)	53	359	93	62	3785	953	1142	6446
Eastern Europe (EEU)	59	1014	25	231	236	4701	441	6707
Other/unknown (O/U)	1295	743	211	1676	561	1041	2819	8345
Total	2906	4705	604	4741	4763	7628	5404	30751

Note: Figures denote depositions caused or experienced by countries; they will usually be differ from emission estimates

Source: Sandnes (1992)

concern in the UK, at a time when coal remained the main energy source for electricity. Controlling NOx entails addressing energy production and the transport sector, and the UK probably felt it had more scope for the latter.

Currently, a new sulphur Protocol is being negotiated – the first one expiring in 1993. Targets are likely to be of the order of 60 per cent reductions in SOx depositions across the UN Economic Commission for Europe region (Europe, Eastern Europe, Scandinavia and the Europe-adjacent parts of the old Soviet Union). But since responsibility for concentrations varies between countries, the target for the UK emissions reductions may be 60 per cent or more. The very long term objective in the Protocol will be 'critical loads', a measure of sulphur deposition at which, basically, no environmental damage is done – see Box 4.1. But the cost of reaching critical loads, which in fact is impossible to achieve everywhere, is unquestionably expensive. The initial agreement will therefore be for 'target loads' expressed as some percentage of critical loads.

EMISSIONS OF AIR POLLUTANTS IN THE UK

Will the UK be able to fulfil its international commitments? The answer hinges on Britain's future use of fossil fuels and in particular of coal. With the exception of VOCs, the emission of air pollutants in the UK is almost entirely linked to fossil fuel use (DTI, 1992), and typically stems from power generation, transportation and various industrial processes – see Table 4.3.

In 1991 SO_2 emissions in the UK amounted to some 3.5 million tonnes. About two-thirds of these were released from power stations, and more than three-quarters were due to the combustion of coal. The EC Large Combustion Plant Directive requires a reduction in SO_2 emissions from large combustion plants of 20 per cent by 1993 and 60 per cent by 2003, compared to 1980 levels. Already emissions from these sources are below the 1993 target, and further reductions should be relatively cheap to achieve. The UK's Environmental Protection Act of 1990 obliges firms to adopt 'best available technologies, not entailing excessive cost' (BATNEEC), to minimise polluting emissions. In practice this typically involves the installation of 'end of pipe' scrubbers like flue gas desulphurisation (FGD) techniques which remove sulphur from releases before discharging them into the atmosphere. The installation of FGD on new plants may raise the cost of generating electricity by some 10 to 15 per cent, according to estimates by Newbery (1990). Compliance with the long run EC target is further facilitated by a continuing shift away from coal to natural gas

Box 4.1
CRITICAL LOADS AND COST-BENEFIT ANALYSIS

A critical load effectively corresponds to a point above which 'damage' occurs to ecosystems or some environmental asset such as soils, trees etc. The load in question is the deposition of a pollutant, for example sulphur dioxide. In the diagram we have converted the physical damage into monetary damage in order to make a comparison between the critical loads approach and the cost-benefit approach. Basically, we assume all physical damage has an economic cost. The 'damage function' begins at a point 'CL', the critical load. Below this point no damage occurs – the ecosystem in question assimilates that much pollution without any problem. The lower diagram shows the same picture but this time it plots the extra damage done from an extra unit of deposition of pollution. This 'extra damage' is known as 'marginal damage' in economic language. The lower diagram also shows a 'marginal cost' curve, ie the extra cost that has to be paid to reduce deposition by one more unit. Note this curve slopes upwards from right to left, indicating that it costs more and more to get less and less pollution.

The 'critical load' approach says that we should aim for point CL, and, interpreted literally, it says we should do this without reference to the cost of achieving critical loads. This is clearly not tenable from a policy standpoint, so policy tends to be formulated in terms of 'target loads', some kind of politically acceptable level of deposition. Another point that could be aimed for is shown by 'CB', the point where marginal costs just equal marginal damages. The idea here is that to the left of CB it costs more to reduce depositions than society gets back in benefits. To the right, costs are less than benefits. So, CB is an 'optimum' in cost-benefit terms. Target loads could be anywhere to the right of CL, such as TL' TL".

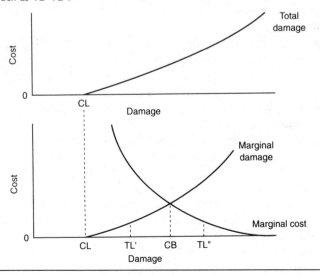

Table 4.3 *The sources of conventional air pollution in the UK, 1991 (%)*

Source	Pollutant					
	SO_x	NO_x	TSP	VOCs	CO_2	CH_4
Power stations	71	37	5	–	33	–
Other industry	16	12	15	2	22	
Road transport	2	34	42	36	19	–
Domestic/commercial	6	6	36	2	21	–
Offshore oil/gas	–	2	–	10	–	–
Processes/solvents	–	–	–	44	–	–
Coal mining	–	–	–	–	–	22
Gas leakage	–	–	–	–	–	11
Landfill	–	–	–	–	–	29
Livestock	–	–	–	–	–	31
Other	5	9	2	6	5	7

Notes: '–' generally means zero or insignificant (< 1%) but occasionally some sources, such as offshore oil and gas, are included in 'other'.

Power stations and road transport are seen to be the major sectors giving rise to air pollution, but in terms of global pollutants the agricultural sector, gas leakage and waste disposal are also important

Source: HM Government, *Digest of Environmental Protection and Water Statistics*, No15, 1992, HMSO, London

and other less polluting fuels, a trend which is unlikely to be significantly halted by the recently raised concerns about the future of the coal industry. The Helsinki target of a 30 per cent reduction seems therefore within Britain's reach, although, ironically, the UK did not sign this protocol.

The NO_x target on the other hand, which the UK is committed to, appears more difficult to meet. The EC Large Combustion Plant Directive requires a 15 per cent reduction in NOx emissions from these sources by 1993, and 30 per cent by 1998. The 1993 target has already been met, and the installation of further low-nitrogen oxide burners should assure compliance with the 1998 target. However, in 1991 releases from large combustion plants accounted for only about a third of all emissions. The dominant emission source is road transport, a sector which has steadily gained in importance over the last ten years. In 1980 transport-related NOx emissions accounted for only about a third of the total, today their share has risen to over 50 per cent. Although the installation of catalytic converters, now compulsory on new cars, may go some way towards curbing emissions there, meeting the Sofia target will therefore prove difficult, unless further measures are introduced.

The introduction of catalytic converters will also help to reduce emissions of VOCs. However, sources of VOC emissions are many, and the transport sector accounts for only about one third of them. VOC emissions have slowly but steadily increased over the last decade, growing at about 0.6 per cent per annum. Under the Long Range Transboundary Air Pollution Convention, Britain is required to reduce these emissions by 30 per cent from 1988 to 1999. Whether the UK will be able to comply with this regulation remains to be seen. Quite predictably, further measures will have to be imposed.

OPTIMAL ABATEMENT AND THE SOCIAL COSTS OF AIR POLLUTION DAMAGE

How important is the control of 'conventional' air pollution? As Chapter 1 indicated, modern environmental policy tends to evolve as a series of reactions to particular issues, rather than as a considered response to an exercise in which priorities are ranked according to agreed criteria. Policy on conventional air pollution is complicated by the transboundary nature of the acidic pollutants, sulphur oxides and nitrogen oxides. Damage done to another country by emissions in one country prompts international attention. Chapter 1 suggested that important indicators would include human health, some measure of excess 'insult' to the environment over its carrying capacity for pollution, and monetary measures of damage. This section reports some very approximate measures of monetary damage.

Chapter 3 reviewed the idea of monetised environmental damage which was discussed extensively in *Blueprint 1* (Pearce, Markandya and Barbier, 1989). Box 4.2 shows some estimates of damage done by sulphur oxides and nitrogen oxides for the United Kingdom.

It is important to note that the figures relate to the UK only: they do not include damage done to other countries in Europe and Scandinavia because of the transboundary movement of UK pollution emissions.

Box 4.2 suggests that damage in the UK from acid rain may well amount to between £1.3 and £3.3 billion each year. The true figure is probably closer to the lower end of this range since the ECOTEC figure for health damage may be suspect: few studies find associations between health damage and acid rain. On the other hand, US research suggests that health damage from suspended particulate matter ('smoke') is significant and any policy that controls sulphur and nitrogen oxides is likely also to control particulate matter since they are jointly produced. The ECOTEC figure may not therefore be an exaggeration.

Box 4.2

MONETARY VALUE OF ACID RAIN DAMAGE IN THE UK

Estimating pollution damages in monetary terms is complex and requires use of 'dose–response' functions. These measure the physical damage done by pollution depositions (the dose). Dose–response functions are disputed. The economic dimension is added by looking at the loss of output or the loss of the asset in question (the response). For example, if we know that air pollution does a certain amount of damage to tree growth then the market price of the timber lost can be used to value the damage. Health costs can be estimated by looking at the health impacts and multiplying them by the 'value of a statistical life' (VOSL) – which is discussed in Chapter 10 – or the economic cost of a day's illness. The estimates below are provisional since the work in question is still under way. They exclude damage from particulate matter. Some studies suggest this could be very large due to the association between particulates and human health damage.

	Cost (£ million pa)	
	ECOTEC (SO$_2$)	CSERGE (SO$_2$ + NO$_x$)
Buildings	408	392
Health	2000	393
Crops	110	165
Trees	790	356
Total	3308	1306

Sources: ECOTEC estimates taken from ECOTEC (1992). CSERGE estimates prepared for this volume and based on unit costs in Pearce (1993a)

Is the £1–3 billion lost to the UK economy? If it were costless to control the pollution then these sums do represent genuine losses. The idea of costless control is not absurd. For example, if capital equipment is replaced and the new equipment is both more productive and cleaner, then the environmental benefits can be thought of as a kind of bonus – a something for nothing. Certainly, a great deal of technical change has these characteristics (a fact that explains why some countries appear to secure both fast economic growth and reduced pollution burdens).

At the other extreme, if pollution is controlled with 'add on' equipment, such as flue gas desulphurisation (FGD) plant, then there will be positive costs to the economy. If the UK had to rely on FGD plant alone to achieve substantial reductions of around 90 per cent in

SO_2 emissions, costs might be in the region of £1.4 billion pa, suggesting that costs and benefits either just balance, or, if the ECOTEC figures are correct, that benefits outweigh costs.

There are several reasons for thinking that such a comparison points to strong support for vigorous acid rain control in the UK:

- In practice, a policy based on FGD plant alone is very inefficient. Other means of reducing emissions are cheaper, including fuel switching (from high to low sulphur fuels) and energy conservation. Hence the costs of control are likely to be much less than £1.4 billion pa.

- Fuel switching and conservation measures affect both SO_2 and NO_x whereas FGD plant affects sulphur emissions only.

- FGD plant actual *lowers* the thermal efficiency of fuel burning, which means that carbon dioxide (a greenhouse gas) emissions actually increase. Looked at one way, this suggests that an FGD policy would be even more expensive than £1.4 billion pa since the additional damage from global warming would need to be added. Looked at another way, FGD policy is clearly to be avoided if there are alternatives, which there are.

- Policies that control carbon dioxide will also tend to be of the fuel switching/conservation type, so that they too will reduce sulphur and nitrogen emissions. An integrated air pollution control policy is therefore likely to be most cost-effective.

- The benefits figures in Box 4.2 omit any damages from transboundary pollution caused by the UK, whereas the costs of FGD, if effected, would reduce transboundary damage. Once mainland European and Scandinavian damages are accounted for, the benefit–cost ratio widens significantly.

All this suggests that the costs of controlling acid rain are likely to be less than the benefits obtained from reduced pollution damage, although more work is needed to verify this provisional conclusion.

A final point to note concerns cost effectiveness and the choice of instruments, both domestically and in a European context. The UK has so far chosen a standards-based approach with the imposition of BATNEEC and similar requirements. It is well known that such approaches are cost effective only in exceptional circumstances and are often inferior to market-based instruments like pollution taxes or tradeable emission permits. More successful may be a system of pollution taxes such as that recently introduced in Sweden, where each pollutant is taxed in accordance with the damage it causes. This would also include a carbon tax, which is essential for global warming control (see Chapter 11). Such an approach would properly account for the various interlinkages between air pollution and other environmental problems, and would thus guarantee that the right mix is found between measures like fuel switching, which are beneficial in several respects, and other techniques like FGD, which basically deal with only one problem, and, as is the case with FGD, may in fact aggravate others.

As far as the international level is concerned it now seems to be understood that equi-proportionate emission cuts in all countries, which has been the practice so far, constitutes the cheapest solution possible. It is more than likely that such a system will require some countries with high abatement costs to undertake action which could more cheaply and to the same environmental effect be carried out elsewhere. A tradeable permit or tax system would not share this weakness and may again be more promising. These issues were addressed in *Blueprint 1* (domestic issues) and *Blueprint 2* (global questions), see Pearce *et al* (1989) and Pearce (1991).

AIR POLLUTION AND SUSTAINABLE DEVELOPMENT

From a sustainable development point of view it is interesting to note that few of the EC and UNECE objectives discussed above are based on sustainability or cost-benefit considerations. They are political targets and thus at best reflect the political sensitivity towards these issues at the time of signing. Recently, the UNECE has come some way towards introducing non-policy oriented targets in the acid rain debate by endorsing the concept of critical loads. Critical loads are defined as the level of deposition below which, according to current scientific knowledge, no damage to sensitive ecosystems will occur (Amann *et al*, 1992, and Table 4.3). Emission levels should then be such that critical loads will not be exceeded. Note that, because different soils have different vulnerabilities, critical loads will generally differ from region to region, and the same will therefore also be true for the required emission levels, which will further depend on the dispersion pattern of a pollutant. Implementing the critical load concept would require significant abatement measures beyond what is already decided, mainly due to the existence of few extremely sensitive territories.

How does the critical load concept compare with the notion of sustainable development? In terms of the concepts introduced in Chapters 1 and 2, the cost-benefit approach is one way of interpreting the 'weak sustainability' rule. It essentially says that some environmental damage is worthwhile because the loss to society of going beyond the 'optimal' amount of damage is greater than the gain. Strict sustainability is closer to the critical loads concept, however, since critical loads have as their underlying objective the idea that the receiving environment should not be damaged overall. But even this interpretation can be questioned, since strong sustainability does not argue (as some commentators have wrongly thought) for the conservation of each and every environmental asset. It may be that the forest stock as a whole should not be sacrosanct, or even that soils should be sacrosanct in this sense. It depends very much on what we think is a 'critical' stock of natural capital.

How one views UK policy on traditional pollutants depends, then, on the view one takes of sustainability concepts. The three options are:

1   adopt goals that are politically determined and unrelated either to critical loads or cost-benefit optima;
2   aim for critical loads (one version of strong sustainability);
3   aim for cost-benefit goals (weak sustainability).

Much depends on just how important the assets in question are, and in the absence of any clear-cut approach to determining environmental priorities, that remains an open question.

Chapter 5

Water and water quality

INTRODUCTION

As was explained in Chapter 2, 'constant capital' definitions of sustainable development differ according to the extent to which they assume that different types of capital, broadly defined to include any asset which provides valuable goods and services, can substitute for each other. Strong definitions tend to stress the life-supporting functions of the environment in arguing that man-made capital is an imperfect substitute for the environment. Hence, strong sustainability requires that the stock of *natural* capital should not decline over time, that is, that there should be no net environmental damage in the long run.

This stance assumes that environmental damage in some sectors can be compensated for by environmental improvement in others. However, some commentators deny even this possibility for certain types of natural capital, because they underpin the very functioning of the environment in some fundamental way. No decline in stocks of this 'critical capital' can be consistent with sustainability (Mäler, 1986). Then, aggregate sustainability requires policies which will not only ensure the maintenance of the aggregate capital stock, but also the maintenance of certain types of capital at the sectoral level, implying a rather more cautionary and 'hands-on' approach to environmental management.

Fresh water has been identified as an example of 'critical capital' (Dubourg, 1992). As a result, sustainability requires that the value of the fresh water capital stock should not decline over time. More generally, we can interpret this requirement as saying that current fresh water use should not impose costs upon future generations, be it directly, via lower health standards from increases in pollution, or indirectly, in terms of opportunities forgone. Hence current water use should not only not impose direct costs upon future users, it should also not foreclose the use options of those future users either.

Fresh water's status as a form of 'critical capital' is based essentially upon the observation that its availability is self-evidently a prerequisite for human life, and underpins the operation of the Earth's ecosystem.

It is quite clearly an ethical imperative that current use of fresh water should not undermine the global ecosystem, as this is likely to have catastrophic consequences for future generations. However, it is also clear that current water use in the United Kingdom is far in excess of the levels necessary for the simple sustenance of human life. Therefore, can water used for everyday domestic and industrial processes really be regarded as 'critical'?

Firstly, it can be argued that, in some sense, uses which might appear 'luxurious' at low income levels can become 'necessary' at higher levels of income and industrialisation. This is not only consistent with concepts of relative poverty (eg Townsend, 1985), but also with the technological relationships which are the foundations of a modern, industrial society. Hence, a lack of water for cooling in power generation might cause severe hardship, at least in the short to medium term, such is the economy's reliance upon electricity.

Secondly, even if we assume that water does have capital substitutes over some restricted range, it is not obvious that we can guarantee sufficient investment in these substitutes to offset any reductions in the water sector. Hence, adopting a sectoral approach can in this case be viewed as an attempt to ensure sustainability in the absence of the institutional arrangements adequate to produce such an outcome without intervention.

If we can thereby justify singling out fresh water as a candidate for individual attention within an aggregate sustainability policy, we need then to consider what sustainable water use might mean in practice.

SUSTAINABLE WATER USE IN THE UNITED KINGDOM – THEORY AND PRACTICE

The water stock has two obvious, physical, dimensions: quantity and quality. Taking quantity first, we can define quantity-sustainable water use by reference to the hydrological cycle and the nature of fresh water as a renewable resource. The quantity of water that is available for use in any particular period is equal to the difference between total precipitation and the amount lost through evapotranspiration, plus any water held in surface or underground storage. We can term the latter the stock of fresh water, and the former (termed 'effective runoff') can be likened to the flow from that stock (in the same way that financial interest is the flow from a stock of financial capital). Then our sustainability rule becomes: water demand should be met out of effective runoff only (Dubourg, 1992). Such water use is clearly sustainable because it does not rely on any finite stocks for support. Effective rainfall is akin to a 'harvest' which can be gathered from the water system whilst still leaving the system as a whole intact. This harvest can be taken from surface water, groundwater, or a combination of the two.

Water use in river systems is sequential. Effluent can be re-abstracted downstream for use by other users, implying scope for natural (and artificial) water re-use. The quantity of effluent depends in turn on the extent to which a particular use is consumptive. Demand for spray irrigation can approach 90–100% consumption, whereas abstraction for cooling in energy generation might be almost entirely non-consumptive. However, effluent recapture is unlikely to be complete. For instance, regions such as Thames with long river lengths have greater re-use opportunities than a coastal region such as Southern (National Rivers Authority, 1991d).

Table 5.1 compares the gross regional resource (the product of effective rainfall and land area) in England and Wales for an average year with 1990 net abstraction (which assumes overall consumption of approximately 40 per cent, with some regional variation, and 50 per cent recapture). There it can be seen that all regions of England and Wales enjoy considerable surpluses of average gross resources over current net abstraction. Regional variations are largely the result of differences in geographical location, which affects rainfall, and in demand, which reflects population, urbanisation and industrialisation. In the United Kingdom, high demand areas tend to be located in the dryer south and east.

Average annual figures mask the considerable variation in rainfall over time. The picture of substantial national and regional surplus changes somewhat when we compare 1990 net demand with 1 in 50 year drought resources, on which planning decisions and reliable yield estimates have historically been based (see, for example, National Rivers Authority, 1992). Surpluses remain substantial in the western regions, such as Welsh and North West, but are greatly reduced in the south and east. Demand in the Thames region is so relatively high that demand can only be met in drought periods via extensive water re-use. While a valid and cost-effective means of increasing effective supply, the scope for re-use is restricted to large, long rivers, and subject to technical and biochemical limits. Any resource deficit can be regarded as unsustainable despite the fact that it would appear to arise only 2 per cent of the time, because water use in excess of reliable yield increases the probability that use restrictions will be required in the future. These restrictions count as costs according to our sustainability criteria, so that such water use can be regarded as unsustainable.

The picture becomes even more uncertain when we consider that water abstraction is, in all regions of England and Wales, far below

Table 5.1 *Regional water resources and demands in 1990*

Megalitres per day	Regions (see key)										
---	AN	NO	NW	ST	SO	SW	TH	WE	WX	YO	E&W
Gross regional resource: average year	9323	8080	25170	18401	7256	17981	8856	40136	8856	11949	156010
Gross regional resource: 1 in 50 year drought	2936	3798	15102	9385	3047	9530	3631	24884	3986	5019	81318
Net demands	1683	821	2715	3445	1912	636	3910	5599	930	1759	23414
Average surplus (deficit)	7640	7529	22455	14956	5344	17345	4946	34537	7296	10190	132596
Drought surplus (deficit)	1253	2977	12387	5940	1135	8894	-279	19285	3056	3260	57904
Licensed demands	4086	4279	5617	11087	4117	3484	7417	23531	1760	5030	70410
'Licensed' average surplus (deficit)	5237	3801	19553	7314	3139	14497	1439	16605	7096	6919	85600
'Licensed' drought surplus (deficit)	-1150	-481	9485	-1702	-1070	6046	-3786	1353	2226	-11	10908

Key: AN – Anglian; NO – Northumbrian; NW – North West; ST – Severn–Trent; SO – Southern; SW – South West; TH – Thames; WE – Welsh; WX – Wessex; YO – Yorkshire; E&W – England & Wales

Source: National Rivers Authority (1991a, 1991b, 1991d)

those levels which are actually licensed. Under drought conditions, six out of ten regions appear to license deficits over gross regional resource (ignoring re-use and recapture). Some caution does, however, need to be exercised in interpreting these data. For instance, many licences are contingent upon actual rainfall, so that their use is restricted to relatively wet periods. On the other hand, some regions do not even have full information on the number of abstraction licences actually granted. Moreover, the granting of a licence bestows a statutory right to abstract on the licensee, so that the National Rivers Authority is obliged to meet increases in demand which are already licensed, or at least compensate those licensees financially or through the provision of alternative supplies.

Turning now to the quality aspect of the water sector, we can refer to the general requirement that current use should not impose costs on future users to arrive at the sustainability rule: water quality should be non-declining over time (Dubourg, 1992; Herrington, 1990). Hence, except in special cases, for instance where effluent levels exceed critical loads, sustainability arguments as such cannot be used to justify improving water quality.

Although not strictly comparable due to varying sampling methods and classification schemes, the results of the last six national water quality surveys are given in Table 5.2. The trend appears to be one of marginal improvement from 1958 up to 1980, with a slight fall-off since then. However, the results of quality monitoring are reported in terms of river length, rather than volume, which almost certainly overestimates the relative availability of clean water (Royal Commission on Environmental Pollution, 1993). This is because the results are distorted by the many miles of small, fast-flowing, relatively unpolluted rivers which account for only a small proportion of the actual quantity of surface water. Changes in water quality between surveys are similarly distorted.

The recent reduction, concentrated mainly in the south east and south west, can be explained by a number of factors, including changes in survey methodology, increased discharges from sewage works, and two hot summers in the late 1980s. Although the last of these could hardly be regarded as being controllable, it is, nevertheless, difficult to argue that the quality dimension of the water stock is being used in a sustainable manner.

The quantity-situation in Northern Ireland is likely to be one of surplus, given its west coast location. Similarly, groundwater development in Scotland has been relatively limited owing to the abundance of easily developed surface water. Hence, quantity sustainability would not appear to be an immediate problem in either of these regions. The

Table 5.2 Water quality in England and Wales, 1958–1990

New classification 1980–1990 Surveys

FRESHWATER RIVERS AND CANALS

Class	1980* km	1980* %	1985 km	1985 %	1990 km	1990 %
Good 1a	13830	34	13470	33	12408	26
Good 1b	14220	35	13990	34	14536	34
Fair 2	8670	21	9730	24	10750	25
Poor 3	3260	8	3560	9	4022	9
Bad 4	640	2	650	2	662	2
X	–	–	–	–	39	–
Unclassified	–	–	–	–	17	–
Total	40630		41390		42434	

ESTUARIES

Class	1980* km	1980* %	1985 km	1985 %	1990 km	1990 %
Good A	1870	68	1860	68	1805	66
Fair B	620	23	650	24	655	24
Poor C	140	5	130	5	178	7
Bad D	110	4	90	3	84	3
Total	2730		2730		2722	

Former classifications 1958–1980 Surveys

NON-TIDAL RIVERS AND CANALS

Class	1958 km	1958 %	1970 km	1970 %	1975 km	1975 %	1980 km	1980 %
Unpolluted	24950	72	28500	74	28810	75	28810	75
Doubtful	5220	15	6270	17	6730	17	7110	18
Poor	2270	7	1940	5	1770	5	2000	5
Grossly polluted	2250	6	1700	4	1270	3	810	2
Total	34690		38400		38590		38740	

TIDAL RIVERS

Class	1958 km	1958 %	1970 km	1970 %	1975 km	1975 %	1980 km	1980 %
Unpolluted	1160	41	1380	48	1360	48	1410	50
Doubtful	940	32	680	23	780	27	950	34
Poor	400	14	490	17	420	15	220	8
Grossly polluted	360	13	340	12	280	10	220	8
Total	2850		2880		2850		2800	

Note: *As revised in 1985

Source: National Rivers Authority, 1991c

recent quality position is shown in Table 5.3. Scotland appears to have witnessed a gradual improvement in the last decade. It is difficult to say anything about Northern Ireland on the strength of one year's survey, although the position appears largely similar to that in England and Wales.

PROSPECTS FOR THE FUTURE

Water demand is a function of several variables which change over time. These include population, income, the household penetration of durable goods, and the level of industrial activity (Kindler and Russell, 1984). In addition, the weather and other non-socioeconomic variables can play a role.

Table 5.4 presents lower bound base line estimates of water demand (assuming a reduction in 'unaccounted-for water' to a maximum of 20 per cent in each region) in England and Wales relative to gross regional resources, for the year 2021. It can be seen from comparison with Table 5.1 that overall demand is actually expected to remain approximately constant over this period. This prediction masks important regional variations, however. Demand reductions are expected to occur predominantly in the north and west of the country, where resources are already plentiful due to high levels of precipitation and a declining industrial base. Demand increases are forecast in Thames (9 per cent) and Anglian (38 per cent), both regions where resources are already relatively scarce. With the present institutional framework, there appears to be no obvious way that these increases can be resisted, since water companies already possess the statutory rights via abstraction licences previously granted but not yet used.

Moreover, we should recognise the impact that global climate change might have upon this scenario. On the demand side, a rise in mean temperatures could be accompanied by an increased demand for water, especially in the domestic and agricultural sectors. Demand for public water supply in the Anglian and Thames regions currently accounts for 80 per cent and 90 per cent respectively of total. The proportion of total demand accounted for by agriculture in Anglian region is 7 per cent, of which 90 per cent is for irrigation (involving 90 per cent consumptive losses). Clearly, both of these regions are vulnerable to increases in demand from these two sectors.

On the supply side, standard climate change models predict higher temperatures leading to higher precipitation, in both summer and winter, across the whole of the British Isles. But if higher temperatures are not only accompanied by greater precipitation but also higher rates of evapotranspiration, with little increase in runoff (Department of the

Table 5.3 Water quality in Scotland and Northern Ireland

Scotland
RIVERS, LOCHS AND CANALS

Class	1980 km	1980 %	1985 km	1985 %	1990 km	1990 %
Class 1	45352	95	45695	96	49452	97
Class 2	2035	4	1723	4	1202	2
Class 3	260	–	272	–	238	–
Class 4	163	–	132	–	71	–
Total	47810		47822		50963	

Northern Ireland
RIVERS

Class	1990 km	1990 %
Good	1033	72
Fair	344	24
Poor	57	4
Bad	3	–
Total	1435	

Source: Department of the Environment (1992)

Table 5.4 *Regional water resources and demands in 2021*

Megalitres per day	Regions (see key above)										
	AN	NO	NW	ST	SO	SW	TH	WE	WX	YO	E&W
Gross regional resource: average year	9323	8080	25170	18401	7256	17981	8856	40136	8856	11949	156010
Gross regional resource: 1 in 50 year drought	2936	3798	15102	9385	3047	9530	3631	24884	3986	5019	81318
Estimated net demands	2325	899	2009	2946	1859	685	4271	4508	1122	1440	22138
Average surplus (deficit)	6998	7181	23161	15455	5397	17296	4585	35556	7734	10509	133872
Drought surplus (deficit)	611	2899	13093	6439	1188	8845	−640	20304	2864	3579	59180

Source: National Rivers Authority (1991a, 1991b)

Environment, 1991), as well as greater variation in actual precipitation around the mean (Intergovernmental Panel on Climate Change, 1990), then this will not necessarily lead to an improvement in the resource situation in those areas facing potential shortage. We might expect more frequent bouts of hot, dry weather, bringing the sort of situation witnessed in the south east of England over the last few years.

In fact, the National Rivers Authority has already drawn up a priority list of rivers suffering from problems of over-abstraction (see, eg Royal Commission on Environmental Pollution, 1992: 162). These are located predominantly in the southern and eastern areas of England where chalk aquifers account for a relatively large proportion of water supply (Department of the Environment, 1992). The costs associated with such over-abstraction are not just in terms of reductions in supply, but also the losses of amenity, wildlife habitat, recreational possibilities and so on. Any environmental damage so caused can take decades to be repaired, bringing a distinctly intergenerational aspect to the low-flow issue. The reparation of certain types of damage might never be fully complete.

The prospects on the quality side are likely to be similar. Gradual improvements since the War have been undermined recently with reductions in water quality in the south and east of England, partly attributed to the effects of two hot, dry summers. If we can expect the frequency of such events to increase with global warming, then quality will suffer as a result. Moreover, the assimilative capacity of a receiving water is a function of its flow. Hence, increases in abstractions will also impact negatively upon river quality. Both of these effects are likely to be more important in the south and east of England.

The discussion presented in this section suggests that the current uneven balance between supply and demand conditions in the United Kingdom water sector is likely to be exacerbated over time. As a result, whereas the water sector in the United Kingdom might appear sustainable at the aggregate level, sustainability at the regional level is much less certain. Acceptance of this imbalance implies the assumption that water 'capital' is spatially substitutable. Then, reductions in the water capital stock in one part of the country can be compensated for by increases elsewhere. Whether or not we can justify this assumption on theoretical or empirical grounds, such a scenario is unlikely to be politically acceptable, as it is unlikely to be free of economic costs. The next section will consider policies to achieve aggregate and regional sustainability.

POLICIES FOR WATER SUSTAINABILITY: THEORY AND PRACTICE

Consider the quantity aspect first. Given our quantity-sustainability rule, sustainability could be achieved by a simple adjustment of the current system of abstraction licences, to ensure that the total quantity of licensed abstraction did not exceed total effective rainfall, as it does at present. Assuming effective enforcement, this would achieve sustainability.

But once we recognise that water is a scarce resource, then allocative efficiency becomes an issue. That is, we need to distinguish between the achievement of sustainable rates of water abstraction, and the efficient achievement of such rates. This would not be ensured by such a simple revision of the current system. Allocative efficiency requires a system of prices which present to abstractors the full social costs of their actions. The principles of efficient pricing in the water sector are well documented elsewhere (eg Organisation for Economic Co-operation and Development, 1991). They involve the estimation of direct, resource costs and any external damage costs, being any costs, broadly defined, imposed upon others as a result of supply provision, including amenity loss, reductions in health, and so on.

Where sustainable pricing differs from standard economic efficiency pricing is in the inclusion of a premium to cover the costs of any resource depletion (Herrington, 1990; Pearce, 1988). In fact, according to our sustainability criteria, this premium would need to be set to ensure that no depletion at all occurred in the long run (Dubourg, 1992, 1993). The size of this premium in practice will depend upon the extent to which intertemporal substitution is permitted, and the level of demand relative to sustainable supply. Given the resource and demand imbalance existing in the United Kingdom, we can anticipate premiums approaching zero in Wales, Scotland and the north of England, rising in the south, and being the greatest in the south east and London.

This distribution of premiums effectively defines a regional pattern of sustainable water use (Dubourg, 1992). It implies that water-using activities which involve low water value-added or which are water-extensive should be located in areas where resources are relatively abundant ie where the sustainability premiums are low.

The current system of allocating fresh water in the United Kingdom cannot ensure an efficient pattern of water use, as the National Rivers Authority has no statutory right to levy charges at any rate higher than that just sufficient to cover administrative costs. However, a complete system of volumetric charging based on economic costs is not a prerequisite for sustainable water use. For instance, even within the existing framework, the current system of allocation could be improved by the estimation of sustainability premiums which could be used to inform licensing policy. 'Net-back' analysis, in which an activity's profitability is judged against the prices it faces, could be used to identify which water-using activities were consistent with sustainability.

Economists tend to use market prices as inputs into their analysis. However, it is not the prices themselves which are important, but rather their function as an indicator of economic value. It is only when we have adequate estimates of the economic value of water that we can begin to make an economically-meaningful attempt at capacity planning and investment appraisal. Otherwise, projects to reduce transportation losses, or to transfer water between regions, will be economically optimal only by chance, and there will be a significant probability that projects will go ahead which would not pass an economic cost-benefit test.

The theoretical requirements for quality-sustainability are simple to identify, their practical analogue less so. Following the standard economic model of pollution, non-declining quality requires that no private incentive exists to increase discharges. This can be ensured by levying a tax on polluting activities, with the level of the tax depending on the cost of pollution abatement (Dubourg, 1992). Sustainability might then be achieved by some high-cost polluters increasing their emissions, while other lower-cost polluters reduced theirs. This would not only result in quality sustainability but also sustainability at least cost.

However, in the same way that volumetric charging based on economic costs is not required to produce quantity sustainability, a full-blown system of effluent charges is not a prerequisite for quality to be non-declining. The current system of discharge licensing, with some revisions, is theoretically capable of ensuring sustainability, given sufficient flexibility and effective enforcement. Efficient sustainability, however, would require that the charges which accompany consents be extended to account more fully for the social costs associated with pollution. Presently, these charges aim only to recover the costs incurred by the National Rivers Authority in granting and monitoring consents. Charge levels thus set are lower than would be the case under a full-cost scheme, and therefore provide insufficient incentive to reduce emissions.

For instance, the charge levied by the National Rivers Authority for consents to discharge to groundwater is subject to a 'groundwater factor' of 0.5, despite their seriousness and potential irreversibility

(Royal Commission on Environmental Pollution, 1992). This is because charging for consents is essentially a cost-recovery exercise, and the 0.5 factor reflects the fact that groundwater consents are cheaper to monitor. The most important means of pollution control is the licensing process itself (Litterick, 1991), but the record on successful prosecutions, and the trend in water quality over the years, testify to its efficacy.

Note that, although we have discussed policies for quantity and quality sustainability separately, this does not mean that they should be formulated in isolation from each other. The physical links between quantity and quality should be fully considered in licensing decisions. For instance, the reductions in river quality experienced in the past few years in the South and East of England have in part been attributed to low river flow as a result of over-abstraction during extended bouts of dry weather. Similarly, the value of fresh water for abstraction and other uses is, to an extent, a function of its quality. Reductions in quality can preclude other uses, in the same way that physical abstraction reduces the amount of water available for other users.

In summary, by requiring water quality and quantity to be non-declining over time, sustainable water management might be seen to have more in common with standards-based approaches to environmental regulation than the usual economic policies. However, we need to distinguish between the achievement of sustainable water use, and its *efficient*, or *least cost*, achievement. The current systems of discharge consents and abstraction licences are capable of ensuring sustainability, given effective implementation and some revision. However, efficient sustainability requires knowledge of the economic value of water and water services. The advantage of efficient markets is that this information is provided automatically in the price signal. Hence, the current systems could feasibly produce efficient outcomes, but at the expense of placing greater (and costly) information-gathering burdens upon regulators and planners.

CONCLUSIONS

Ultimately, it might be argued that the need to recognise the economic value of water and water services is immediately more urgent than the issue of sustainable water use. Current water use is, or is very close to being, sustainable in all parts of the country, in both the quantity and quality sectors. Further, the institutional requirements for future sustainability are not taxing, and to a certain extent already exist. There is ample scope, however, for future inefficiency in the water sector, and inefficient sustainability. This is largely due, not just to an absence of economic pricing of water services, but to a lack of knowledge of the economic value of water and water services. It is not difficult to demonstrate, both in theory and empirically, how this can lead, and has led, to inefficiency, especially in the area of capacity planning. Whereas the costs of sustainability *per se* will occur in the future, if they occur at all, these costs of inefficiency have been felt in the past, and will continue to be felt into the future, so long as the basis for resource management remains non-economic.

In fact, placing fresh water use and planning on a more economic footing might well be expected to produce the classic 'double dividend': it will not only greatly facilitate efficient and sustainable water use in the future, but it will also significantly reduce costs now. The economic value of the United Kingdom's fresh water needs to be recognised.

Chapter 6

Solid and hazardous waste

INTRODUCTION

The laws of thermodynamics dictate that economic activity inevitably creates waste in the form of materials and energy flows. Too much waste entering the environment rather than being recycled or re-used will over-stress the assimilative capacity of the environment to handle such waste safely. The result will be a range of pollution and resource degradation impacts and consequent economic damage costs. This chapter looks at municipal solid waste and other hazardous waste flows that are generated in the UK economy.

The strong sustainable development approach would prescribe that persistent wastes should not be allowed to accumulate and thereby disrupt nutrient and material cycles in the environment. It also recommends that waste emissions/discharges are limited to rates that are significantly less than natural, or human augmented, assimilative capacity (the precautionary principle). At the same time, the costs of achieving these objectives must be taken into account. In order to fulfil these objectives an integrated waste management system is required which combines together as efficiently as possible, waste minimisation, recycling and re-use policies. Market based instruments can play a significant role in this policy.

WASTE ARISINGS AND DISPOSAL OPTIONS

Total waste arisings in the UK are estimated to be around 400 million tonnes of which mining and quarrying waste accounts for 27 per cent. About a third of total waste arisings is defined as 'controlled waste' and includes household and commercial waste, some sewage sludge, demolition and construction waste and industrial waste. Special wastes in the UK (ie controlled wastes which are 'dangerous to life') are estimated to be around 2.5 million tonnes and growing. The remainder of the total waste flow is made up of waste from agricultural premises and radioactive waste. In addition, some 40 to 50 million tonnes of hazardous waste are imported (for specialised treatment) into the UK each year (HM Government, 1992).

This waste must be disposed of somehow, and at a cost. The environment has a large waste assimilation capacity, but it is not infinite. Landfill is the main method of disposal for controlled waste accounting for 85 per cent of the total, it also accounts for 70 per cent of special waste. Other disposal routes include incineration, sea dumping and physical or chemical treatment. About half of sewage sludge is used as a soil conditioner and nutrient on farm land and horticultural areas (see Box 6.1).

Box 6.1
DISPOSAL ROUTES FOR UK WASTE

The UK is almost self-sufficient in the disposal of waste from all sources but there is some international movement of metal-containing residues and other industrial by-products. Most controlled waste may be treated or disposed of only under a licence.

Number of UK waste disposal facilities

Type	Number of disposal licences
Landfill	4,196
Civic amenity	559
Transfer stations	936
Storage (remote)	274
Treatment plants	122
Incineration	212
Other	366

The disposal picture for controlled waste, special wastes, sewage sludge, and imported hazardous waste is summarized below.

Disposal Routes (% of total waste accounted for by each route)

Waste category	Landfill	Incineration	Sea dumping	Other
Controlled waste	85	4	4	7
Special waste	70	5	10	15
Sewage sludge	13	7	28	46 (farmland)
				7 (other)
Imported hazardous waste	–	29	–	7 (solidification)
				58 (physical chemical treatment)
				6 (other)

Source: HM Government (1992)

While there is a variety of sources of data on waste arisings, no single database exists that is national, comprehensive, extensive and current. The UK lacks acceptable projections for the quantities and composition of waste streams which are essential for the planning of an effective and economically efficient waste management system. Warren Spring Laboratory has, however, undertaken detailed waste arising and composition surveys of household, civic amenity and certain commercial and industrial arisings. Its best estimate of UK waste arisings and characteristics is summarised in Table 6.1.

Table 6.1 UK waste arisings (controlled waste) and disposal

Waste type	Arisings (mt/yr)	Landfilled (mt/yr)	Incinerated (mt/yr)
Household	15.5	13.3	2.2
Civic amenity	3.6	3.6	0.0
Commercial	15.1	14.3	0.8
Sewage sludge	1.4	1.2	0.2
Construction and demolition	13.2	13.2	0.0
Asphalt planings	1.6	1.6	0.0
Industrial (blast)	1.8	1.8	0.0
Industrial (PS ash)	6.5	6.5	0.0
Industrial (general)	9.0	9.0	0.0
Industrial (misc. proc.)	15.3	15.3	0.0
Industrial (food proc.)	14.4	14.4	0.0
Clinical	0.3	0.1	0.2
Hazardous	3.5	3.5	0.0
Fragmenter residues	0.5	0.5	0.0
Meat proc. residues	1.2	1.2	0.0
Poultry wastes	1.8	1.4	0.4
Mushroom compost	0.3	0.3	0.0
Tyres	0.3	0.3	0.0
Wood waste (proc.)	0.6	0.5	0.1
TOTAL	105.9	102.0	3.9

Source: Warren Spring Laboratory, personal communication

Poor information has compounded the difficulties that the public, industry and government all face in the vexed and often conflict ridden context of waste (particularly hazardous waste) and its 'proper' management.

WASTE DISPOSAL: THE EXTERNAL COSTS

All the available disposal options carry with them 'externalities'. These are costs and benefits that are borne by, or accrue to, society in general and which are not accounted for in the decisions made about waste. For example, landfill results in methane emissions and methane is a greenhouse gas. The main example of an external benefit is associated with the energy recovery that occurs if the methane is captured and used. The value of the energy is not an external benefit because it is already accounted for in the costs and revenues of the site owner, but the energy recovered will displace energy elsewhere in the economic system, eg by making it less necessary to have power from, say, a coal fired power station. The pollution avoided in this way is then an external benefit of the methane capture at the landfill site.

The negative externalities include social costs such as site disamenity – noise, smell, unsightliness, air and water pollution, health impacts, and congestion costs.

The net externalities from waste disposal (assuming energy recovery is practised) can be calculated as follows:

Waste disposal externality =
Site externality + Variable externality

The site externality tends to be 'fixed', ie it is not closely related to the amount of waste going through the site. There is a cost whatever the scale of the site. The variable externality is related to the amount of waste going through the site – the more the tonnage the bigger the cost (or the benefit).

The variable externality tends to comprise:

Global pollution costs (related to greenhouse gas emissions such as carbon dioxide (CO_2) and methane (CH_4)) +

Conventional air pollution costs (related to sulphur dioxide (SO_2), nitrogen oxides (NO_X)) and particulates (TSP) +

'Air toxics' (such as dioxins) +

Water pollution costs +

Transport costs (air pollution, congestion and accident costs) –

Displaced pollution damage (because of energy recovery systems).

Environmental health risks, natural or of human origin, are an ever-present feature of human life. As economies have industrialised, the nature of these risks has changed from past concerns over infectious diseases, through more recent chemical and radiation exposures in the workplace, to current worries over 'environmental' (non-occupational) toxic exposures. This shift in public health focus has inevitably meant a shift in concern away from acute illness arising promptly after relatively high doses of toxic exposure, toward concern for delayed (perhaps years later) health effects resulting from low dose exposure. Risk assessment (typical of hazardous waste facilities) with respect to this latter situation can be quite an ambiguous process and will not produce the precise answers that society seems to demand.

Frequently, analysts have to resort to extrapolations of the results of high-dose animal toxicity experiments to forecast the outcomes of human exposures. The uncertainties involved in this sort of chemical risk analysis should not be shrouded from public view and debate by over-elaborate formal analysis. It is a problem that is increasing in severity as time passes because the rate at which new chemicals and mixtures enter the environment (one thousand new chemicals a year), combined with the rate of 'new' exposures from 'old' chemicals (for instance old dump site releases), is greater than the capacity of toxicity research to test for effects.

As society demands more definitive risk management knowledge, a difficult balance will have to be maintained between attempts to formally model and forecast hazardous waste related risks, and the concealment of inevitable uncertainties behind a mass of jargon and statistics. It is now a well-established psychological research finding that expert and lay opinion of the riskiness of things often differ considerably. Opinion polls show that chemical waste disposal is at the top of public concerns. Yet risks from such sites (active and inactive) only rank eighth and thirteenth on the US Environmental Protection Agency's list of 31 cancer risks.

Waste disposal facilities in particular have suffered from the NIMBY (not in my backyard) syndrome, with health risk perception usually at the centre of people's concern. But why it is that people perceive the health risks to be unacceptable when formal analysis does not confirm these perceptions? Experts tend to use the 'relative-risk' approach – the risk posed by toxic chemical exposure from a waste site versus risks like smoking, alcoholism, poor diet, traffic accidents. On this basis the chemical hazard can be shown to be a relatively low risk (Petts, 1992).

Individuals, however, continue to see risks as absolutes and often involuntary, perhaps because of misinformation and misperception. There is on the other hand a psychosocial basis for the NIMBY syndrome. Waste facilities defined as hazardous are inherently stigmatised and therefore classed as undesirable. Deeper and wider social-concerns may also underlie local opposition, including invasion of homelife and territory, loss of personal control, stress and lifestyle infringement, loss of trust in public agencies and lack of accountability of the 'system'. Here the waste site is merely the catalyst for unlocking concerns about trends in society in general.

WASTE MANAGEMENT SYSTEMS

The three ways in which the flow of materials waste to the environment can be reduced are:

1 waste minimisation, ie reducing the amount of material per product;
2 re-use;
3 recycling.

An effective system will have to integrate waste minimisation, recycling and re-use, processing, transport and final disposal activities. Historically, a significant percentage of all wastes have been disposed of via landfill sites (see Box 6.1). Only a small percentage of total waste is incinerated and an even smaller amount is incinerated in facilities with an energy recovery capability. However, EC and IPC (Integrated Pollution Control) legislation requires operators of existing incineration plants to meet new emission standards by 1996. It is also probably the case that income from energy recovery will be vital for the financial viability of any future waste incinerator plant.

The UK now has a legacy of abandoned and operational landfills containing a variety of wastes whose exact composition is often unknown. Standards of operation, maintenance and monitoring have been and continue to be variable; many sites probably pose significant environmental risks. In a study of 100 UK landfill sites 54 per cent performed no monitoring of ground water and 50 per cent had no gas monitoring boreholes. Of those who monitored more than half found surface or ground water contamination and half detected gas migration (Croft and Campbell, 1990). Surface and groundwater contamination by leachate discharges from landfill sites is a particularly costly problem to mitigate. Retrofitting costs for such problem landfill sites can range from £500,000 to £4 million. Monitoring costs for all sites (probably around 9000) have been estimated to be some £91.3 million. Increasingly stringent environmental protection legislation will serve to put severe pressure on the UK's stock of disposal facilities (see Box 6.4). Landfill sites will become a scarce resource in the future, not because of any absolute shortage of holes in the ground, but because of a relative shortage of environmentally sound and socially acceptable sites. In the light of all this the selection of the appropriate future waste management system will be of paramount importance. The cost rise, reflecting the true social costs of waste disposal, will have important positive ramifications for waste minimisation and waste recycling. Currently the cost to the nation of disposing of some 102m tonnes of controlled waste that is landfilled is approximately £510m–£2040m per year, and the cost of incinerating 3.9m tonnes of controlled waste is £780m–£1170m per annum.

WASTE RECYCLING IN THE UK

In 1990 the UK Government declared its target for the recycling of household waste as 25 per cent, or 50 per cent of the recyclable component. These targets are to be reached by the year 2000 (HM Government, 1990). Government publications (HM Government, 1990; HM Government, 1992b) state that the current average recycling rate for household waste is 5 per cent. However, a survey carried out by Friends of the Earth (FoE, 1992) found that the average recycling rate for household waste is 4.4 per cent in England and Wales and 3.7 per cent in Scotland, suggesting that the government estimate is a little generous. Section 49 of the Environmental Protection Act 1990 requires local waste collection authorities to prepare recycling plans to ensure that the 25 per cent recycling target is met. The deadline for the submission of the plans was 1 August 1992, but by the end of 1992 some of the collection authorities still had not completed draft plans. The FoE survey also revealed that only 54 per cent of Scottish councils and 36 per cent of councils in England and Wales expected to meet or exceed the government's recycling target. For the remainder, proposed targets have been set as low as 10 per cent. However, these targets for recycling rates are an average for all household waste. Some elements of municipal waste, particularly packaging, are more recyclable than others and are already achieving higher recycling rates than the average, see Box 6.2.

Potentially Recoverable Waste

Given the difficulties of achieving the 25 per cent target, the question arises as to whether the target is reasonable. Since its introduction, the 25 per cent target has been criticised on two fronts. The first focuses on a technical aspect. The UK Government's Environmental White Paper, *This Common Inheritance* (HM Government, 1990), claims that dry recyclables account for about 40 per cent of household waste and wet recyclables constitute a further 10 per cent, making a total of 50 per cent of household waste potentially recyclable. However, another government publication (HM Government, 1991b) reporting research

Box 6.2
UK RECYCLING RATES FOR SELECTED MATERIALS

| | Recycling rate (%) | |
	1990	1991
Glass	20.6	21.4
Paper	33.3	33.4
Steel cans	9.5	10.0
Aluminium cans	5.3	8.0
Plastic	0.1	0.7

Source: *ENDS Report* 207 April 1992, p12

As the government target of 25 per cent recycling of all household waste is based on 50 per cent recycling of recyclables, these materials are under pressure to reach even higher recycling rates. In order to meet these targets, the packaging and retail industries (COPAC) have submitted a plan to the government which proposes that they could recycle 42 per cent of all used packaging by 1999 (see table below). However, this figure includes planned recycling by industry, commerce and institutions. The fact that COPAC's planned overall recycling rate for household packaging, which by the government is considered 'recyclable', only comes to 33 per cent, illustrates the problem of reaching the government targets.

COPAC's recycling plan

| | H | ICI | Total | H | ICI | Total |
	Recycling rate (%) 1992			Recycling rate (%) 1999		
Glass	17	–	17	51	–	51
Metals	8	18	10	45	47	45
Paper	9	51	44	10	56	49
Plastics	–	11	5	8	34	19
Total	11	43	27	33	51	42

H = Households, ICI = Industry, commerce and institutions

Source: *ENDS Report* 213 October 1992, p14

results from the Warren Spring Laboratory, claims that household waste contains 38 per cent dry recyclables and 30 per cent wet recyclables, making a total of 68 per cent potentially recoverable. Thus, given the Government's wish to recycle 50 per cent of potentially recoverable waste, the overall target should, on this analysis, be 34 per cent rather than 25 per cent.

The optimal recycling level

A more fundamental criticism concerns the target of 50 per cent. Why 50 per cent? Why not 100 per cent? – Or 20 per cent? The 50 per cent appears to be the outcome of a balancing act designed to consider both the views of environmental groups and 'green consumers' on one side, and industry and business on the other, rather than a clear attempt at identifying the best or 'optimal' level. But how would one identify the optimal recycling level?

To determine the optimal level of recycling it is necessary to consider the costs and benefits associated with recycling. Contrary to common belief, not all recycling is beneficial. There are cases where the associated costs exceed the environmental benefits gained. The condition for optimal recycling is that the extra benefits ($\triangle B$) of recycling should just equal the extra costs ($\triangle C$), see Box 6.3.

RECYCLING AND 'MARKET FAILURE'

Current 'free market' levels of recycling are less than the optimal level of recycling (see Box 6.3). This is due to the way waste disposal is financed. Under section 12 (1 and 3) of the Control of Pollution Act 1974, implemented in 1988, local waste collection authorities are under a duty to collect household waste free of charge. This means that the individual household faces no direct cost for the removal of waste. It is financed from the general funds of the local council.

Thus, when waste is recycled, the saved disposal cost will accrue to the local authority rather than to the recycler. The result is that in the 'free market' recycling will only take place when the revenue to be obtained from recycled materials is greater than the costs associated with recycling, whereas we have shown that recycling activities should be subsidised. On the other hand, the government recycling target may or may not represent an economically efficient level of recycling.

Waste management policy has traditionally been secured through the use of the command-and-control regulatory standards approach in most industrialised economies and not just the UK. Under this approach the regulatory authority sets an environmental standard (target) and the polluter is required to honour the standard, under the threat of some penalty system.

Box 6.4 summarises some of the waste recycling standards that have recently been adopted, or are under consideration, in industrialised economies.

Box 6.3
THE OPTIMAL LEVEL OF RECYCLING

The condition for optimal recyling is that extra benefits ($\triangle B$) of recycling should just equal the extra costs ($\triangle C$). The extra benefits are approximated by:

$\triangle B$ = Price of recycled material
  + Avoided cost of disposal (eg to landfill)
  + Avoided environmental costs of disposal

The extra costs are approximated by:

$\triangle C$ = Cost of any separate collection
  + Costs of the recycling process
  + Environmental costs of recycling

After some manipulation, it turns out that optimal recycling can be defined as that level of recycling which would emerge if all recycling were subsidised by an amount equal to the avoided costs of waste disposal where these avoided costs include the environmental damages done by waste disposal. If this cost is, say £20 per tonne, then recycling should be subsidised by £20 per tonne.

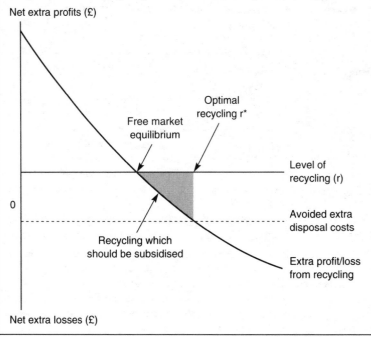

Box 6.4
EXAMPLES OF THE REGULATORY APPROACH TO RECYCLING

Country	Regulatory standard (target)
Austria	Has passed a regulation which mandates the following refilling/recycling rates for glass and cans: Beer: glass 80% by 1992; cans 90% by 1994; Carbonates: glass 60% by 1992; cans 80% by 1994; Juices: glass 25% by 1992; cans 40% by 1994.
Belgium	Target level of 30% of waste to be recycled by 1995; the balance to be incinerated; landfill to be used only as a last resort.
Canada	National Packaging adopted in 1990 – aims to reduce packaging in the MSW by 20% (from 1998 levels) by 1992 and by 50% by the year 2000.
France	50% recycling target (undated), either involving materials recycling or energy production.
Germany	64% recycling target by 1995, bias towards materials recycling rather than energy production.
Holland	10% reduction in all waste target; 50% minimum reuse/recycling target for MSW, up to 30% of which could be for energy recovery; landfill to take a maximum of 10% of waste by the year 2000 (intermediate targets to be achieved by 1994).
Italy	Legislation has laid down a 50% recycling target for both glass and cans, to be achieved by the end of 1992. From April 1993, containers which have not met this target will have a penalty tax imposed on them.
Switzerland	Legislation has laid down that the amount of beverage packaging in the waste stream must not exceed 10% by the end of 1993. PVC bottles are banned, and a 50% recycling rate for aluminium beverage cans must be met by the end of 1991.
United Kingdom	50% of recyclables (25% of total MSW) to be recycled by the year 2000.
United States	1998, EPA national goal of reducing waste disposal by 25% by 1992 via recycling and source separation.
EC	Packaging Directive is under consideration; proposals include a packaging waste 'standstill principle' which would operate five years after adoption and be related to a 1990 base level. After five years materials recycling should encompass 60% of waste, with a maximum of 30% as energy recovery and a maximum landfill requirement of only 10% of total waste.

Note: MSW is municipal solid waste

Source: Pearce and Turner (1993)

This target-setting process is well intentioned but may not always represent a feasible policy objective because of information deficiencies and the lack of a proper 'systems' perspective. In the USA, Alter (1991) has concluded that a proper analysis of the municipal solid waste (MSW) data that are available suggests a future decrease in the amount of recyclable items in MSW, hence a change in the economics of recycling. He further claims that an analysis of the intensity of waste generation leads one to query whether the generation rate of MSW in the USA is likely to increase as the economy grows. Even if recycling scheme participation rates and collection system efficiency improve, Alter believes that national recycling targets much in excess of 25 per cent of MSW are unobtainable.

Target setting may also represent a very inefficient form of policy response. Let us take the example of municipal solid waste and analyse the situation from the individual household perspective. Households pay for waste collection and disposal through a local property-based tax system that is unrelated to the quantity of refuse discarded, or to the full costs actually imposed on society. The result is that households face a marginal cost of refuse disposal equal to zero. As a consequence the likelihood is that the demand for the solid waste service will be too high and recycling rates too low (there is an undervaluation of the waste disposal service of the environment).

For the quantity of waste not only to decline (and recycling rates to increase) but also to be at an economically efficient level, the price charged for waste collection/disposal should reflect the full social cost of such services. The argument here is not that any increase in recycling is undesirable. We have shown that current recycling activity levels are below the economic optimum level, but target setting in the absence of any economic cost-benefit analysis can incur unnecessary costs.

The United Kingdom Government is committed to the introduction of economic instruments for achieving environmental goals. Thus:

> Economic instruments are an inherently more flexible and cost effective way of achieving environmental goals. The Government believes that the time has now come to deploy them more fully to achieve environmental objectives.
>
> (HM Government, 1992: para 3.44)

Economic instruments have special attractions in the field of solid waste management. Since there are various options for waste disposal – recycling re-use and for the reduction of waste at source – changes in the cost of one disposal route should encourage the diversion of waste to other routes. The government has already begun a process of using the price mechanisms to change the flows of waste going to different disposal routes, with a presumption in favour of more waste recycling, through the introduction of 'recycling credits'.

A system of recycling credits was introduced in April 1992 under Section 52 of the Environmental Protection Act of 1990. It provides for Waste Disposal Authorities (WDAs) to pay Waste Collection Authorities (WCAs) and, at the WDA's discretion, others engaged in recycling activity, a sum equal to the avoided waste disposal cost of the WDA. Sums payable are either estimated directly or are based on the standard values below where no direct estimation is possible. The 1993/4 figures are simply the 1992/3 figures adjusted for inflation. From April 1994, these figures should be increased substantially as avoided cost becomes based on estimates of the long run marginal cost of disposal – see Table 6.2.

In general, the recycling credit is equal to the avoided private costs of disposing of waste to landfill and incineration. For example, if it costs £10 per tonne to dispose of waste, then a Waste Collection Agency that avoids this disposal by recycling a tonne of waste is entitled to a payment of £10 per tonne. But as long as the recycling credit reflects only the market costs of disposing of waste, it will ignore the other benefits of recycling, including the avoided external costs of waste disposal. This demonstrates that a further adjustment is required, ie there needs to be a charge on conventional disposal options to reflect their environmental damages, or there needs to be a further subsidy to recycling to reflect the fact that recycling avoids those damages.

Table 6.2 *Recycling credits*

| Area | Payments (£ per tonne) | | |
	1992	1993	1994
Inner London	16.50	16.93	35
Outer London	14.00	14.36	30
Manchester, Merseyside, Metropolitan districts	11.00	11.29	23
Others (where WDA incurs transport costs in disposing of similar waste)	8.00	8.21	17
Remainder	4.50	4.62	10

Source: SI 1993 No. 445, The Environmental Protection (Waste Recycling Payments) (Amendment) Regulations 1993, HMSO, London. 1993/4 estimates based on government statement that long run marginal cost pricing would approximately double the payments

Solid waste charges, including a landfill levy, are possible candidates in this context. A landfill levy has been discussed, and generally supported, in the report on waste incineration by the Royal Commission on Environmental Pollution (RCEP, 1993), and by the Advisory Committee on Business and the Environment (ACBE, 1991). A levy is also relevant to the 'aftercare' provisions of the European Community Draft Directive on Landfill.

In principle, a levy on landfill sites should reflect the external costs associated with landfill. The levy should be equal to the marginal external cost of landfill net of any marginal external benefit. 'Marginal' here simply means 'extra', so the levy should be equal to the loss of well-being associated with disposing of an extra tonne, or extra cubic metre, of waste. The principles underlying this rule can be found in any text on environmental economics (see, for example, Pearce and Turner, 1990).

Box 6.5 shows the relationship between the market for recycled products, the recycling credit, and the externalities from landfill/incineration. Strictly, each waste disposal route should attract a levy or charge equal to the net marginal external costs of the specific disposal route. There would then be a landfill levy and an incineration levy. Since recycling tends to generate external benefits it should attract a negative levy or subsidy. However, great care has to be taken in formulating a complete set of such levies and subsidies. It would not be correct, for example to put a levy on landfill and incineration and a subsidy on recycling if the recycling subsidy already reflected the externalities from landfill and incineration. This would amount to correcting for the same externality twice, and that would be inefficient. Additionally, the external benefits from waste disposal through incineration are quite significant.

At the time of writing (Autumn 1993) the UK Government is considering the introduction of a landfill levy designed to act as a stimulus to increased recycling and to divert waste from landfill to incineration which many regard as an environmentally preferable disposal route. If introduced, the levy would mark a cautious first step on the road to adopting market based instruments for the achievement of environmental policy, something other countries have already done with considerable success.

PACKAGING WASTE

One component of the waste stream, packaging waste, has become a focus for attention by policy makers in a number of countries. This concern is revealed in measures implemented or being considered by

Box 6.5
RECYCLING CREDITS AND A LANDFILL LEVY

In the diagram the downward sloping line is the marginal profit from recycling, ie the extra profit secured by recycling an extra tonne of waste. If recycling was left entirely to market forces, then the amount of waste that would be recycled is W, ie that amount corresponding to the point where marginal profits are zero and hence total profits are maximised. This amount is not optimal because the structure of the waste disposal industry is such that waste disposers do not bargain with recyclers to avoid the cost of disposal. Hence government intervenes through the medium of recycling credits which equal the marginal *private* cost of disposing of waste (MC_L). The effect of the credits is then to expand recycling beyond its privately profitable level to W_{RC}. But even this level of recycling is still not socially optimal because recycling credits do not account for the environmental costs of landfill (and incineration). The effect of placing a levy equal to MEC_L on landfill/incineration (or of making payments to the recycling industry equal to this amount) is shown in the figure as the shift from W_{RC} to W_{RC+E}. This is then the socially optimal level of recycling.

If there are external costs associated with recycling, then W_{RC+E} will be too high and MEC_L should be reduced. MEC_L is also computed here as the differential externality between landfill and incineration if incineration is not to be subject to a separate levy.

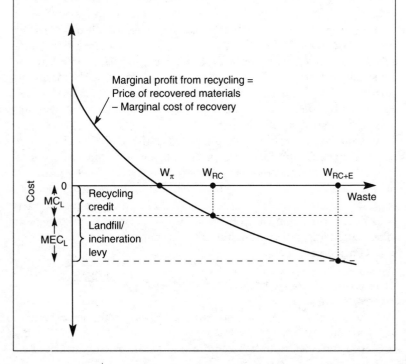

Germany and the European Commission to secure (a) source reduction of packaging; and (b) increased recycling of packaging waste. Table 6.3 shows broad estimates of packaging waste arisings in the European Community: there is, however, extensive uncertainty about the true magnitudes.

Command-and-control approaches such as recycling and source reduction targets are most likely to be cost-ineffective and dynamically inefficient, as firms will have little or no incentive to develop new technologies which facilitate high recycling rates or light-weighting. Compared to this, market-based instruments are found to be both cost-effective and dynamically efficient. By internalising the external effects associated with the disposal of packaging, firms will include them in their decision making and thus are provided with an economic incentive to develop technologies which to a greater extent facilitates recycling and 'light-weighting' (ie reducing weight of materials at source).

Three command-and-control approaches aimed at packaging waste have been taken by Germany, the European Community and the Netherlands. The Packaging Ordinance mandates the take back and recycling of packaging in Germany. However, Brisson (1993) argues that the Ordinance is far too rigid and inflexible and creates new economic inefficiencies and in addition is an impediment to trade. Also, the costs of reaching the very high recycling rates are not taken into account, just as insufficient consideration has been given to the resulting recycled materials, some of which have no markets.

The proposed EC Directive on packaging waste repeats some of the misconceptions of the German Packaging Ordinance by also setting recycling targets for all Member States. Again, no attempt has been made to determine the optimal recycling level. Furthermore, the Directive also prescribes that landfill should be used as a last resort only. This is done without any mention of the current underpricing of

Table 6.3 *Packaging waste arisings in the European Community*

Sector	Total (m tonnes)	Non-recycled (m tonnes)	Recycled (m tonnes)	Recycled (%)
Domestic	25.0	22.5	2.5	10
Commercial	15.0	12.5	2.5	17
Industrial	10.5	6.0	4.5	43
All	50.5	41.0	9.5	–

Source: European Commission

landfill disposal, which, if corrected, may lead to the market forces arriving at the optimal level of landfill disposal. The Directive does encourage the use of economic instruments by individual Member States, only to obstruct this possibility with conditions which effectively rule out any use of economic instruments after a transition period of five years.

The Netherlands is another example of a country which has set arbitrary recycling and source reduction targets. It does, however, allow for renegotiation of the terms in the Packaging Covenant, if the costs associated with reaching the goals set out turn out to be unacceptable.

Under an alternative economic instruments approach a packaging charge reflecting disposal costs associated with packaging waste could be introduced. On the basis of the concept of life cycle analysis, it can be argued that external effects occurring earlier in the life cycle of packaging (such as external costs associated with energy use in the production of packaging) are more efficiently dealt with at the point of occurrence rather than attempting to bundle all such external costs together in one all-encompassing packaging charge. In fact, since some externalities are already dealt with through regulatory policies, including them in a packaging charge would merely result in double taxation, which would be economically inefficient. It can be argued then that a packaging charge should only include marginal collection costs (MCC), marginal external waste disposal costs (MDC), litter costs (MLC) and perhaps some allowance for marginal landfill 'user costs' (MLUC). User costs measure the true scarcity of a resource, in this case the scarcity of the landfill site. Consideration should be given to the amount of recycling taking place and source reduction, as both result in less waste being landfilled.

The basic principles of a packaging charge, then, are that:

- the charge should be larger, the heavier or more voluminous the waste is;
- the charge should be lower, the higher the rate of recycling.

One such formula that is both simple and feasible to estimate and which reflects these principles is:

$$t = (100W/Lk).(MCC+MDC+MLC+MLUC)$$

where 't' is the levy on the packaging, applied in this instance to beverage containers (cans, cartons, bottles); W is the weight of the container; 100/L simply standardises the formula for a charge per 100 litres of containers; MCC, MDC and MLUC are as explained above; k is the number of trips made by the container, ie the number of times it is re-used. If the container material is recycled rather than re-used then r, the recycling rate, can be expressed in terms of k as $k=1/(1-r)$. Brisson (1993) reports empirical estimates of such a product charge for various countries, including the UK. Table 6.4 sets out the results for the UK. Note that the charge achieves the purposes set out above: it is higher the less recycling there is, and lower the more source reduction there is, thus rewarding environmental improvement. Note also that the results are not quite as many would expect. Cartons, which often strike the environmentalist as environmentally the most 'unfriendly' (because they are hardly recycled at all) attract the lowest charge rate. If energy recovery potential is allowed for, cartons might attract an even lower charge rate (they have high calorific value).

CONCLUSIONS

The polluter pays principle lays down that both producers and consumers should pay the full social costs of their actions. It has been argued in this chapter that the full social costs are not currently reflected in the prices of products or in the charges made for waste-related services. This market failure means that the receiving capacity of the environment is underpriced: there will be too large a demand for waste disposal services and too low a level of recycling activity. However, the setting of recycling targets without regard for the costs and benefits of recycling is likely to lead to inefficiency and a waste of resources. The UK Government is now committed to the introduction of economic instruments for the achievement of solid waste management goals. This we argue is likely to improve the efficiency of waste management policy. The recycling credits scheme is under way and the introduction of a landfill disposal levy has been debated in official and other circles. However, neither of these instruments will directly encourage the reduction of waste at source (both householder and commercial/industrial waste generators). Other instruments such as charging households for the removal of waste according to quantity and the use of deposit-refunds or product charges could augment the instruments portfolio (Pearce and Turner, 1993; Brisson, 1993).

In the context of packaging waste, a simple packaging tax has much to recommend it. Such an instrument offers a more cost-effective solution to the problem of packaging waste and litter than regulatory legislation of the type introduced, for example, in Germany. Waste management should be viewed as an integrated system encompassing, waste minimisation, recycling and final disposal activities (Turner, 1992). Formally identifying the most effective and efficient system components and overall system configuration is, however, a

Table 6.4 Devising a packaging charge for the UK

| | PET bottle | Aluminium can | | Steel can | | Aseptic carton | Gable top carton | Glass bottle | | | |
		CSD 33 ml	Beer 44 ml	CSD 33 ml	Beer 44 ml						
Recycling rate	5%	8%	8%	10%	10%	0%	0%	0%	86%	90%	93%
[1] Weight (kg/100 litres)	3.00	5.15	4.32	8.48	7.50	2.70	2.90	36.00	45.00	45.00	45.00
[2] Trips	1.05	1.09	1.09	1.11	1.11	1.00	1.00	1.00	7.00	10.00	14.00
[3]=[1]/[2] Weight per trip (kg/100 litres)	2.86	4.74	3.97	7.74	6.75	2.70	2.90	36.00	6.43	4.50	3.21
[4] Collection and disposal costs (£/tonne)	20.00	20.00	20.00	20.00	20.00	20.00	20.00	20.00	20.00	20.00	20.00
$[5]=[3]\times[4]/10^3$ Packaging charge (£/100 litres)	0.06	0.09	0.08	0.15	0.14	0.05	0.06	0.72	0.13	0.09	0.06

Source: Brisson (1993)

formidably complex and resource-intensive task. Economic analysis (and economic instruments) can make an important contribution to this policy/options evaluation process. Currently, the UK lacks an integrated waste management policy and has instead opted for arbitrary recycling targets which (a) have no particular rationale in themselves and (b) have not been put into the context of an integrated policy. Some of the ingredients of policy towards waste have a sound economic basis, but there is no coherent economic framework for policy as a whole.

Chapter 7

Biodiversity

INTRODUCTION

The term biological diversity, often shortened to biodiversity, is used to describe the number, variety and variability of living organisms. Biodiversity therefore embraces the whole of 'life on earth'. Decline in biodiversity includes all those changes that have to do with reducing or simplifying biological heterogeneity, from individuals to regions. It is common to think of biodiversity in terms of the number and diversity of species, and indeed it is the influence of one species, human beings, which now threatens global biodiversity. Extinction of species is now taking place at an unprecedented rate, possibly 1000 times greater than the background or natural rate and these losses are almost all human induced (Wilson, 1988). This massive extinction of living organisms is of economic concern because it may impose large costs on both present and future generations.

Extinction is an irreversible process, unless we envisage a biotechnological revolution such as portrayed in *Jurassic Park* (Crichton, 1991), where long-extinct organisms can be cloned from preserved fragments of genetic material. Extinction threatens sustainability for a number of reasons, but particularly because it may affect the stability of economically important ecosystems, and it may entail the losses of plants, animals and micro-organisms that would otherwise have become important resources in the future (Bishop, 1993). This chapter sets out some of the problems in defining and measuring biodiversity; outlines the status of biodiversity in the UK and the policies enacted to protect biodiversity. Are we using our biological resources in a sustainable way in order to conserve adequate biodiversity for future generations?

DEFINITIONS AND MEASURES OF BIOLOGICAL DIVERSITY

Biological diversity incorporates the idea of distinctiveness at every level of life, from molecules, to cells, to individuals, to species, to assemblages of species, and to ecosystems. Biodiversity may be described in terms of genes, species, and ecosystems, corresponding to three fundamental and hierarchically-related levels of biological organisation.

Hierarchical definitions

Genetic diversity is the sum of genetic information contained in the genes of individuals of plants, animals and micro-organisms. Each species is the repository of an immense amount of genetic information. The number of genes ranges from about 1000 in bacteria, up to 400,000 or more in many flowering plants. Each species is made up of many organisms, and virtually no two members of the same species are genetically identical (although this is relatively common in some types of plants). This means for example that even if an endangered species is saved from extinction, it will probably have lost much of its internal diversity.

Species diversity refers to the number and variety of species, which are regarded as populations within which gene flow occurs under normal conditions. Within a species all normal individuals are capable of breeding with the other individuals of the opposite sex belonging to the same species, or at least they are capable of being genetically linked with them through chains of other breeding individuals. By definition members of one species do not breed freely with members of other species. Although this definition works well for many animal and plant species, it is more difficult to delineate species in populations where hybridisation, or self-fertilisation or parthenogenesis occur. Arbitrary divisions must be made, and indeed this is an area where scientists often disagree. Within the hierarchical system used by scientists to classify organisms, species represent one rung on the ladder of classification. In ascending order, the main categories, or taxa, of living things are: species, genus, family, order, class, phylum, kingdom. We do not know the true number of species on earth, even to the nearest order of magnitude. Wilson (1988) estimates that the absolute number of species falls between 5 and 30 million, although some scientists have put forward even higher estimates, up to 50 million. For example, one recent survey of the deep ocean floor gave rise to an estimate of perhaps 10 million new species. At present approximately 1.4 million living species of all kinds of organisms have been described.

Ecosystem diversity relates to the variety of habitats, biotic communities and ecological processes in the biosphere as well as the diversity within ecosystems. Diversity can be described at a number of different levels and scales. Functional diversity is the relative abundance of functionally different kinds of organisms. Community diversity is the number, sizes and spatial distribution of communities, and is sometimes referred to as patchiness. Landscape diversity is the diversity of scales of patchiness. No simple relationship exists between the diversity of an ecosystem and ecological processes such as productivity, hydrology, and soil generation.

A better understanding of biodiversity can be obtained when we examine exactly what we measure in order to assess biological diversity. However, this also serves to highlight further the range of interpretations, and the importance placed on different hierarchical levels of biodiversity by scholars of different disciplines, and by policy makers. There is no clear consensus over how biodiversity should be measured.

Measurable indicators

Genetic diversity can be measured in terms of phenotypic traits, allelic frequencies, or DNA sequences, and recent advances in genetics produce new findings each day. However, despite the technology now available, the sheer magnitude of genetic diversity means that gathering information takes time; for example, although warranting many million dollars funding and an international coordinated effort, the 'Human Genome Project' will take decades to crack the human genetic code.

Species diversity is a function of the distribution and abundance of species. Often, species richness (the number of species within a region or given area) is used almost synonymously with species diversity. However, technically, species diversity includes some consideration of evenness of species abundances. In its ideal form, species richness would consist of a complete catalogue of all species occurring in the area under consideration, but this is not usually possible, unless it is a very small area.

Community diversity is less easy to define, as many different 'units' of diversity are involved at the supra-species level, including the pattern of habitats in the community, relative abundance of species, age structure of populations, patterns of communities on the landscape, trophic structure, and patch dynamics. At these levels, unambiguous boundaries delineating units of biodiversity do not exist. Given the complexities of defining biodiversity at ecosystem level, there are a range of different approaches to measuring ecosystem diversity. As Reid *et al* (1992) explain, any number of community attributes are components of biodiversity and may deserve monitoring for specific objectives. There are several generic measures of ecosystem level diversity. These include biogeographical realms or provinces, based on the distribution of species, and ecoregions or ecozones, based on physical attributes such as soils and climate. These definitions may differ according to scale, for example, the world has been divided into biogeographical provinces, or more fine-grained classifications which may be more useful for policy-making. More policy orientated measures include the definition of 'hotspots', based on the number of endemic species, and 'megadiversity' states.

This demonstrates that biodiversity may be measured at a number of different levels, and also at different scales, and it is unclear just how useful a national scale approach is in scientific terms. Indicators are needed in order to monitor and develop policy, and Noss *et al* (1992) suggest a number of indicators at the species level which can be easily monitored. These include *keystone species*, those species of pivotal importance in their ecosystems and upon which the diversity of the community as a whole is strongly dependent; and *umbrella species*, relatively wide-ranging species, such as large carnivores, whose protection would assure adequate amounts of habitat for many other species. Five categories of species have been used to justify special conservation effort: ecological indicator, keystone, umbrella, flagship (charismatic) and vulnerable species.

THREATS TO BIODIVERSITY

The main cause of loss of biodiversity in the UK, as in most of the world, is the conversion of land from natural vegetation to agricultural and other uses. A recent analysis predicts a loss of two to 13 per cent of all currently existing species in the next 25 years, inferred from rates of destruction of natural habitat alone (Reid, 1992). Other losses are due to pollution, the use of pesticides, chemical contamination, and the introduction of exotic species. The forces driving the loss of global biodiversity can be characterised as proximate causes, which include the conversion of land use such as deforestation; and fundamental causes which include the global specialisation of production (see Swanson, 1992). This is exacerbated by the failure to demonstrate and appropriate the value of biodiversity as a cause of biodiversity loss (Pearce *et al*, 1993), compounded by a series of market and institu-tional, and policy and information failures.

Land use conversion has certainly been a major cause of biodiversity loss in the UK and the process is ongoing. Data presented in Chapter 8 on agriculture show how semi-natural vegetation now accounts for less than 10 per cent of the area of England and Wales, and that this has declined by more than a fifth in the last 45 years, since the Second World War. The Council for the Protection of Rural England (CPRE) has recently estimated that over 10,000 ha – more than twice the figure cited by Government statistics – is converted from countryside to urban use each year in England alone (*Guardian*, 1993).

CURRENT STATUS OF BIODIVERSITY IN THE UK

Even in a well-studied country such as the UK, there is no one comprehensive catalogue of our resident flora and fauna. Despite this, more is probably known about the natural history of the UK than any other country. Such studies have a long tradition, starting with Gilbert White's letters, published as the *Natural History and Antiquities of Selborne*, in 1789, a pioneering work describing the ecology of a parish in Hampshire. Only about three per cent of the global total of recorded terrestrial species are found in these islands, which represent 0.007 per cent of the planet's land area. However, species new to science, as well as those new to the UK, are discovered each year. There are an estimated 30,000 species of animals (excluding marine microscopic and less well-known groups), and 3,200 plant species according to HM Government (1993b). Approximately 22,000 of these animal species are insects. Not all of these species are native to the UK. Table 7.1 shows the number of native species, and those which are at risk (as defined by the World Conservation Union) in the UK.

Table 7.1 *UK native species at risk, 1991*

Species group	Native species	Extinct	Endangered[1]	Vulnerable[2]	Rare[3]
ANIMALS					
Mammals breeding on land[4]	44	1[5]	n/a	n/a	n/a
Birds	c560[6]	6[5]	n/a	n/a	n/a
Non-marine reptiles	6	–	2	–	–
Amphibians	6	–	1	1	–
Freshwater fish[7]	41	2	2	3	2
Flies	c6000	13	208	223	312
Bees/wasps/ants	520	31	27	20	54
Beetles	c3900	64	132	84	266
Butterflies/moths	c2400	22	21	22	55
Caddis flies	196	2	7	7	8
True bugs	540	7	13	6	53
Grasshoppers/crickets/ cockroaches	30	–	3	2	1
Stoneflies	33	1	–	1	–

Dragonflies/damselfies	41	3	1	2	3
Mayflies	47	–	1	2	1
Spiders/harvestmen/ pseudoscorpions	c670	–	22	31	29
Larger non-marine crustaceans	c70	1	2	1	2
Non-marine molluscs	c200	–	10	7	11
Leeches	16	–	–	–	1
PLANTS					
Seed plants	1425[8]	19	48	91	151
Ferns and related plants[9]	69	–	3	2	3
Liverworts/mosses	c1000	16	30	59	117
Lichens	c1500	25	57	63	176
Stoneworts	29	2	4	6	6

Notes:

n/a Comparable data are not available for birds and mammals because their status is considered in the international not national context

1 IUCN Red Data Book category defining, in a national context, species in danger of extinction and whose survival is unlikely if the causal factors continue operating

2 IUCN Red Data Book category defining, in a national context, species believed likely to move into endangered category in the near future if causal factors continue operating

3 IUCN Red Data Book category defining, in a national context, species with small populations that are not at present endangered but are at risk

4 Includes seals but not cetaceans

5 Breeding species which have become extinct in Great Britain since 1900, and remain so

6 Total recorded in Britain, including 237 regularly breeding species and a further 54 common passage migrants and winter visitors

7 Includes fish which leave the sea to breed in freshwater (eg salmon)

8 This figure excludes certain groups such as hawkweeds, dandelions, and blackberries, for which the number of species is not certainly known

9 Including clubmosses and horsetails

Source: HM Government, 1993b

Biodiversity in the UK is influenced by a number of factors, particularly the relatively short time since the last glaciation, which means that there are relatively few endemic species (those that are found only in the UK). High human population density and long history of intensive land use has determined the vegetation cover. Woodland once covered 80 per cent of the area of Great Britain, and consequently plants and animals characteristic of forest conditions predominate. However, most of the forest and woodland cover was cleared centuries ago, so that forest covered only five per cent of the area at the turn of the century, and species characteristic of more open habitat such as heath, grassland and wetlands, have colonised cleared areas. This has resulted in the development of distinctive assemblages of plants and animals, in most cases shaped by traditional countryside management practices, for example, hedgerows hundreds of years old provide havens for a variety of plants, insects, birds and small animals.

Although tropical areas form the natural habitats for a greater proportion of the world's species (for example, one hectare of coastal forest in northeastern Brazil was recently found to contain 450 different species of tree), and most media attention has focused on destruction of tropical forests and coral reefs, the UK nonetheless has habitats and sites of global significance. The UK has a rich and characteristic biodiversity for an island of its size, isolation and geographical position. Table 7.2, for example, shows the international importance of British estuaries. British estuaries are especially important for migratory bird species, as the geographical position of

Table 7.2 *Number of birds dependent on British estuaries*

Estuary	Waterfowl	Wildfowl	Waders	Internationally important bird species
Wash	280,000	52,000	228,000	12
Morecambe Bay	202,000	27,000	175,000	11
Ribble	191,000	69,000	122,000	13
Thames	129,000	35,000	95,000	11
Humber	123,000	19,000	104,000	10
Solway	122,000	43,000	79,000	10
Dee	118,000	26,000	92,000	10
Severn	85,000	22,000	63,000	6
Forth	72,000	31,000	42,000	6
Strangford Lough	65,000	23,000	41,000	3
Mersey	64,000	28,000	36,000	5
Alt	61,000	2,000	60,000	2
Lindisfarne	58,000	30,000	28,000	6
Swale	58,000	25,000	33,000	4
North Norfolk marshes	56,000	34,000	21,000	4

Note:
The international importance of British estuaries
At least 56 estuaries in the UK are of international importance for waterfowl, and British estuaries support some 40 per cent of wading birds that winter in Europe. This is illustrated in the table, which shows the numbers of waterfowl, wildfowl, waders, and internationally important bird species in 15 British estuaries. Thirteen species of wading birds and seventeen species of estuarine wildfowl occur in sufficient numbers, and are under sufficient threat to justify inclusion in the list of Red Data birds.

Source: RSPB, 1993

the British Isles lies at the junction of a number of migration routes, but many estuaries are under threat from water pollution and urbanisation.

The importance of UK estuaries for wading birds and wildfowl is attributable to three main factors. First, estuaries are productive habitats, providing invertebrate food resources which can support high numbers of birds. Secondly, unlike much of Europe and Africa, our coastline experiences a large tidal amplitude, and this exposes extensive areas of intertidal habitat. Thirdly, the comparatively mild winter climate provides ice-free conditions at a northerly latitude (RSPB, 1993).

Other important habitats include heather moorlands, ancient woodland, lowland and upland bogs, and chalk grasslands which, together with certain wetlands, are recognised internationally through designations such as Biosphere Reserves and Ramsar Sites. English Nature has recently highlighted the importance of marine reserves to Britain's coast, and identified 27 areas which were under threat and required special protection (English Nature, 1993).

MONITORING AND PROTECTING BIODIVERSITY

This section briefly describes the policies implemented in the UK to conserve biological diversity, by referring to the three 'levels' of biodiversity – genetic, species and community – which were introduced earlier in the chapter. It then examines the effectiveness of those policies and highlights the degree of scientific uncertainty concerning measuring and monitoring effective policy implementation.

Conservation of genetic diversity

All species vary in many characters, but in most cases this variation remains little known or undocumented. There are many examples of geographical variation amongst Britain's plants and animals, which may give rise to geographical subspecies or races. Some of the most well-known cases of genetic variation are those associated with domesticated species. In Britain there has been a long and successful history of plant breeding and selection of domesticated animals for preferred characteristics. For example, the many varieties of domestic apples, descended from the wild crab apple, show different characteristics according to their use; for eating, cooking, cider-making and so on. Over 40 breeds of sheep occur in Britain, with some found only on small islands, such as North Ronaldsay in the Orkneys, where the sheep have adapted to eating seaweed. Much of this diversity associated with traditional uses is now rapidly disappearing, as consumers and processors demand uniform products. The erosion of genetic diversity is also occurring as a result of introduction and restocking with 'alien' genes, and because of extensive planting of exotic species such as ryegrass.

The *in situ* (in its natural habitat) conservation of biodiversity through the protection of ecosystems and habitats may not be sufficient to maintain genetic stocks of some species for a number of reasons. These include the natural rarity of the species themselves; if their natural habitats are particularly threatened; if they are difficult to obtain from the wild. *Ex situ* (outside of its natural habitat) conservation may play a vital role in supporting species through crisis periods, as well as providing resources for research. *Ex situ* collections are used especially to provide reservoir populations or stocks used to support the survival of species in the wild, for example in reintroduction or restocking programmes, and most importantly to maintain genetic stocks and as an insurance policy through holding stocks in long term storage (germplasm banks).

There are more than 50 botanic gardens and arboreta in the UK; indeed, the UK ranks third in the world for the number of accessions in cultivation, with over 200,000 species of plants. The most famous are the Royal Botanical Gardens at Kew, established in the 1780s by George III. Although traditionally associated with the collection, preservation and scientific investigation of specimens collected from overseas, Kew is now responsible for the propagation of endangered plants such as the Lady's Slipper (*Cypripedium calceolus*), and is home to the Seed Bank, funded to collect seeds from most of the English flowering plants protected under Schedule 8 of the Wildlife and Countryside Act, as well as many species as possible of the native British flora (Prendergast, 1992).

Species conservation policies

Within the UK specific protection is provided for a number of species of wild animals, as well as broad protection for wild birds by making it an offence to kill, injure, take or possess them, disturb them, destroy places used for shelter or protection, or offer them for sale. Table 7.3 shows native species protected in the UK under the Wildlife and Countryside Act. This shows increased numbers of species protected between 1981 and 1991, but it is unclear whether this reflects greater numbers at risk, or a higher level of protection.

Table 7.3 *Native species protected under the UK Wildlife And Countryside Act*

Species group	Fully protected		Partially protected	
	1981	1991	1981	1991
ANIMALS				
Mammals breeding on land	20 (a)	24 (a)	(b)	(b)
Whales/dolphins/porpoises	3	25 (c)	–	–
Birds	(d)	(d)	35	35
Reptiles	2	7 (e)	4	4
Amphibians	2	2	4	4
Fish	1	3	(f)	1 (f)
Beetles	1	2	–	–
Butterflies/moths	9	9	–	22
True bugs	–	1	–	–
Grasshoppers/crickets	3	3	–	–
Dragonflies	1	1	–	–
Spiders	2	2	–	–
Crustaceans	–	3	–	1
Sea mats	–	1	–	–
Molluscs	3	2	–	1
Leeches/other worms	–	2	–	–
Sea anenomes and allied animals	–	2	–	–
PLANTS				
Higher plants	62	92	(g)	(g)
Lower plants	–	1	(g)	(g)

Notes:
(a) Includes all species of bat; badgers have full protection under other legislation
(b) Seals and deer are partially protected under separate legislation
(c) All species which have or may occur in British waters
(d) All those which have occurred or may occur in Britain, excluding those listed as partially protected
(e) Includes five species of vagrant marine turtle
(f) In addition, all other fish breeding in freshwater including eel are protected by other legislation
(g) All plants are protected against uprooting

Source: HM Government, 1993b

Conservation at the ecosystem level

In Britain, conservation is primarily concerned with intervention and the active manipulation of the environment, aiming to maintain a given habitat at a particular successional stage in perpetuity: the objectives are therefore determined by a human cultural perception of biodiversity and the natural environment which shows a demand for managed or semi-natural landscapes and habitats. This contrasts markedly with the North American conservation ethic based on the purity and inviolability of wilderness (see Henderson, 1992, for a comparison of the UK and North America). In effect, there is no *wilderness* in Britain and nature conservation is generally focused on semi-natural areas. Indeed, two different studies by Willis and Garrod (1993), and O'Riordan *et al* (1993) examining conservation options in a semi-natural upland area, the Yorkshire Dales National Park, reached the same conclusions: that public opinion favours a conserved and planned landscape, rather than one allowed to revert to a more natural, climax state.

UK conservation policy is based primarily on the protection of representative areas. According to the UK Government's latest environmental policy document, a discussion paper on sustainable development, nearly 20 per cent of the UK is covered by special designations intended to 'help conserve its character and natural features on which wildlife are dependent' (HM Government, 1993c: 20). These designations, which include National Parks, Areas of Outstanding National Beauty and Sites of Special Scientific Interest (SSSIs), are shown in Table 7.4.

Designated and statutory protected areas in the UK

The primary purpose of the UK system for designating areas is to 'identify and protect the finest landscapes and the most important nature conservation sites and areas of recreational interest throughout the country' (HM Government, 1993b: 87). Table 7.4 shows the areas designated as National Parks, Areas of Outstanding Natural Beauty (AONBs), and their equivalent, National Scenic Areas in Scotland. National Parks comprise some nine per cent of the total area of England and Wales, AONBs 14 per cent of England and Wales, 13 per cent of Scotland, and 20 per cent of Northern Ireland. Various other categories of statutory protected areas have been established for the protection of natural conservation features; the main ones are shown below.

The most widespread designated areas are Sites of Special Scientific Interest. There are more than 5800 SSSIs in Great Britain; most of these are notified under the 1981 Wildlife and Countryside Act, while a smaller proportion, though still increasing over time, is covered by management agreements between site owners and the national bodies concerned with countryside and conservation – English Nature, the Countryside Council for Wales, and Scottish Natural Heritage. Under

Table 7.4 *Designated and protected areas in the UK, March 1992*

Designated areas	Number	Area (sq km)
National Parks (England and Wales)*	10	13,729
AONBs[1] (England and Wales)	40	20,428
AONBs[1] (Northern Ireland)	9	2,849
National Scenic Areas (Scotland)	40	10,173
Protected areas		
National Nature Reserves	297	1,763
Local Nature Reserves[2]	307	185
SSSIs	5,852	18,161
– notified under 1981 Act	5,770	17,594
– S15 Management Agreements	(a)	1,225
Areas of Scientific Interest[3]	46	634
Areas of Special Scientific Interest	36	75
Special Protection Areas	48	1,488
Biosphere Reserves	13	443
'Ramsar' Wetland Sites	53	1,441
Environmentally Sensitive Areas	19	8,387

Notes:
Some areas may be included in more than one category. For example, in Great Britain NNRs, SPAs, Biosphere Reserves and Ramsar Sites are all SSSIs
* This does not include the Norfolk and Suffolk Broads, which although not designated a National Park under the 1949 National Parks and Access to the Countryside Act, is afforded virtual National Parks status by the Norfolk and Suffolk Broads Act, 1989
1 AONBs are Areas of Outstanding Natural Beauty
2 Great Britain only
3 Northern Ireland only
(a) 2271 agreements

the 1981 Act, these bodies have a statutory duty to notify site owners and local planning authorities of SSSIs.

The latest policy documents from English Nature, the government's statutory advisor on conservation, advocate a more integrated approach and focus on 'Natural Areas' (English Nature, 1993a, 1993b). However, there are few concrete proposals for action suggested. As scientists understand more about the complex interactions of species and their habitats, so a more scientifically rigorous approach to land use is required. Such a strategy has recently been set out for the Pacific Northwest of the USA, the 'Wildlands Project' (Mann and Plummer, 1993), utilising a mix of wildlife corridors, buffer zones and protected areas to maximise wildlife benefits. Such an approach may not be appropriate nor feasible in the UK given the density of population and intensity of land use, but it does stand as a model for more sustainable land use. As part of its commitment to the Convention on Biological Diversity (further examined in Chapter 11) the UK has now to develop a Biodiversity Action Plan which it is hoped will consider the integration of biodiversity into a sustainable development programme.

Monitoring biodiversity

Table 7.1 showed the numbers of species which are endangered and also those estimated to have become extinct this century. This of course says nothing about historical extinction before 1900 (and we expect large numbers of extinctions of many plants and invertebrates, and especially beetles associated with ancient trees and deadwood as a result of forest clearance in the past 5000 years), but also examining species richness tells us little about what is happening to genetic variations within remaining populations. Whilst comfort might be taken from the fact that 'only' one per cent of Britain's invertebrate species has become extinct this century, that fauna has become markedly impoverished in terms of the size and distribution of species populations. Once genetic variation is lost from within a species, for instance because the population has declined to a few closely related individuals, it takes many generations to be regained.

National recording schemes for wildlife species are carried out by several organisations, and data exist for a number of mammal species, including seals, otters, and squirrels (HM Government, 1993b). More extensive data exist for bird species, and the monitoring of birds has a longer and more intensive history. Insects such as butterflies and moths are monitored, and rare and threatened species of plants, animals and birds are recorded in Red Data Books for Britain.

Earlier sections have identified the main focus of UK conservation policy as being on protected areas. Despite containing little of what might be described as 'wilderness' or 'wildlands', it appears that the UK has a comprehensive system comprising a hierarchy of designated areas affording different kinds of protection; to individual species as well as habitats, but this policy remains relatively ineffectual in terms of conservation and sustainable use of biological diversity. According to categories defined by the World Conservation Union, none of the designated protected areas in the UK qualify as 'fully protected', all designations, equivalent to 18.96 per cent of land area, falling under the category of 'partially protected'. Table 7.5 shows this in comparison with some other countries.

Under the World Conservation Union classification, all UK designations are defined as either Category IV, Managed Nature Reserves/

Table 7.5 *National protected areas: land area protected by IUCN categories*

Country	Totally protected (%)	Partially protected (%)	All categories (%)
UK	0.00	18.96	18.96
Norway	12.00	0.89	12.89
Europe average	0.99	7.01	8.00
USA	4.10	6.38	10.49
Costa Rica	9.50	2.74	12.24
World average	3.04	2.12	5.17

Source: World Conservation Monitoring Centre, 1992

Wildlife Sanctuary (44 sites, 136,877 ha), or Category V, Protected Landscape or Seascape (96 sites, 4,502,829 ha). So even SSSIs are not categorised as Scientific Reserves or Strict Nature Reserve (Category I), neither are English and Welsh National Parks classed as National Parks (Category II).

English Nature, the government's statutory advisor on nature conservation in England, recognises in its latest policy document:

> Society's past failure to adopt the principle of sustainable land use has resulted in the national decline of most of England's wildlife and natural features. It has led to the local extinction of many species, not just the rare, but also the commonplace. Society now needs to recognise that it depends upon the natural environment and has a duty to secure it for future generations.
>
> (English Nature, 1993c: 5)

The effectiveness of past protection policies is inadequate when the condition of SSSIs is examined, as shown in Table 7.6.

Agricultural activities are the greatest cause of all sorts of damage (Department of the Environment, 1993b); recreational activities, insufficient management, and miscellaneous activities including pollution, unauthorised tipping and burning were also important. In addition, more than 1000 Sites of Special Scientific Interest are likely to suffer from acidification damage within the next decade (ENDS Report, 1993).

The limited monitoring systems in place, which may detect some aspects of biodiversity, but not others, indicate that the level of protection is not adequate to prevent undermining of biological diversity. Amongst the threats to British biodiversity can be identified the continuing loss and fragmentation of key habitats, particularly

Table 7.6 *Damage to Sites of Special Scientific Interest (SSSIs)*

	1986	1987	1988	1989	1990	1991	1992
Number of SSSIs	4842	4729	4996	5184	5435	5671	5852
Area (10^6 hectares)	1.43	1.52	1.58	1.64	1.71	1.78	1.82
SSSIs lost or partially lost	2	24	21	21	7	11	7
SSSIs with long- or short-term damage	172	212	146	220	317	262	313

Sources: Department of the Environment, 1993b, 1992; Usher, 1992

SSSIs, due mainly to unsustainable agricultural practices and pollution. In addition there is a narrowing of the genetic base of not only the domesticated species, in terms of crop varieties and livestock breeds, but also dwindling populations of wild species. Many of these processes are still not fully understood, and this scientific uncertainty on certain aspects of biodiversity has particular implications for sustainable development policy on biodiversity.

SCIENTIFIC UNCERTAINTY AND SUSTAINABLE DEVELOPMENT POLICY

If biodiversity is so difficult to define and measure, and there remains so much scientific uncertainty – for example, simply the number of species which exist, and the exact nature of services and functions from communities – then the formulation of appropriate policy, and the assessment and evaluation of its effectiveness is difficult.

For example, applying a safe minimum standard of environmental quality, or an area of representative habitat, will not safeguard critical biodiversity capital. MacGarvin (1993) highlights the difficulty of setting safe minimum standards for pollution in the Northeast Atlantic and North Sea, as well as in estimating the minimum viable population and 'optimal depletion' of fish stocks. In the past, population predictions have proved highly inaccurate, and there have been huge differences between model predictions and observations. During the 1980s, theoretical ecologists became increasingly frustrated at their inability to produce a 'grand unifying theory' to explain how population regulation worked. For example, uncertainty abounds on the relative importance of competition or natural enemies, flaws in experimental design and statistical analysis. In addition the possible influence of chaotic fluctuations and random events further reduces the possibility of predicting the effect of human interaction on marine and other ecosystems.

Such scientific uncertainty therefore supports the adoption of a precautionary approach to biodiversity conservation, at least until better knowledge is gained. This view is endorsed by Hohl and Tisdell (1993) who argue that safe minimum standards for the conservation of species do not exist and that no standard ensures the continued existence of any species. This obviously creates difficulties for policy makers who hope to use the findings of natural scientists to inform policy.

CONCLUSIONS

The UK clearly lacks a coherent policy on biodiversity, to the extent that we find biodiversity as a term rarely mentioned in policy documents in the British context. Biodiversity is something that tropical countries have; in Britain the focus remains on 'nature conservation'.

Serious consideration of biodiversity has failed to take place for a number of reasons. First, because of the lack of a clear definition of biological diversity, and therefore of measures and indicators for monitoring. This makes the formulation and assessment of effective conservation policies very difficult. Secondly, scientific uncertainty, which is related to this lack of a clear definition, makes the application of a safe minimum standard difficult, and therefore recommends the adoption of a precautionary approach which may be expensive and politically unpopular. Thirdly, conservation policy has traditionally relied on the designation of protected areas which has neither afforded a sufficient level of protection, nor proved to be the most appropriate policy, given both the lack of knowledge and historical patterns of land use.

Conservation and sustainable use of biological resources and biodiversity is intrinsic to the concept of sustainable development and a more integrated approach to land use is therefore required. At present policies in other sectors, especially forestry and agriculture (see Chapters 8 and 9) have been highly detrimental to biodiversity. For example, although forest cover has risen from five per cent to around ten per cent of land area since the end of the First World War, most of the new planting, which was mainly initiated under the auspices of the Forestry Commission, has consisted of introduced coniferous species. A policy making use of mixed stands of indigenous broadleaved species would enhance rather than deplete the biological diversity of wooded areas. Likewise, North Sea fishing policy has not taken biodiversity needs into consideration and fish stocks continue to be depleted. Agricultural policy is often at odds with nature conservation; for example in the past, subsidies were given to destroy hedgerows. There may be opportunities to integrate biodiversity needs into agriculture policy; for example, the EC Set-Aside regime could be adapted to maximise conservation benefits (Wilson and Fuller, 1992).

A 'strong sustainability' approach to conservation of biodiversity, where the precautionary principle is adopted and biodiversity considerations are integrated into all areas of public policy is vital in order to maximise conservation and minimise extinction of species. Given the lack of information on values, uses and ecological functions of diverse biological resources, an optimal rate of depletion of biodiversity cannot be estimated. The present system of weakly enforced protected areas does not even match 'weak sustainability' criteria and results in continual erosion of the UK's biological diversity.

Chapter 8

Agriculture and the environment

INTRODUCTION

The agricultural sector is vital to sustainability and conserving the natural environment. The current activities of the agricultural sector are not sustainable because of their impact on critical natural capital, and the international ecological footprint of EC support for agricultural production. The agricultural sector produces pollutants itself, but also acts as a sink for pollutants from other sectors. Indicators presented in this chapter demonstrate that changes in land use and management in recent decades have increased pollution and have acted as one of the major pressures causing loss of biodiversity.

To minimise these unsustainable impacts, public support of agriculture should be given to environment-enhancing activities rather than intensive production. The implementation of reform is likely to be resisted by existing group interests, as evidenced in protests against Common Agricultural Policy reform in the EC. Indeed, as shown throughout this volume, policies in many sectors are marked by similar disregard for sustainability and for catering to organised interests.

CONDITIONS FOR SUSTAINABLE AGRICULTURAL DEVELOPMENT

The prime objective of the agricultural sector is the production of food and fibre, but due to the interaction of land use, human well-being and culture, the sector has a unique relationship with sustainable development. The importance of the sector to the environment is much greater than the indicators of the number of people employed in agriculture or of agriculture's contribution to the economy would suggest. The agriculture sector combines the classic factors of production – land, labour and capital. It is the extensive use of the land factor which determines the unique influence of agriculture, along with forestry, on the natural environment. In the UK for example, agriculture accounts for around 77 per cent of the total area, with forestry about 10 per cent and the remainder being urban. Indeed the significance of agriculture is recognised by the UK Government: 'Farming remains the main force shaping Britain's rural economy, and the appearance of our countryside and landscape' (HM Government, 1990).

The agricultural sector has an effect on many aspects of environmental quality. In the previous chapter on biodiversity it was explained that the species and habitat diversity and distribution of the UK has been determined not only by ecological factors but by the evolution of human intervention and agricultural practices in the past millennia. Agriculture poses one of the greatest immediate threats to its decline. The population of Britain derives amenity from the existence of the countryside as well as from recreation and direct use of the countryside. As outlined in Chapter 5, the management of the rural environment also directly affects pollutant loading in ground and surface water and hence the quantity and quality of drinking water.

In the wider sense, sustainability and environmental change in rural Britain is conditional on many social and demographic factors (Hodge and Dunn (1992) review the diversity of factors in sustainability in the rural context). The maintenance of the aspects of rural Britain which would constitute environmentally unsustainable changes, such as in natural habitats or landscapes, depends on the structure and diversity of the rural population and economy. In short, the physical environment interacts with the human population, and ignoring social equity considerations may lead to unsustainable outcomes. The review here focuses on the maintenance of the natural capital stock, and its definition in the agricultural sector, as a prerequisite for sustainability.

Agricultural production combines the factors of production in different ways. Agriculture is a system consisting of: present land use and technology; external inputs such as energy and chemicals as well as labour; and a set of outputs, essentially food and fibre. For sustainability to be achieved it would seem that the inputs, the outputs and the system itself must be sustainable, and the links between the agricultural sector and 'natural' habitats as well as with other sectors of the domestic economy must be recognised. In the following sections the mechanisms of agricultural policy and their influence on sustainability are described. Indicators of environmental change and impacts are shown for the UK. If agriculture is to reduce its environmental impact and be sustainable, as defined by social and generational equity and non-declining natural capital, the agricultural policy signals, as well as the whole emphasis of land use policy, need to be revised.

AGRICULTURAL POLICY AND ITS ENVIRONMENTAL IMPACTS

The pattern of rural land use in the UK has been fundamentally affected by agricultural and other planning and regional development policy. For example, both the Agriculture Act of 1947, which set out the expansionary agricultural production policy of the following 40 years, and the Town and Country Planning Act of 1947, which essentially limited urban growth in rural areas through designation of Green Belts and other planning procedures, are major influences on the pattern of agricultural development. Entry into the Common Agricultural Policy of the EC in 1973 changed the mechanism of agricultural support and increased the pace of change. In the period since 1973 the UK has become 80 per cent self-sufficient in temperate foodstuffs, with the EC having fulfilled the food security objectives of the Treaty of Rome many times over and being in surplus in most commodities.

EC Agricultural policy

The tenets of the Common Agricultural Policy were determined by the original treaty of the European Community, the Treaty of Rome, in 1958. The objectives of the Common Agricultural Policy as set out in Article 39 were to increase agricultural productivity by promoting technical progress and by ensuring the rational development of agricultural production and the optimum utilisation of the factors of production, in particular labour; thus to ensure a fair standard of living for the agricultural community, in particular by increasing the individual earnings of persons engaged in agriculture; to stabilise markets; to assure the availability of supplies; and to ensure that supplies reach consumers at reasonable prices.

Many other industrialised countries and regions, which are prepared to subsidise agricultural sectors, have similar objectives, though the EC is probably unique in having a 'written constitution' for its policies. In general, developed countries subsidise agriculture and developing countries tax their agricultural sectors. This has variously been explained across countries by how organised farm lobbies are; by self-interested politicians realising that urban populations are more central to their support hence creating urban-rural biases; and by other cultural and historical contexts (Olson, 1985; de Gorter and Tsur, 1991).

The mechanisms instituted to meet agricultural policy objectives in the EC are, for the main commodities and 'regimes', variable import levies and export restitutions. Variable import levies set a threshold price each year in the EC for commodities such as wheat. As a result, wheat imported into the Community is subject to a levy to bring it up to the threshold price from the world market price which generally has been much lower. The overseas producers receive only the world market price with the revenue from the import levy accruing to the EC. Export restitutions are similar for produce going in the opposite direction, in that producers not able to sell their produce domestically due to surpluses are still guaranteed the threshold price for exporting outside the EC.

Table 8.1 illustrates the extent of this support in OECD countries, as measured through the numeraire of producer subsidy equivalent (PSE). This is a measure of the proportion of the revenue of farmers which accrues to them as a result of price support. The higher the PSE, the greater the proportion of farmers' income which comes from state support. For the EC for example, across the agricultural sector, nearly one half of farmgate revenue in 1990 resulted from price support. The EC, the USA and Japan have the highest levels of price support, which have also been growing in the past decade. The aggregate support of these countries and regions also varies between commodities, and with domestic agricultural support. The PSE of rice for Japan has reached over 90 per cent, and sheepmeat in the UK has a PSE over 70 per cent, a proportion of which is due to domestic price support.

Table 8.1 *Agricultural support for OECD countries and regions (net percentage producer subsidy equivalents)*

Country/region	1979–86	1987	1988	1989	1990	Annual % change 1979–90
EC	37	49	46	41	48	+3.5
US	28	41	34	29	30	+4.9
Canada	32	49	42	37	41	+6.0
Japan	66	76	74	71	68	+1.6
Australia	11	11	9	10	11	+1.8
New Zealand	24	14	7	5	5	–11.3
OECD	37	50	46	41	44	+3.9

Note: EC is 12 members post-1986; 10 members pre-1986

Source: Rae (1991) from OECD data

These policies have achieved the objectives of price stability in the EC. However, the system fuelled an expansion of production to levels greater than self-sufficiency. Consequently impacts on world markets were inevitable. The impacts of these policies on the environment, and hence on sustainability, include:

- increased intensity of input use for agricultural production;
- destabilisation of international commodity markets which negatively affects resource allocation and the structure of agriculture in many other parts of the world;
- the distorting effects of agricultural policy, which affect the ability of other policies for environmental protection to work, and their cost.

CAP reform

Inevitably the budgetary and environmental pressures of this system, and the need for trade reform, led to the 1992 CAP reforms (called the MacSharry reforms after the Agriculture Commissioner). The main principles of the reforms were:

- price reductions to reduce oversupply incentives;
- supply control measures in the form of set-aside requirements and cuts in production quotas;
- direct income support decoupled from production.

The major regimes of cereals, dairy products and beef were all reformed, though the market organisations for olive oil, fruit, vegetables and wine remain as before. The environmental impact of these measures are primarily in the cereals sector where price cuts and set-aside will affect the hectarage and the intensity of production; and in the afforestation and other environmental protection measures, which are to date unspecified but are primarily the responsibility of member states. In the UK, such policies already independently undertaken include Nitrate Sensitive Areas and Environmentally Sensitive Areas, where producers are compensated for lost income for not polluting or for enhanced conservation practices.

Of the reforms, set-aside has created the greatest controversy. Cereal producers in the EC who produce over 92 tonnes are only paid the guaranteed prices for their cereals if they designate 15 per cent of their land to be set aside from production. A fundamental problem with agricultural policy, highlighted by the set-aside part of the CAP reform and by Nitrate Sensitive Areas payments is that farmers are being compensated for not producing surpluses and avoiding the impacts of agricultural practices on the environment – this is in effect paying the polluter. In the words of Bromley and Hodge (1990), the EC confers a 'presumptive policy entitlement' to compensation which goes against such principles as making the polluter pay. Indeed this principle is enshrined in the UK Government's commitments in the

Environmental Protection Act. One major implication is that environmental quality in the rural environment may be lower than if the property rights regime was fundamentally different. This is due to it becoming increasingly more costly, in terms of foregone revenue, for farmers to reduce their polluting activities as subsidies increase.

Coase's (1960) theorem states that the efficient level of abatement of an externality will be achieved no matter where the property rights lie. However this has been shown not to hold in the real world for various reasons such as income effects and transactions costs of abating pollution. Because Coase's theorem does not hold, the environmental quality supplied by the present situation will always be less than if the property rights were reversed.

Figure 8.1a shows that the level of abatement achieved in any situation depends on the cost of abating each extra unit of the externality (say nitrate pollution) and on the marginal benefit of the party afflicted by the pollutant. According to the Coase theorem (Coase, 1960) if the victim bribes the polluter not to pollute (victim pays) or if the polluter compensates the recipient for suffering the externality (polluter pays), the solution is the same amount of abatement (optimal level of abatement Q^* at price P). One central assumption of the Coase theorem is that the amounts of compensation paid by the recipient or the polluter do not affect their overall economic position (their budget constraint). However, this has been shown not to hold. In Figure 8.1a, the revenue changing hands is equivalent to the amount $0P \times 0Q^*$. This is potentially a large sum and will make either the recipient or the polluter better off and change their demand and supply schedules for environmental quality. This is shown in Figure 8.1b where the level of abatement achieved with the polluter paying $0Q^{pp}$ is greater than with the victim paying $0Q^{vp}$ because the demand for environmental quality has changed with changing incomes.

In 1993 initial estimates are of 600,000 hectares of land set aside, making it the seventh largest 'crop' in the EC after wheat, barley, olives, fodder, vines and maize. The set-aside total compares with a maximum in 1991 of only 130,000 ha when the set-aside and guaranteed prices were not linked and the scheme was essentially voluntary. However the main objective of the scheme, to reduce surplus production, is not likely to be effective because some land would not have been cropped even in the absence of the scheme; that the land set aside tends to be of the lowest quality and yield potential; and that set-aside allows better operational efficiency of labour and capital and creates some advantages in the planned rotation of land (Buckwell, 1992). The previous set-aside scheme on 2 per cent of arable land

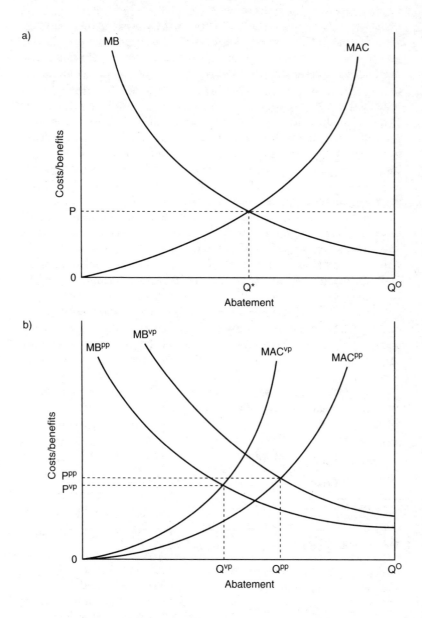

Source: Pearce and Turner (1990)

Figure 8.1 *Optimal level of abatement of an external environmental effect and income effects of changing property rights*

brought about a reduction in production of cereals of only 0.75 per cent as a result of these factors.

Set-aside has only mixed benefits to the environment. Although some aspects of the interaction of agricultural production with the ambient environment, such as the reduced use of inputs such as pesticides and fertiliser, will have positive effects on soil, aquifers and the products themselves, other features may not be enhanced. As indicated in Chapter 7 on biodiversity, little or no wilderness exists in Britain, biodiversity being concentrated in semi-natural or even managed ecosystems. If farming becomes less profitable then possibly less investment will occur in managing the privately owned non-productive parts of the rural environment. This strengthens the argument for paying land users for providing the environmental services which the wider society demands.

Some environmental policy options at the national level are already in place, acting in conflict with the intensification of agriculture as encouraged by the CAP. These include the designation of Environmentally Sensitive Areas (ESAs), where a primary objective is the maintenance of agricultural landscapes, mainly in upland areas of the UK. Designation of land for conservation and amenity objectives is one policy mechanism for ensuring a minimum standard and quantity of the particular resource. Table 8.2 aggregates the land use designations loosely by objective, though some of the areas overlap, or are subsets of each other, illustrating the complex nature of multiple land use in the UK.

Areas designated for use and for non-use values confer value to visitors and users of these areas which generally go unrecorded in the market-place. The use value derived by visitors and residents of a recently designated ESA of the South Wessex Downs, have been elicited with results showing that visitors derive use value of £19 per

Table 8.2 *Area of land designated for different purposes*

Designation	Area (000 ha)	As % of area of GB
Recreation designations	5,251	23.1
Green belt	1,963	8.6
Conservation designations	2,243	9.9
Environmentally Sensitive Areas	786	3.5
Total land area of Great Britain	22,744	100.0

Note: many areas are designated in more than one category

Source: based on HM Government (1992a)

household per year and residents derive £27 per household per year on average (Willis and Garrod, 1994). The crux of these schemes is direct payment, unrelated to agricultural commodity production, for maintaining and enhancing the environment. Thus for example there are per hectare payments for allowing hay meadows to flower and seed wild flowers, and for the maintenance of stone walls in the particular areas. The overall area of Environmentally Sensitive Areas has increased to approximately 1.7 million hectares with 1993 new designations and planned designations for 1994 (Whitby, 1994). This is almost 10 per cent of the total surface area of the UK. However, the consequences of creating designated areas is possibly to encourage a two track rural environment with intensive production taking place only on a decreasing proportion of land.

In summary, the driving forces behind the intensification of land use, with its negative environmental impacts, has been the entrenched system of high support prices. It is not clear that the linking of support price payments to set-aside will halt or reverse specific aspects of environmental decline.

The Impacts on External Economies

Agricultural price support in industrialised countries also impacts on both the level and stability of world agricultural commodity prices. Economic models of these effects estimate the effects on production and economic welfare of simulated reductions in agricultural support. Tyers and Anderson (1988) for example forecast that the welfare gain to producers in developing countries of trade liberalisation in the EC alone, would be in the order of $30 billion (US$ 1985) in terms of higher prices, four times the welfare loss to consumers in those aggregated countries. More recently, their model has simulated the effect in 1990 of both production and welfare of regions, given that agricultural price support had not existed up to that period (Anderson, 1992). Some results are presented in Table 8.3 to show that grain production in most regions would be greater under trade liberalisation, except in those with the strongest comparative disadvantage in food production, such as the Middle East.

At present, the Uruguay Round of the GATT negotiations, which tries to implement free trade through multilateral agreement on tariff barriers and other trade-distorting mechanisms, is being stalled by the major hurdle of agricultural trade as agricultural protection is such a sensitive political issue in the major trading blocs as evidenced by French farmers' demonstrations against proposed GATT deals. The present system of agricultural protection leads to economically

Table 8.3 *Effects on net economic welfare and food production of liberalising agriculture in the EC, the US and Japan, 1985*

Effect on:	Net welfare (US$ billion)	Grain production (percentage)	Beef and sheepmeat production (percentage)
Industrial countries	46.6	−5	−15
Developing Asia	4.6	2	21
Latin America	12.7	9	28
Africa and Middle East	−0.7	0	12
Total developing countries	16.6	3	22
Total world	62.4	−0.2	2.6

Notes: the liberalisation of agricultural trade scenario is zero agricultural protection in EC, US and Japan in 1990. Net welfare measures in the study are the usual changes in producer and consumer surplus. The results do not include estimation of impacts on the environment

Source: based on Anderson (1992)

depressed agricultural sectors in other countries, as estimated in Table 8.3. But what would be the environmental implications of freer trade in agricultural commodities?

The environmental implications of liberalising agricultural trade are complex. As highlighted above, a major objective of CAP reform is to reduce trade distortions, but the implications on UK and EC's rural environments depend on the instruments used. Developing countries are not an homogeneous group, and the impact of trade liberalisation on their environments would depend critically on whether the country is an agricultural importer or exporter and on the economic and social conditions prevailing in the country. Exporting countries may benefit economically with access to industrialised country markets, but agricultural intensification, with increased fertiliser and pesticide use, has been a root cause of negative environmental impacts in the EC and the pressures would be similar for the agricultural exporter. The agricultural industries in food importing countries would also be boosted due to liberalisation, but more intense use of marginal land may result. The impacts will be mixed and depend upon the scale of resource use and the domestic agricultural policies.

INDICATORS OF ENVIRONMENTAL CHANGE IN AGRICULTURE

Given the policy context and the impact of agricultural policy on sustainability some indicators of these impacts on the UK rural environment are now presented. Sets of indicators of environmental quality, such as those assembled by the OECD (OECD, 1991), generally follow a model of presenting data on pressures on the environment, state of the environment and response to environmental change. Most of the data presented here are of the pressure and state type. The agricultural sector produces pollutants and agricultural and other lands are sinks for the pollutants of other sectors of the economy. Agricultural land is also a source of recreational and amenity benefits, and interacts with the habitats of all the species in the UK.

Changes in land use

Land use has changed in the UK as a result of the policy context described above. Table 8.4 shows changes at discrete intervals in the past 50 years, of the main land uses *in England and Wales only*. There is a lack of data on aggregate land use, except for data collected as part of the agricultural census, which does not cover all of the UK. England and Wales land use change has therefore to be regarded as a proxy for the trends for the whole of the UK.

Urban growth has increased the proportion of total land area in the 'urban and other' category by 3.5 per cent, also explained by the land take of the road building programme. There has been an increase in forestry area, though the aggregated data hide the change in composition of the forest stock. This has been changes from old growth forest, which has been lost to coniferous forest and improved grass-

Table 8.4 *Land use change in Great Britain, 1947–1985*

	1947	1969	1980	1985
% of total area				
Woodland	7.0	7.9	7.9	–
Semi-natural vegetation	12.6	10.1	9.2	–
Farmed land	72.7	72.1	71.8	–
Water and wetlands	1.3	1.1	1.1	–
Urban and other	6.4	8.8	9.9	–
Linear features *(000 km)*				
Hedgerows	796	703	653	621
Woodland fringe	241	241	243	243

Source: HM Government (1992a)

land, increasing the proportion of the forest area under monoculture exotic species. There has also been a decline of 3.4 per cent of the total area from semi-natural categories; again the major new use has been as improved grassland and as coniferous forest. Linear features, such as hedgerows, have been declining by 175,000 km in the period 1947 to 1985, in England and Wales. Since then the trend seems to be increasing with the preliminary results of a 1990 countryside survey estimating 121,000 km of hedgerow lost between 1984 and 1990 (Bunce, 1993).

Although there seems to be a slight decline in the farmed area in England and Wales (although the area of land held on farms is closer to 80 per cent because of on-farm forests, water and roads), the mix of crops and land uses has been evolving to a more intensive agricultural system. Table 8.5, for example, shows the change in crop areas in the period since the UK's entry into the Common Agricultural Policy. This shows that the total area under crops has increased by over 10 per cent, with the largest additions being in the area of wheat, peas and beans and of oilseed rape planted. The most striking effect on the

Table 8.5 *Agricultural land use in the United Kingdom, 1972 and 1992*

Land use (000 ha)	1972	1992	% change
Total cereals	3801	3485	−8.3
of which:			
wheat	1128	2066	+83.2
barley	2289	1297	−43.3
oats	315	100	−68.3
Total other crops	468	1140	+143.6
of which:			
potatoes	237	180	−24.1
sugar beet	190	197	+3.7
oilseed rape	7	421	+5914.3
peas and beans	28	208	+642.9
Horticulture	273	197	−2.8
Total tillage	4542	5033	+10.8
Temporary grass	2359	1558	−34.0
Permanent grass	4913	5225	+6.4
Rough grazing (private and common)	6619	5909	−10.7

Source: MAFF (1974, 1993)

landscape has been the nearly 6000 per cent increase in oilseed rape which has radically changed the colour of the UK countryside in early summer. Less crop rotation occurs and hence the decline in temporary grassland, though permanent grassland has increased by improving what was previously rough grazing. Rough grazing is low fertility and usually non-fertilised upland, and both the private and commonly owned parts have declined in area with implications for access to upland areas and for the habitats of some upland species.

Agricultural pollution

The cycles of nutrients such as nitrogen and phosphorus are essential to the processes of agriculture. Both these processes occur naturally, nitrogen being fixed by plants direct from the atmosphere, and a major, though variable, component of soils. The application of nitrogen-based fertilisers is intended to speed up natural processes and allow plant growth on less fertile soils. The nitrogen cycle of the UK is summarised in Table 8.6, based on a study by the Royal Society

Table 8.6 *The UK nitrogen cycle, 1978 and 1988*

Inputs	1978	1988 (kt N)	Outputs	1978	1988 (kt N)
Wet and dry deposition	275	372	Crops and grass	1358	1503
Seeds	14	14	Straw burning	–	26
Fertilisers	1150	1525	NO_3 leaching	326	998
Sewage	26	25	Livestock products	244	259
Livestock waste	1020	1065	Livestock excreta	1020	1065
Silage effluent	9	26	Livestock waste leached	52	49
Straw	15	13	NH_4 volatilisation	595	400
Biological N_2 fixation	150	196	Balance by difference*	380	481
Animal feed	1316	1545			
Total	3975	4781	Total	3975	4781

Notes: * includes denitrification and immobilisation in soil

Sources: Royal Society (1983) and CSERGE calculations based on 1988 land use

(1983), with updated balances based on changes in crop area and livestock numbers in the period 1978 to 1988. Agriculture acts as both a sink and source of nitrates, for example as a sink for increasingly large amounts of human sewage. The leaching of nitrates to water courses is perceived as a major pollution source from agricultural practices. The impacts of nitrate pollution are disputed, but links with stomach cancer and other diseases have led to an EC Directive limit on nitrates in drinking water of 50 mg/l.

Nitrate leaching has probably increased significantly in the period 1978 to 1988 as shown in Table 8.6, as the area under crops such as wheat and oilseed rape, which have high fertiliser application rates, has dramatically increased (Table 8.5). However, not all leaching is a pollution problem, as it is the location and timing of the leaching in relation to river catchments and aquifers which determines impact. Estimates of the potential area of arable land which could be designated as vulnerable to leaching are up to 4 million ha (Hanley, 1991). Pilot Nitrate Sensitive Areas covering 14,600 ha have been created to limit application and hence leaching in particularly sensitive areas of England. Again compensation for revenue lost due to avoidance of this pollutant is paid to farmers, with the implications for property rights discussed above.

Table 8.7 shows that agriculture is a net source of phosphate which reaches water courses as a result of leaching processes. Eutrophication of water courses and the promotion of plants in water with harmful effects on water quality result from this addition of nutrients. Phosphorus is a non-point pollutant with sources from both agriculture and the household sector, with some point sources from industrial outputs. Compared with nitrogen, much smaller quantities of pollutant are involved, and environmental impacts in the UK are generally less damaging than from nitrates, or than the large problems in some North Sea basin countries.

Table 8.7 *Environmental impacts of phosphorus from UK agriculture, 1988*

	Phosphorus (kt)
Net sink for sewage	11
Addition to soil P stock (maintaining soil fertility)	134
Creation of organic P for human consumption	91
Sink for P-deposition	1
Soil losses of P to water courses (eutrophication risk)	40

Source: based on Centre for Agricultural Strategy (1978), updated for 1988 land use

Additionally, agriculture involves fluxes of both CO_2 and non-CO_2 greenhouse gases. Emissions of NO_x from straw burning were 26 kilotonnes per year in 1988 (Table 8.6), though straw burning is now banned primarily because of its localised nuisance and air quality impacts. Table 8.8 shows a carbon balance for Great Britain for 1980, in carbon equivalent. This is the result of a model of historical land use change in Great Britain with secondary information of the carbon fluctuations associated with agriculture and forestry operations (see Adger *et al* (1992)). This was undertaken by modelling the organic carbon fluctuations associated with land use in Britain from 1947 to 1980. Estimates of the carbon and methane from the operation of the agriculture and forestry sectors, such as the energy input, were then combined to give the annual balance. The results show that land in Great Britain constitutes a small net sink for carbon dioxide, equivalent to reducing the UK's net CO_2 emissions by around 0.72 per cent. The emissions of methane (CH_4) from livestock however constitute 30–40 per cent of the UK's net CH_4 emissions.

The greatest net emissions of carbon in these estimates occur from changing land use through the draining of land for arable use or for plantation forestry. This is despite the sequestration of much aboveground biomass in trees. Present agricultural policy reform seeks to encourage new forestry plantation on marginal agricultural land,

Table 8.8 *Carbon emissions and fixations by Great Britain land use sector, 1980*

Fixed	Kilotonnes Carbon	Emitted	Kilotonnes Carbon
Crops for consumption	5091	Fossil fuel	894
As meat	297	Liming	348
Livestock products	212	Peat wastage	500
Harvested timber	737	Land use change	903
Retained land use	2224		
Total	8561	Total	2645
		CH_4 from livestock	1194
		CH_4 from soil	201

Notes: retained land use refers to fixation on land retained in the same use (eg maturing forests) over the period 1947–1980. Land use change net emission is on land which has changed out of its original use during the period. CH_4 emissions are kilotonnes CH_4. Livestock emissions include direct emissions as well as from stored slurry

Source: based on Adger *et al* (1992)

though it seems that the greatest instant impact on the carbon balance may be from preventing loss of deep peatland and from the maturation of the presently immature forestry estate. In summary, the agricultural production processes by their nature assimilate and emit levels of various potentially polluting substances. The use of pesticides and their potential impact in the food chain, and the costs of soil erosion, are other environmental impacts of UK agriculture not considered in detail here (see Conway and Pretty, 1991). The aggregate pollution loads have in general increased with increased agricultural intensification during the recent past. The changes in land use and land use practices also have implications for the amenity of the rural environment which is constantly evolving and is subject to interactions with the other sectors of the UK economy.

CONCLUSIONS

Agriculture has a direct and incontrovertible role in achieving sustainable development in the UK. The evidence of the physical indicators of environmental impact points to the agricultural sector being unsustainable. Fundamental to moving towards sustainability in this sector will be the minimisation of environmental impacts both within the UK environment and externally. Sustainability includes equity in both present and future generations and policies to promote these social objectives have to be part of agricultural policy.

The mechanisms for delivery of sustainability objectives will be wide ranging. The impacts of the Common Agricultural Policy on developing countries can best be minimised through non-trade-distorting domestic protection. Domestic support requires the decoupling of the social, environmental and conservation objectives from production of food and fibre. So for example, environmental quality should be promoted by paying farmers directly to provide environmental public goods. However, present policies are sending the wrong signals to farmers who need to be re-directed towards the objectives which would secure sustainability in agriculture.

Chapter 9

Forestry

INTRODUCTION

Growing interest in defining and measuring sustainability in British forestry coincides with a transition period in which a new multipurpose role is slowly being defined in both public and private sectors. Multipurpose forestry involves forestry for timber, recreational use and environmental services such as carbon fixing. This chapter evaluates forestry policy in the context of recent approaches to measuring sustainable development. Considering even the narrowest definition of harvest rates relative to growth, it is far from clear whether the sector is or ever has been on a sustainable path. A broader focus on all aspects of forestry will help to redress this situation and should form the basis of future planning strategies.

HISTORICAL CONTEXT

Even in the absence of consistent policy, recent forest expansion in Britain has been a minor success story. A combination of direct state activity and indirect state incentives has, since 1919, succeeded in doubling UK land area under forestry to 10 per cent (FICGB 1993), reducing import dependency in softwoods and fostering a highly sophisticated processing capacity. Although the timber crises which characterised the traditional *laissez-faire* approach to policy in early years may now be a thing of the past, they serve as a periodic reminder of the extent of import dependence and a prescient example of resource exploitation on an unsustainable basis.

Albeit laudable, the current level of forest cover means that the UK is still denuded relative to European neighbours (see Table 9.1); a result of differing historical trends in agricultural development and perhaps a narrower view of the socio-economic role of the forest stock.

As substitute and complementary priorities, forestry's interaction with agriculture and the environment has been a recurrent and inescapable theme in sectoral planning. Periodically marginalised by concern for food security and a reduced strategic reliance on timber, the resulting spatial distribution of afforestation – towards poorer

Table 9.1 *Relative forest cover in EC countries, 1992*

Country	Total area (million hectares)	% Forest cover*
Portugal	9.2	40
Spain	49.9	31
Germany	34.9	30
France	55.0	27
Italy	29.4	23
Belgium/Luxembourg	3.3	21
Greece	13.1	20
Denmark	4.2	12
United Kingdom	24.1	10
Netherlands	3.4	9
Ireland	6.9	5
EEC	233.4	25

Note: * forestry areas include unproductive woodlands

Source: Forestry Industry Committee of Great Britain (1993)

quality land – would at once be at odds with conservation objectives. More recently such trade-offs have been accentuated by fiscal incentives to coniferous monocultures and shortcomings in the planning and consultation process to resolve the growing areas of conflict. Simultaneously a growing recognition of the value of forestry *per se* – a wider total economic value (see Pearce *et al*, 1989) – is steadily manifesting itself in government thinking. A switch of emphasis toward amenity forestry and consideration of regionalised Indicative Strategies for forest planning (see for example MacMillan, 1993a) reflect a continuing shift away from the primacy of timber production. It is in this climate that policy making encounters the growing need of a formalised approach to measure progress. One approach involves the development of forestry accounts for use in conjunction with conventional national accounts.

SUSTAINABILITY AND FORESTRY

Strictly speaking the definition of sustainability appropriate to forestry should recognise that any man-made capital is always an imperfect substitute for the total economic value of the national forest stock and the critical role forest resources play in global biogeochemical cycles. The requirement of a non-declining capital stock (see Chapter 3) then implies a strictly defined concept of sustainable income whereby the rents derived from forest resources are limited to non-extractive consumption of recreation, carbon storage plus aesthetic and other indirect benefits such as soil protection.

In practice an approximation of current forestry practice requires relaxation of some of these assumptions and a move to a weaker definition of sustainability, accepting that man-made forestry can in some respects substitute for what we may define as the natural forest stock. Such a definition does not invalidate a constant capital rule, but only widens the flow account to include some consideration of timber depletion. On this concept of sustainability then, the focus is broadened to the intertemporal value of a multipurpose resource which can be consumed extractively and non-extractively. Depreciation in the value of forest capital can take two forms: resource depletion and environmental degradation. In the former it is the change in the value and quantity of assets provided by forestry which is measured. In the latter it is the change in the quality of the stock or flow which is of interest (see Chapter 3).

Recall from Chapter 3 that the net price method was deemed appropriate to measure depreciation in renewable assets such as forestry. It was suggested that a simplified definition of sustainable income was annual timber yield, and implicitly depreciation equalled the excess of the rate of harvest over growth. Note that growth of existing stands is not the only way in which change in the physical stock may be brought about. New planting may also be interpreted as an annual increment, although there is likely to be a value loss (quantitative and qualitative) in substituting new growth for old. Such a definition is perfectly reasonable provided value is derived solely from timber. In fact such a definition may be comprehensive if annual harvest exceeds annual increment (sustainable income), since related non-market benefits will be simultaneously depleted. The accounts could be expressed in physical units or converted to monetary terms. For the latter, the value assigned to depletion – and which might be used in an hypothetical account adjustment – is simply the total rent per unit multiplied by the physical units extracted over the accounting period.

However, acceptance of multi-purpose forestry implies a broader concept of wealth. In particular the notion of sustainability encapsulated in the concept of non-declining welfare dictates that a number of heterogenous forest values be incorporated into accounts and monitored through time. A common numeraire for comparative purposes is money. The use of valuation techniques such as contingent valuation or travel cost can then be viewed as central to the process of making non-market adjustments (Pearce, 1993a). In what follows, an

Table 9.2 *Value of forests in the UK, 1985/6–1988/9*

Year	Forestry Commission		Private woodland	
	Area ('000 ha)	Value[1] (£ million)	Area ('000 ha)	Value[2] (£ million)
1985/86	898	1137	1333	5292
1986/87	900	1220	1356	5367
1987/88	899	1330	1386	6710
1988/89	898	1450	1409	7324

Notes: 1 market value; 2 book value

Source: Forestry Commission, reproduced in ERL (1992)

overview of existing and suggested satellite methodologies is discussed. Notwithstanding the uncertainty surrounding the status of green adjustments and the sophistication of current satellite systems, we show how some progress may be made through valuation of some basic indicators of forest value.

FORESTRY ACCOUNTS FOR THE UK

A comprehensive accounting approach should attempt to make deductions for depletion and degradation of the forest stock. Of the

Table 9.3 *Stocks and flows of forest resources in England and Wales[1]*

	Forestry Commission			Private woodland		
	Conifer	Broadleaf	Other[2]	Conifer	Broadleaf	Other
Stock @ 1/1/90	na	na	na	12,435	na	na
Annual increment	na	na	na	na	na	na
Natural losses	−9	0	0	−7	0	0
Gross removals	−3,460	−97	0	−2,000	−1,025	0
Land transfers[3]	−480	−400	0	+480	+400	0
Stock @ 31/12/90	17,865	810	5,100	10,926	na	na

Notes:
1 '000m³ overbark
2 other woodland refers to land not managed for timber as primary objective. Some 25,000 ha of Commission woodlands are currently classified as such
3 Transfers from the Commission to private ownership
na = not available

Source: Forestry Commission, reproduced in ERL (1992)

two, the latter is likely to be more complicated since stock depletion is more closely associated with market prices. Degradation on the other hand deals with the value associated with stock or flow of quality: for example, damage from poor air quality and reduced aesthetic or landscape quality resulting from inappropriate species mix. Table 9.4 provides figures of forestry value in recent years and demonstrates how monetary and physical information can be broken down in stock flow accounts.

Such accounts are limited, yet even here there is a basic consideration between valuing timber volume or forest land or both. Evidently large divergences in value can occur considering two areas with forest of differing maturity.

Table 9.4 reproduces a simple stock flow account of Forestry Commission resources for an accounting period 1990–1991. Although data would seem to suggest some stock depreciation (8,431+ 656 – 8,629) some caution is required in interpreting these results since they include cost and grant figures which are not strictly relevant to the calculation of net forest income. Data limitations prevent reproduction of a separate account for private woodlands, though it is suspected that, adjusting for grant payments, the year on year monetary value equivalent to sustainable income may be negative. In other words, the net monetary value of harvest exceeds that of growth and new planting.

Similar data limitations prevent the extension of Table 9.3 into a complete disaggregated species account. Norwegian accounts devel-

Table 9.4 *Forest stocks for Forestry Commission land and private woodland in the UK, 1990–1991*

Monetary value	£ million
Opening stocks (31 March 1990)	8,431
Revaluation to current prices	656
Expenditure on forest costs	253
Net investment in plantations	−817
Grants	−20
Growth in value	330
Sales of timber	−136
Land disposed of	−5
Closing stocks (31 March 1991)	8,629

Source: Forestry Commission, reproduced in Bryant and Cook (1992)

oped along similar lines (OECD, 1990) are useful in providing an aggregate view of the sustainability of the forest estate although can be deceptive. In particular such figures say little about forest management. Clear felling and replanting may for example be consistent with a sustainable volume; but such practice takes little account of visual impacts.

OTHER INDICATORS OF SUSTAINABLE FORESTRY

The multiplicity of forest benefits necessitates a wider focus on alternative indicators of sustainability. Concern for non-declining welfare suggests an interest in all aspects of value. In the context of current UK environmental policy, several indicators may be of relevance although data requirements for monitoring purposes are likely to be the main limitation. In this section three potential indicators are considered for which existing data availability may eventually permit some assessment of intertemporal value.

Forest health

A growing concern with the effect of declining atmospheric quality – in particular acid rain – has prompted considerable effort to ascertain the extent of potential adverse effects on trees (Innes, 1992; ECE, 1993). Ideally forest health data would be recorded in the form of stock and flow accounts for defined health quality categories (ERL, 1992), areas being reclassified through periodic damage monitoring. In practice the difficulties involved in monitoring the entire forest stock leave considerable scope for biased sampling. There is also considerable uncertainty surrounding existing damage indicators. The Forestry Commission has monitored tree health since 1984. The 1992 survey of a total of 8856 trees on 369 plots covers five species distributed throughout Britain. Although several indicators can be employed, a measure of defoliation – 'crown density' – seems to be a common index throughout Europe. On this basis ECE (1993) appears to suggest the appearance of a trend of deteriorating tree health in the UK; the yearly increase in defoliation in 1991/2 was only surpassed by declines in the Netherlands, Spain and Italy among EC member states (Table 9.5).

Such evidence is however hotly disputed on several grounds, not least the relative monitoring effort of countries included in the survey. While not ruling out the potential for long term – as yet unmonitored – air pollution damage, numerous alternative explanations can be advanced to explain tree condition. Innes (1992) cites biotic and

Table 9.5 *Changes in defoliation of all species, 1986–1992[1]*

Participating countries	All species, defoliation classes 2–4						No. of sample trees	% change 1991/92
	1987	1988	1989	1990	1991	1992		
Belgium			14.6	16.2	17.9	16.9	2,384	−1.0
Denmark	23.0	18.0	26.0	21.2	29.9	25.9	1,558	−4.0
France[2]	9.7	6.9	5.6	7.3	7.1	8.0	10,113	0.9
Germany[3]	17.3	14.9	15.9	15.9	25.2	26.0	103,422	0.8
Greece		17.0	12.0	17.5	16.9	18.1	1,912	1.2
Italy					16.4	18.2	5,857	1.8
Luxembourg	7.9	10.3	12.3	–	20.8	20.4	1,152	−0.4
Netherlands	21.4	18.3	16.1	17.8	17.2	24.5	32,875	7.3
Portugal		1.3	9.1	30.7	29.6	22.5	4,518	−7.1
Spain		7.0	3.3	3.8	7.3	12.3	11,088	5.0
United Kingdom	22.0	25.0	28.0	39.0	56.7	58.3	8,856	1.6

Notes:
1 percentages of trees surveyed in defoliation classes 2–4; damage classes ranging from moderate to severe
2 change in sampling procedure in 1988
3 1986–90 only includes Western Germany

Source: adapted from ECE, 1993

climatic disparities as significant determinants of apparent damage: yearly variation which might obscure detection of any long term trends in atmospheric damage. As an appropriate index, the use of crown density is also questioned. The higher yield class of softwood coniferous species in the UK's relatively mild climate, for example, produces greater branch spacing and thinner crowns than would ordinarily be the case in less favourable climates.

Table 9.6 demonstrates species trends disguised by aggregate measurement of the type advanced by UN/ECE. Biotic factors (winter moth and oak decline) explain deteriorating oak condition while the jump in Scots Pine damage is due mainly to storm damage (Redfern *et al*, 1993).

Given doubts about pollution being uniquely involved in damage to the forest stock, the existing physical evidence is insufficient basis for proposing any quality adjustment to stock accounts. If it is the case however that forest damage (real or illusory) does cause a welfare loss to users and non-users, it is of some interest to consider how this may be accounted for.

Table 9.6 *Change in crown density during the period 1990–1992**

Species	1990	1991	1992
Sitka spruce	48.6	49.1	43.9
Norway spruce	36.3	48.0	49.5
Scots pine	40.7	56.8	63.6
Oak	54.3	71.0	80.6
Beech	49.4	59.0	51.7

Note: * each figure is the proportion of trees in the Commission sample in which the crown density was reduced by more than 26% compared to a tree with full foliage

Source: Redfern *et al* (1993)

Table 9.7 presents some empirical estimates of the economic value of environmental quality as deduced through hypothetical market transactions of willingness to pay for environmental improvements or willingness to accept environmental damage. The feasibility of peri-

Table 9.7 *Empirical estimates of the economic value of environmental quality*

Type of environmental quality variable	Value	Economic value		Authors
		Exact welfare measure	Valuation technique	
Reduction in aesthetic damage to forest caused by geothermal development	$4.96 US (1988) per household per visit	Willingness to pay	Contingent valuation	Thayer (1981)
Reduction in moderate gypsy moth damage to trees	$36 US (1988) per tree	Willingness to accept	Contingent valuation	Heuth *et al* (1981)
Reduction in air pollution damage to trees	$2.48 US (1988) per household per visit	Willingness to pay	Contingent valuation	Croker (1983)
Additional trees in a public park	$0.36 US (1988) per tree	Willingness to pay	Contingent valuation	Brookshire and Coursey (1987)
Preservation of visibility at a recreation area	$6.08 US (1988) per household per visit	Willingness to pay	Contingent valuation	Brookshire *et al* (1976)
Reduction in acid rain damage on sensitive ecosystems	£52 (1992) per person	Willingness to pay	Contingent valuation	MacMillan (1993b)

odically assessing damage through such valuation procedures is primarily constrained by the cost of extensive surveying. At best, such an approach might help establish a fixed value scale of standard quality adjustments.

Forest quality

Broadleaf forests now occupy just over half of the forest area in England while in Scotland they account for less than 10 per cent. It is perhaps in reaction to the excessive 'coniferisation' of the uplands, that broadleaf prevalence has become an accepted index for amenity value. The reaction against the favourable tax treatment of woodland which culminated in the fiscal reforms of 1988 was as much a rejection of coniferous monocultures as of the alleged social injustice of tax breaks for the wealthy. Forest characteristics seem to matter in welfare terms and should therefore be a consideration when planning the forest legacy of future generations.

Both the Forestry Commission and Ministry of Agriculture include broadleaf incentives in afforestation grant schemes, and planting composition data provide a fairly accurate picture of national species patterns. Box 9.1 gives some indication of changing species prevalence

---

Box 9.1
FOREST TYPE DISTRIBUTION AND RELATIVE IMPORTANCE OF CONIFEROUS SPECIES AT THREE SURVEY DATES[1]

Forest type	1947 Area	%	1965 Area	%	1980 Area	%
Mainly coniferous high forest	397	27	922	53	1317	62
Mainly broadleaved high forest	380	26	352	20	564	27
Total high forest	777	53	1274	73	1881	89

Year	1st	2nd	3rd	4th
1947	Scots pine	Sitka spruce	Norway spruce	European larch
1965	Scots pine	Sitka spruce	Norway spruce	Jap./Hybrid larch
1980	Sitka spruce	Scots pine	Lodgepole pine	Norway spruce

Note: 1 minimum woodland area 0.25 ha, areas in thousands of hectares

Source: Forestry Commission (1987)

up to the last comprehensive national survey of the UK forest stock. The growing influence of fast-growing exotic species such as Sitka spruce is not unrelated to fiscal incentives which prevailed over much of the period and the need for a quick return on investments. Extending these data we might expect to see the changing attitudes to visual amenity reflected in increased broadleaf planting on Commission estate and grant aided planting on private and increasingly agricultural land. Table 9.8 provides data on state and private planting patterns for broadleaves and conifers since 1981. Diminishing state involvement in planting is increasingly apparent; a pattern set to continue with the sale of Commission estate.

So is forest quality improved by broadleaf stocking and an emphasis on species diversity? Hanley and Ruffell (1993) show that diversity can be identified as a significant variable in explaining survey respondents' willingness to pay. In particular, responses to photographic comparisons of specific forest attributes revealed that around 94 per cent of 884 (usable) responses preferred mixed woodland over no broadleaves, with a mean incremental willingness to pay to access the mixed forest type of £0.49. In other words, the presence of broadleaved trees results in significantly higher visitor valuation per visit. An alternative approach to gauging an economic measurement of the value of broadleaf forest is by determining the effect of diverse woodland sites on local residential or business infrastructure. Garrod and Willis (1991) determine the potential extent of this so-called hedonic price

Table 9.8 *New planting: Great Britain, 1981–1992 (hectares)*

| Year | Forestry Commission | | Private woodland | | Total |
	Broadleaf	Conifer	Broadleaf	Conifer	
1981	92	11,542	7,918	482	20,034
1982	51	10,927	12,068	394	23,440
1983	84	8,802	11,911	600	21,397
1984	51	8,331	15,995	678	25,055
1985	61	5,044	15,434	595	21,134
1986	56	4,277	18,170	849	23,352
1987	270	5,072	17,799	1,348	24,489
1988	373	4,579	21,326	2,495	28,773
1989	274	3,831	22,339	2,643	29,087
1990	261	3,820	9,642	3,125	16,848
1991	201	3,314	8,273	3,586	15,374
1992	245	2,754	7,310	3,472	13,781

Source: Forestry Industry Committee of Great Britain (1993)

effect by examining the effects of proximate Forestry Commission estate on a subset of UK residential property transactions handled in 1988 by a nationwide mortgage lender. Their finding of a 1 per cent increase in local mature broadleaved tree cover leading to increased property prices (1988) of £42 has interesting implications for ongoing plans for a new national forest and other community and urban fringe schemes.

Recreation

The need to account for woodland recreation has long been recognised and indeed, was the first non-market benefit element to come under official scrutiny in a bid to justify the Forestry Commission's operating deficits (HM Treasury, 1972; NAO, 1986). There is to an extent some overlap with quality in valuation in that we can assume that the recreational experience is probably increased in a diverse (and indeed healthy) forest. The recreational value of existing forest areas may be dependent on a range of variables some of which are endogenous to policy decisions such as access and site facilities, while others are exogenous, such as the aesthetic qualities of the surrounding area. Here we present some evidence to suggest trends in aggregate recreational value of the national forest estate. For accounting purposes an annual approximation of such a value may be relatively straightforward. Monitoring any year-on-year change in recreation value is more challenging.

Worldwide forest recreation studies abound since forests are a common subject of contingent valuation studies and travel cost measures using transportation costs as proxy values of recreational experience (Walsh, 1986; Navrud, 1992). In Great Britain, Benson and Willis (1992) estimate a total value for the Forestry Commission estate of approximately £53m in 1988 prices with an average value of £47 per hectare. These figures are partially derived from estimates of 'consumer surplus' per visit inferred from travel costs to a representative number of forest areas (Table 9.9). A reworking of these figures by Garrod and Willis (1991) revises the total recreation value down to £9 million per year. Although a significant reduction, the figure is still equivalent to around 12 per cent of Commission timber sales in 1990. Both estimates are restricted to the Forestry Commission estate only, and therefore underestimate total recreation value derived from private woodlands including those held by conservation bodies.

Since recreation value is essentially a use value, our main indicators of interest are visitor numbers and actual access.

Table 9.9 *Travel cost consumer surplus estimates for representative forests*

District	Consumer surplus per recreational visitor (£ 1988)
New Forest	1.43
Loch Awe	3.31
Buchan	2.26
North York Moors	1.93
Newton Stewart	1.61
Dean	2.24
Thetford	2.66

Source: adapted from Benson and Willis (1992)

Total visits to the Forestry Commission estate alone are reckoned to be in the region of 50 million per year (Cunningham, 1991); while an estimate of leisure day visits to all woodlands suggested that as many as 351 million visits were taken between April and September 1992 (Countryside Recreation Network, 1993). Allowing for error in these estimates it is clear that woodland provides an important leisure focus in Britain.

A likely determinant of forest use is ownership. Currently the ownership structure of high forest areas in the UK is split roughly 43 per cent Forestry Commission and 57% private areas including woodland held by conservation bodies with an environmental interest. This split is however not stable. Since 1981, against a background of financial pressure, the Forestry Commission and its Enterprise successor have been disposing of significant areas of plantations and plantable land (Table 9.10). Since 1989 this policy has been stepped up with the Commission being required to sell around 100,000 hectares by the end of the century, on top of the 58,622 hectares sold between 1981 and 1989. Subject to section 39 of the 1981 Wildlife and Countryside Act, sales are supposed to be safeguarded by the use of management agreements which rely on local authorities entering into agreement with new owners on a site-by-site basis. Among other things such agreements are for the protection of access rights. Agreements are not however costless to local authorities, and there is increasing evidence that deals are breaking down, resulting in the loss of access (Countryside Commission, 1993b).

Such regulatory failures might not be of significance if purchasers of Commission sales are sympathetic to their conservation value. Special arrangements to permit the possibility of sales of land to voluntary

Table 9.10 *Land acquisition and disposal by the Forestry Commission, Great Britain*

Year	Acquisitions (ha)		Disposals (ha)		Net
	Plantable forest land	Other land	Plantation/ planting land	Other land	
1980/81	1,623	279	688	1,552	−338
1981/82	4,194	579	2,347	8,076	−5,653
1982/83	3,422	764	6,362	5,746	−7,922
1983/84	2,765	88	28,615	28,063	−53,825
1984/85	695	160	16,072	12,785	−28,002
1985/86	935	171	8,314	8,259	−15,467
1986/87	2,395	1,245	6,186	4,770	−5,056
1987/88	1,635	80	6,387	2,542	−7,214
1988/89	1,820	461	4,328	3,347	−5,394
1989/90					−7,346
1990/91					−4,458
1991/92					−4,991
Total					−145,666

Source: Colman (1991), Forestry Commission (various years)

bodies at a District Valuer's (rather than market) price were a potential safeguard for the continued maintenance of environmental benefits. Of sales carried out between 1981 and 1989 however, only 4 per cent went to conservation bodies with a further 30 per cent being identified as going to financial institutions (O'Carroll, 1993).

The transfer of land and potential loss of access have two not unrelated implications for the intertemporal recreation value of domestic forestry. Firstly, the fragmentation of the public estate is likely to bring about (however subtly) a change in management priorities, with greater emphasis on financial rather than economic viability. In other words, since the non-monetary benefits associated with forests are rarely captured by private owners, there is little incentive to take them into account in planting and management decisions. Existing grant structures for amenity improvement on private land may be insufficient to offset this definite amenity loss. Secondly the potential reduction in access rights implies a reduced recreation value.

Of course it is difficult to be unequivocal about the overall direction of recreation value, since rising visitor numbers to remaining accessible woodland areas obviously attenuate the second effect. Value effects resulting from altered forest characteristics remain to be determined.

INTEGRATING SUSTAINABILITY IN FOREST PLANNING

So far we have looked at how sustainability might be monitored in a macro sense, considering appropriate indicators and their possible use in a national accounting framework. We now turn to consider the role of forestry at a microeconomic level and suggest what sustainability might mean for practical planners. More particularly, we consider the complementary role that forestry might play in the planning of sustainable investment programmes using cost-benefit analysis.

Investment drives economic growth and the use of effective selection criteria facilitates efficient investment choices. The simple criterion underlying cost-benefit analysis dictates that an action is judged acceptable if the benefits accruing from it outweigh the costs. For most investment decisions costs and benefits are financial flows of money occurring over the complete lifetime of the project. A wider focus can be taken however to encompass all costs and benefits resulting from the investment, including those – such as environmental services – not commonly associated with monetary flows. For many projects that impact on the environment, it is not uncommon for financial benefits to outweigh costs but for the costs to outweigh benefits when (in this case) damaging environmental effects are included in the appraisal. In the absence of some form of compensating reinvestment it follows that a succession of such projects will be running down the natural capital base over time.

One way to control for depletion is by the use of offset shadow projects. Barbier *et al* (1990) show one way in which cost-benefit criterion can be adapted to operationalise something akin to a sustainability rule in the project context. Overall, this may be achieved by formulating investment programmes to include a requisite number of environmentally compensating projects designed specifically to counter known environmental damages from other projects in the programme portfolio. Such an approach can be shown to be approximately consistent with a weak or strong sustainability constraint depending on whether the objective is the attainment of a non-positive present value for damages or that every project in any time period be associated with non-positive damage (Barbier *et al*, 1990).

Aside from definitional rigour the concept of offsets is not altogether novel. The flexibility of forestry has traditionally made it the ideal candidate as an environmental compensator of small scale industrial damage. What is new in the British context is consideration of such a role when national development impacts on the global environment. Increased responsibility for the global commons, particularly the impact of global warming, adds a further value category to those we have already considered above, namely the carbon value. Table 9.11 shows the amounts of CO_2 per hectare released through conversion of representative forest stands in Britain (Adger *et al* 1992). These can be translated into monetary benefits or carbon credits using an estimated shadow price of avoided damage (Fankhauser, 1993).

Commitments to stabilise emissions under the Framework Convention on Climate Change provide one obvious albeit modest rationale for continued expansion of multi-purpose woodlands in Britain, as a cost effective method of moving toward abatement targets. Forecast availability of surplus agricultural land is an added impetus for ongoing woodland schemes – such as those for the new national forest – and provide real opportunities for 'win – win' scenarios.

DISCOUNTING

Given the intergenerational dimension to both sustainability and forestry it would be impossible to escape from a consideration of how the future benefits and costs are to be factored into planting decisions we take now. In other words should we discount the future, and if so what rate do we use and how does this influence our forestry legacy?

Ethical, philosophical and economic arguments abound as to the rationale of discounting and have been exhaustively covered elsewhere (Pearce *et al*, 1989; Broome, 1992; Lind, 1982). Since few investments are as time-dependent as forestry it suffices to point out that the apparently innocuous investment criteria we use now may have profound implications for well-being over the lifetime of a single timber rotation. There is therefore a special case to be made for forestry which is more creditable when the resource is considered as a social as opposed to solely financial investment.

Table 9.11 *Carbon emissions for land use change out of forestry[1]*

Woodland type	Broadleaf	Coniferous	Mixed
Carbon credit (tonnes C/ha)	74.1	33.33	40.22
Value per hectare £[2]	963	433	523

Notes:
1 Based on assumed felling age of 55 years for conifers and 100 years for broadleaves
2 Based on shadow value of damage avoided \$20t/C $\approx$ £13t/C; Fankhauser (1993)

Source: adapted from Adger *et al* (1992)

Public decision making implicitly recognises the pay back handicap encountered in forestry investment. Currently the Forestry Commission is allowed to work with a lower 3 per cent rate of return on plantations – the difference between this rate and the required rate for other public investments being the forest subsidy. Although it has been argued that environment friendly discount rate reductions are unnecessary if we already operate a strict non-declining natural capital constraint, the potential imprecision of designing shadow investments or assuring reinvestment to maintain constant capital may mean that a reduced rate approach is more practical than working with standard rates within the modified CBA framework. Of the two approaches it may be argued that a lower rate is more likely to act as the greater incentive to invest, while the concept of devising balanced project portfolios may be considered an investment barrier. Providing lower rates are opted for, it still however remains for decision makers to define what is and what is not an environmental investment.

SUSTAINABLE FORESTRY IN AN OPEN ECONOMY

With nearly 90 per cent of wood requirements (currently worth around £6 billion per annum) being imported, Britain ranks as the second largest importer of wood in the world. Given the current state of knowledge in tropical forest management it is likely that the majority of tropical hardwood imports originate from forests being harvested over growth. In these circumstances the UK may be effectively importing unsustainability and it is of some interest to consider how this might be recorded.

Quite simply a representative adjustment to the forestry account (Table 9.4) would show a negative item equivalent to the resource depreciation of the exporting countries. For each exporter this would be calculated as the export price less the marginal cost, multiplied by the export volume. In the case of Britain it is not inconceivable that such an adjustment would offset any growth in value achieved in the domestic stock. Moreover, we can go further and ask what the outcome might be if the adjustment was required to account for market and non-market welfare losses to exporters? Clearly the recording may become highly convoluted; particularly if there is disagreement about whether the exporter or importer makes an adjustment. It would seem that if such deductions were workable then some convention on trade responsibility would be required to arbitrate adjustments and avoid double counting. If the ultimate conclusion then becomes a retrenchment into self sufficiency by some countries in a bid to maintain respectable trade balances, then the overall environmental benefit becomes highly questionable.

For practical purposes it seems that trade adjustments are some way off. However even if green adjustments never go beyond national boundaries importers cannot be blind to the effects of domestic demand and additional economic pressures driving exporters. Timber certification schemes and the transfer of forest management expertise may be effective ways of exporting sustainable practice, but some analysis of macroeconomic pressures facing exporters may show that importers should bear some responsibility for foreign resource depletion.

TOWARDS A NATIONAL FORESTRY PLAN

The failure to agree anything binding at the UN Conference on Environment and Development (UNCED) leaves global forestry in a state of flux. While most concern is still rightly concentrated on the fate of the world's tropical forests, the compromise collection of Sustainability Principles, which emerged amidst the much publicised disagreements, contain much that should be taken on board by temperate regions planning a response to Agenda 21. Most notably, calls for a forest use consistent with the non-declining provision of goods and services – implicitly the maintenance of a non-declining capital stock – and 'comprehensive assessment of economic and non-economic values of forest goods and services' (Section 6c), are central tenets of the sustainability which has been broadly outlined here.

As part of its commitment to sustainable development in Britain, the government is bound to outline a strategy for the sustainable development of the forestry sector. Much of the likely tone of the plan has already been set by a Department of the Environment consultation document (HM Government, 1993c) which begins by endorsing one of the most widely accepted definitions of sustainable development (WCED, 1987) and follows up with a reference to the importance of a sustainable income (HM Government, 1990). It is of some interest to consider the substance of this plan and how it might be reconciled with the apparent inconsistencies in current forestry policy.

The plan might usefully begin, for example, in outlining the government's vision for forestry in the context of the espoused ideals of non-declining welfare and constant capital. More particularly some explicit rationale must be provided for the ongoing transfer of existing public estate to the private sector. Whose interest is such a policy designed to serve, and, if as discussed above, the totality of economic (as opposed to purely financial) value cannot be safeguarded, how is such a policy to be reconciled with the UNCED undertakings? The ambiguity of the sales policy deserves closer scrutiny for a number of reasons. Firstly, the operating deficit of Commission activities, often highlighted as a rationale for divestment, is not easily justified when forestry is economically appraised. Indeed, as Pearce (1991) shows, several types of forestry expansion can yield economic rates of return in excess of the 6 per cent rate of return currently used to assess public sector investments. Whether or not such a criterion could possibly help to form the basis of a truly rational sales policy is far from certain. Secondly, and related, the endorsement of any definition of sustainable development is an implicit recognition of the need to avoid actions which might compromise the welfare of future generations. Given that private ownership will on the whole be limited to timber production, welfare potential is likely to be compromised. Thirdly, on this basis, the sale of public estate can hardly be justified on the grounds of enhanced efficiency. In economic terms, private provision is more likely to be less efficient (and less concerned) in delivering the multiple demands increasingly put on forestry.

The current private ownership of high forest area in Britain is arguably sufficient to contain plantation forestry. It seems ironic that the Forestry Commission is under pressure to sell land at a time when there is some support for the notion of public purchase of areas of high environmental value as a cost effective alternative to grants in perpetuity to encourage environmentally sound practice (O'Carroll, 1993; Colman, 1989). If sales must continue, then more effective safeguards are necessary to preserve the environmental interest of divested areas. Sales of land with attached conditions – conservation covenants – may be one approach although the administration and monitoring of such agreements is problematic. In particular, drawbacks in the current legal framework for land transfer mean that the administration of such agreements could in the long run be as expensive as grant schemes in conjunction with private ownership.

CONCLUSIONS

This chapter has reviewed a number of indicators of forest value with a view to their potential use in an accounting framework. Where possible a monetary numeraire was adopted to facilitate intertemporal comparisons. Taken together these indicators may offer some clues as to the sustainability of British forestry.

We conclude that publicly owned forestry may be generating a sustainable income, but that subsidised private forestry may not be meeting even the most basic sustainability indicator of annual increment value relative to harvest. If this is the case, then it follows that a whole array of non-market benefits are being simultaneously lost.

Various indicators of the quality of British forests can be used to determine whether, even with the stock of forests remaining constant, sustainable management is being practised. Some of these indicators also reflect external influences such as air pollution on the forestry sector. This may be viewed as another form of 'imported' unsustainability which illustrates the interrelationship of the environment with the economy and the limitations of sustainability indicators for each individual sector.

Indicators of forest health seem to present conflicting evidence. Data series are too recent to give a long term picture but irreversible damage may yet become apparent. Forest quality, loosely defined in terms of broadleaf prevalence, seems to be moving in the right direction, albeit slowly. The transfer of forest land from public to private ownership suggests that future growth of this index will depend increasingly on grant incentives. Finally, what can be said of recreation value? The current failure of safeguards on access to former Commission estate suggests a real potential for decline. Whether this can be offset by a renewed push for national and community woodland areas remains to be seen.

On balance it is difficult to be unequivocal about the overall sustainability of British forestry. The basic indicator of value of timber produced does not show sustainability. The indicators of quality show that although some non-marketed services from forestry may be increasing over time, as expected given the greater demand for such services in a high income country, forest quality in general is declining. Moreover, even if this subset of presented indicators did paint a favourable picture for British forestry in isolation, a question mark would still remain over the issue of imported unsustainability.

Chapter 10

Transport and the Environment

INTRODUCTION

Transport is one sector of the UK economy in which almost everything has gone wrong. Previous transport policy has resulted in too much pollution, too much congestion, too much investment in 'profitable' roads, too little investment in public transport and planning decisions being taken on the basis of misleading price signals. Without a fundamental change in policy it is inevitable that the transport sector will continue to impose large and growing costs on the natural environment, human health and the competitiveness of the British economy. At the root of these problems lies the free access nature of the roads and the atmosphere, enabling motorists to impose costs on others which they do not bear themselves. Any policy to tackle these problems must involve confronting the motorist with the true cost of his or her journey. Road pricing is likely to be an integral part of the solution and the government must quickly initiate pilot schemes to facilitate this transition. Road pricing will reduce the disamenity from traffic and increase the financial viability of investment in public transport.

TRENDS IN THE TRANSPORT SECTOR

For passenger traffic the period 1961 to 1991 has shown a marked increase in the relative share and absolute volume of private transport matched by a correspondingly precipitous decline in public transport (see Table 10.1). The trends in freight transport are more mixed, but once again the relative share and absolute volume of freight hauled by rail has fallen sharply (see Table 10.2). However, there are strong reasons for believing that the modal split does not reflect the relative costs and benefits associated with each mode, but rather regulatory failure. With a few notable exceptions past policy has been to treat the roads and the atmosphere as an open access resource. Without the

Table 10.1 *Passenger transport by mode, 1961–1991*

	1961	1971	1981	1991
Bus and coach				
Passenger kms (bn)	76	60	49	45
Percentage	25	14	10	7
Cars and vans				
Passenger kms (bn)	164	314	396	590
Percentage	54	75	80	86
Rail				
Passenger kms (bn)	39	36	34	38
Percentage	13	9	7	6

Source: DoT (1992a): Table 9.1

threat of exclusion from the roads or the atmosphere, car drivers need not pay either for the congestion costs which they inflict upon other road users or the pollution which their journeys create. This has encouraged an excessive reliance upon private transport. Furthermore, the omission of key costs and benefits from calculations also distorts price signals which are used for the basis for investment infrastructure. If motorists had always paid the full cost of their

Table 10.2 *Freight transport by mode, 1961–1991*

	1961	1971	1981	1991
Road				
Tonne kms (bn)	53	86	94	130
Percentage	50	64	54	61
Rail				
Tonne kms (bn)	29	22	18	15
Percentage	28	16	10	7
Water				
Tonne kms (bn)	22	22	53	56
Percentage	21	16	20	26
Pipeline				
Tonne kms (bn)	1	4	9	11
Percentage	1	3	5	5

Source: DoT (1992a): Table 9.3

journeys urban geography and commuting patterns might be very different to those observed today.

THE SOCIAL COSTS OF ROAD TRANSPORT

Economic efficiency requires that the number of journeys by each mode of transport be pushed to the point where the marginal social costs equal the marginal social benefits. Part of the marginal social cost of a journey by road will be the direct cost of the fuel, wear and tear on the vehicle, the driver's time and the risk of an accident. These are the private costs of motoring paid for by the motorist himself. Were these the only costs involved then road transport would operate efficiently in the absence of government intervention. But permitting virtually free access to the road network and the atmosphere allows road users to impose a variety of additional costs on the rest of society. These external costs include the costs of traffic congestion, physical damage to roads, air pollution, noise pollution and the cost of accidents. Accordingly there may be journeys undertaken where the social costs exceed the social benefits. Higher taxes would close the gap between private costs and social costs and curtail wasteful journeys. This section attempts to quantify the external costs of road transport for which road users should be made to pay.

The 'road lobby' is frequently apt to point out that road users already pay more in tax than they receive by way of expenditure on road construction and maintenance (see Table 10.3). The implication seems to be that motorists are paying more than enough tax already. However, whether motorists pay sufficient taxes to cover the costs of road construction and maintenance is something of a red herring.

Table 10.3 *Road tax revenue and track costs, 1992/3*

Vehicle class	Road tax (£m)	Road costs (£m)	Taxes to cost ratio
Cars, light vans & taxis	11,865	3,785	3.1:1
Motorcycles	70	25	2.8:1
Buses and coaches	295	260	1.1:1
HGVs	2,230	1,835	1.2:1
Other vehicles	240	120	2.0:1
Total	14,700	6,030	2.4:1

Source: DoT (1992a): Table 1.20

What matters from an economic perspective is whether individual road users pay the full marginal costs of their journeys.

It turns out that road users do not pay nearly enough in this respect even leaving aside the questions of whether the users of the road network should be asked to pay the cost of the provision of the network or whether it is justifiable to tax motorists even more heavily in order to raise additional tax revenues for the government.

Congestion costs

Any vehicle on the road imposes a cost on other vehicles by slowing them down and hence increasing journey times. Goods whose delivery is urgent or people whose time is valuable are delayed by drivers on relatively unimportant journeys. By charging all users of the road a fee equal to the additional congestion costs which they impose on other road users, congestion costs are reduced. This occurs primarily by dissuading those whose journeys are relatively unimportant from travelling by road or by encouraging them to reschedule their journeys away from peak times. Some may decide to cancel their journeys altogether. This problem can be illustrated with the aid of Figure 10.1.

Abstracting from the issues of air pollution and noise damage etc the costs of using a road have three elements: the own costs of using the uncongested road (time, fuel, own risk assumptions etc) represented

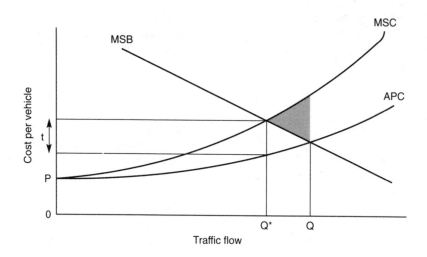

Figure 10.1 *The costs of road congestion*

by distance 0P in the diagram, the congestion cost faced by the marginal road user (which increases with the flow of traffic due to slower journey times), and the congestion costs imposed by the marginal road user on everyone else. The first two costs are internal and represented by the average private cost curve (APC).

The tendency is for traffic flows to expand to point Q where the APC curve cuts the marginal social benefit (MSB) or demand curve. At that point the private cost incurred by the last motorist is just equal to the benefit which he obtains from his journey. In other words he is indifferent towards the journey despite the fact that he is imposing positive congestion costs on other road users. By contrast the efficient flow of traffic is where the marginal social cost (MSC) curve crosses the MSB curve at Q^*. The MSC curve lies above the APC curve because it includes the congestion costs imposed on other road users as well as the private costs of motoring. At Q^* the net benefit enjoyed by the last motorist is equated with the additional time costs imposed on all other motorists. This may only be achieved by the imposition of a tax t as illustrated in the diagram and results in a welfare gain equal to the shaded area. Note that as the demand for the use of the road increases (during the rush hour) the demand curve shifts out and the optimal tax increases.

Newbery (1990) suggests that the *average* congestion cost across all roads in 1990 was 3.4p/PCUkm (although urban roads at peak periods have an average congestion cost of 36.37p/PCUkm). If this fee were charged to all road users then the revenue raised would have been £12.75bn. Adjusting Newbery's estimate for a unit value of 3.4p per passenger car unit (PCU) to 1991 values and multiplying by the 380bn PCU kms in 1991 gives a conservative congestion tax estimate of £13.5bn. This is the payment necessary to internalise all congestion cost externalities.

Road damage costs

The manner in which the maintenance costs are shared between different road users is important. Each road user must be made to pay a charge equal to the damage that they cause. The damage done depends upon the nature of the road surface and the axle weight of the vehicle. The damage done rises extremely rapidly as weight increases (by a power of four). Thus heavy vehicles should pay a considerably greater fraction of the costs than cars per kilometre travelled. If it is assumed that the expenditure on structural maintenance can be equated with damage costs then for the local roads in England alone damage caused was £766.5m in the year 1990/91 and for motorways and trunk roads in England it was £527.3 – this is an estimate due to incomplete statistics in the DoT report and may not include all structural maintenance (see Table 1.18, DoT, 1992b). Thus damage costs are at least £1.3bn per annum even excluding policing costs.

Air pollution

Table 10.4 illustrates the extent to which the transport sector is responsible for air pollution in the UK. Vehicle emissions account for about one fifth of the UK's CO_2 emissions, half the emissions of NO_x, Volatile Organic Compounds (VOCs) and Black Smoke and almost all emissions of lead and CO. Automobile emissions are also responsible for low level ozone pollution in cities caused by the action of sunlight on NO_x and VOCs. Ozone is widely thought to be responsible for the increasing incidence of asthmatic attacks. In 1981 the number of asthma deaths was 1603. By 1991 the number of deaths reached 1884. Over the same period the number of asthma deaths in the 5 to 34 age range rose by 60 per cent despite improvements in the treatment of asthma victims (see *The European*, 19 August 1993). With the exception of lead, emissions of all types are growing rapidly over time reflecting the growth in traffic generally. The rate of increase in pollution has almost matched the growth in traffic. The damage estimates provided in Table 10.4 are calculated on the basis of unit valuations in Pearce (1992c), Fankhauser (1993) and additional estimates.

The total is dominated by the figure for particulates which is

Table 10.4   *The cost of air pollution from road transport, 1991*

Pollutant	Emissions (tonnes)	Unit value (£/tonne)	Damage costs (£m)
CO_2	30,000,000	13.33	400.0
CH_4	10,000	70.00	0.7
SO_x	58,000	220.69	12.8
NO_x	1,400,000	190.00	266.0
CO	6,000,000	10.43	62.6
VOCs	970,000	n/a	n/a
Particulates	208,000	9,778.84	2,034.0
Pb	1,800	n/a	n/a
Total			2,776.0

Source: CSERGE

unfortunately one of the least well-researched. Nonetheless the figure used is well below that found in other studies (eg Glomsrod *et al*, 1992). Altogether then, air pollution damage may account for £2.8bn of damage annually in the UK.

Noise

Transport noise is responsible for productivity losses caused by an inability to concentrate at work or disrupted sleep resulting in tiredness. Extreme exposure to loud noise can cause stress and even hearing difficulty. These costs may be measured by considering either the relative reduction in house prices which can only be explained by the noise levels or by the use of surveys. Such an approach however fails to account for the distress caused by noise whilst outdoors and away from home. Based on a survey of the available literature Quinet (1989) suggests that traffic noise may give rise to damages in the form of productivity loss and annoyance amounting to 0.1 per cent of GNP. In 1991 for the UK this was equivalent to £0.6bn. Quinet further suggests that almost all of this damage is caused by road transport, the majority of the noise coming from HGVs.

The cost of accidents

There is some uncertainty as to whether the cost of accidents constitutes an external cost to road traffic or not. Each driver carries in his own mind a subjective evaluation of the risk which he faces. External accident costs arise only to the extent that an additional motorist increases the probability of any other motorist having an accident. If however the presence of an additional motorist makes no difference to the likelihood of any other motorist encountering an accident then there is no externality. Evidence regarding whether there exists a link between the accident rate per PCU kilometre and traffic flow is ambiguous. There are however two definite external costs of accidents. In the first place it is clear that the costs of clearing up the aftermath of an accident is a cost not borne directly by the motorist and neither is the cost of his medical treatment. Secondly, the deaths and injuries of pedestrians and cyclists is external since it is not borne by the motorists responsible. Yet to regard the injuries suffered by pedestrians and cyclists as a fair reflection of the social costs would be perhaps to severely underestimate the social costs. Many people for example refuse to let their children walk to school or ride a bicycle or themselves feel physically intimidated. So one social cost has been partially offset by another one – the need to restrict individual freedom.

The Department of Transport publishes monetary estimates of the

Table 10.5 *UK road accident casualties, 1981 and 1991*

	1981	1991
Pedestrians		
Killed	1,870	1,488
Seriously injured	16,494	13,334
Lightly injured	40,657	38,089
Pedal cyclists		
Killed	310	242
Seriously injured	5,179	3,903
Lightly injured	19,439	19,227
Motor cyclists		
Killed	1,131	548
Seriously injured	21,198	7,953
Lightly injured	46,800	22,235
All other road users		
Killed	2,535	2,290
Seriously injured	35,388	26,415
Lightly injured	133,839	175,545

Source: DoT (1992a): Table 4.13

cost of accidents based upon an individual's willingness to pay to reduce risks. The value of a statistical life (VOSL) is taken by the Department of Transport (1992b) to be £786,500. Although to many the idea of putting a value on life seems absurd it is important to remember that many activities increase or decrease the probability of a fatal accident. If life were infinitely valuable all resources would be devoted towards its preservation. But the fact that no individual or nation behaves in such a way suggests that there are acceptable degrees of risk. Finding out how people behave with regard to risk enables researchers to calculate the willingness to pay to reduce risk to be calculated.

From this the VOSL can be deduced. Studies aimed at eliciting this figure have been made in the context of industrial risks by considering the element of compensation in the wages paid to those employed in dangerous occupations (the Hedonic wage approach). Other studies question people directly regarding their willingness to pay regarding risk (the contingent valuation approach) whilst others look at behaviour in actual risk contexts such as the wearing of seat belts (the discrete choice approach). From all these studies it is possible to argue that the VOSL is closer to £2m, several times higher than the figure

Table 10.6 *The value of injuries to pedestrians, cyclists and motor cyclists, 1991*

	Number	(a) Cost (£bn)	(b) Cost (£bn)
Killed	2,278	1.8	4.6
Severely injured	25,190	2.2	2.2
Slightly injured	80,551	0.7	0.7
Total		4.7	7.5

Notes: (a) DoT valuations, (b) CSERGE valuations

used by the DoT (Pearce *et al*, 1992). The Department of Transport's estimate of the cost for a serious injury is £86,000 and for a non-serious injury, £9,290, all measured in 1991 prices.

The calculations made in Table 10.6 suggest that the social costs of road traffic accidents, even excluding injuries caused to motorists, is unlikely to be less than £4.7bn.

Aggregate social costs

Drawing together the various cost estimates in Table 10.7 indicates that the social costs of road use were at least £22.9 – £25.7bn in 1991. This was twice the revenue obtained from taxing road users. The argument that road users already pay for the costs of roads and road use is untenable.

CHARGING FOR ROAD USE

As the previous section explained, in order to achieve economic efficiency each road user must be confronted with the full costs of his or her journey. This requires the use of charges to make up the difference

Table 10.7 *The external costs of road transport (1991 estimates and prices)*

	Costs (£bn)
Congestion	13.5
Damage	1.3
Pollution	2.8
Noise	0.6
Accidents	4.7 to 7.5
Total	22.9 to 25.7

Source: CSERGE

between the private costs of the journey and the full social costs. However, the government can only charge for what it observes and it cannot for example readily observe individual journeys made on congested routes or the mileage of HGVs resulting in damage to the surface of roads. It is not possible to use the existing tax system of fuel duty and Vehicle Excise Duty (VED) to proxy for congestion costs and road damage costs: fuel consumption is not highly correlated with congestion costs because these vary with the road on which the vehicle is travelling whilst road damage depends on the weight per axle of the vehicle raised to the power four. VED has virtually no power to confront the road user with the full costs of their journey. In effect once the VED is paid, the marginal cost – the extra cost of a journey – of all subsequent journeys is zero. To charge road users for the congestion costs they inflict on other road users and the road damage they cause the government must develop an ability to directly monitor both flows of traffic on congested roads and the total distance travelled by vehicles.

Charging for congestion costs

To deal with traffic congestion it must become possible to exclude certain sorts of road users from the road network – specifically those for whom the value of a journey is less than the value of the delays they would inflict on other road users. Which road users have valuable journeys and which do not is revealed by their willingness to pay an amount equal to the marginal congestion costs they impose on other road users. But using conventional tolling involving lanes and booths to collect such a payment is not a very attractive option, particularly for the United Kingdom. These tolling systems create backlogs of traffic and delays during peak times. To deal with the high volume of traffic, toll plazas would require perhaps up to thirty lanes or even more. Such plazas would require a considerable area of land and be costly to construct. Nevertheless this system has found uses in some countries, most notably France. Switzerland currently operates a system of motorway permits. This system requires all drivers wishing to use Switzerland's motorways to purchase a permit allowing access for a given duration (normally a year). Although relatively easy to implement and enforce, the scheme is unattractive because it cannot restrict demand during congested periods and it is not related to use. After the first journey has been made all subsequent journeys are 'free'.

Given the unattractive features possessed by both the use of manned toll booths and the permit entry system the majority of attention has now turned to the possibility of electronic direct charging (eg see DoT,

1993). Electronic tolling could work by an electronic tag inside the car which communicates with a beacon on the side of the road. By observing the passage of individual vehicles a charge can be related to the stretch of the road along which the vehicle is travelling as well as to the time and day on which the journey is made. Either a centralised system of billing can be used to process the charges due or the electronic tag can be loaded with credit which is gradually spent as the vehicle passes more beacons. If the beacon fails to detect a signal from the car it assumes that the driver has contravened the rules and the vehicle's number plate is photographed. Eventually this system might be extended to provide a two-way flow of information between the car and a central computer.

The set up costs of road pricing are said to be substantial but so are the potential benefits. Hong Kong's experiment with electronic road pricing for example resulted in an increase in road speeds of some 40 per cent (Hau, 1990). Unlike the permit system the charges paid relate to the use of the road made by each individual motorist. Charges may be differentiated according to vehicle class since some vehicles (HGVs) create more congestion on hilly stretches. Unfortunately, direct electronic charging on all routes is not a practical proposition, but is perhaps possible on urban and inter urban routes. Because not all routes can be monitored there is likely to be a problem in preventing traffic diversion from tolled roads to non tolled ones. This tends to reduce the relative attractiveness of road pricing.

It is important not to confuse road pricing with the tolls which were historically charged for the use of roads (or still today for some bridges). The purpose of these tolls was to ensure a sufficient rate of return on investment and thereby to guarantee the continued private provision of roads. A second argument used to justify tolls was that the people who used the road were the ones who paid for it. Tolls set by the private investors would have the objective of maximising the revenue taken. Whilst all this relieves the pressure of road construction programmes on the public purse there is no reason to believe that setting tolls in such a manner would result in an efficient amount of traffic moving along the road. Apart from the desire to raise government revenue the only economic justification for charging for road use is to prevent congestion.

Unfortunately road pricing has, for a variety of reasons, been strongly opposed by several groups. There are many who wrongly perceive that the toll on roads represents a real resource cost to the economy. In fact the revenue raised by road tolls does not represent a cost to the economy at all but instead replaces existing taxes. It is simply a way of efficiently rationing the demand for an over-utilised resource and should improve economic efficiency. There are also those who object to road tolls as an infringement of the right of freedom of movement and the recording of individual journeys as an invasion of privacy. However, it is not necessary to record the identity of individual road users unless they fail to comply with the regulations, and as for the argument that road pricing infringes the right to travel, congestion charges are simply a charge for a scarce resource: road space. One might just as well complain that the fact that petrol and cars are not free constitutes an infringement of the freedom to travel.

Charging for road damage

Any charge made for road damage must be related to the distance which a vehicle travels since those travelling greater distances cause more damage (although it also depends on the nature of the roads on which particular types of vehicles will travel). A tax on fuel cannot be used for this purpose because the damage caused is not by any means proportional to the quantity of fuel burned. Only one kind of tax appears to give a fair reflection of the variable costs of HGV road traffic (ie the noise and axle weight): the kilometre tax. Odometers have been successfully used in some countries (eg New Zealand, Finland, Sweden and Norway). Given the dominance of HGVs in causing road damage the kilometre tax might be confined to this class of vehicle. The tax should be related to the weight of the vehicle and to the number of axles it possess. Since road pricing can also measure the distance a particular vehicle travels, electronic direct charging might eventually replace odometers.

Recently the maximum permitted weight of HGVs allowed on UK roads has been increased to 44 tonnes. These lorries however have to have more axles than normal in order that the damage does not become excessive. Under a system of a kilometre tax related to axle weight, private road hauliers would automatically be encouraged to use vehicles which constitute an efficient choice from a social perspective.

Charging for air pollution

With fuel taxes superseded by congestion charges as a way of reducing traffic levels it might be that the level of fuel taxes would need to be reduced. One of the main tenets of market based instruments is that the tax on pollutants should be the same across all sectors of the economy and, relative to fuel used in other sectors of the economy, the duty on motor fuel is probably higher than can be justified on pollution prevention grounds alone. In any case there is no fixed link between the consumption of fuel and the emissions of most pollutants. It is necessary to use traditional command and control devices to control these pollutants because the government cannot observe individual vehicles' emissions of these gases. In order to comply with EC regulations all petrol engine vehicles have to be fitted with a catalytic converter after 1992 – catalytic converters reduce emissions of CO, NO_x and VOCs. Unfortunately by stipulating that only new vehicles require catalytic converters the rate of turnover of the vehicle fleet may slow and hence possibly increase emissions in the medium term.

Although specifically directed at relieving congestion, road pricing schemes also contribute to reducing pollution by decreasing private road traffic generally as well as by encouraging a switch to mass rapid transit systems which have lower pollution emissions per passenger kilometre (see Table 10.8). Another advantage of road pricing over fuel taxes is that persons in peripheral and uncongested areas with few public transport alternatives are not unduly disadvantaged.

Charging for noise pollution

It is extremely difficult to devise a satisfactory way of charging for noise pollution. Apart from restraining the use of vehicles (particularly HGVs) in residential areas by road pricing the only other alternative appears to be the use of command and control regulations covering the design and construction of motor vehicles. The maximum limits for noise are currently 84dB(A) for HGVs and 77dB(A) for cars. There is no metered testing of the noise levels of vehicles in the UK either in the MOT test or at the roadside.

Aircraft require a noise certificate before being permitted to use British airports showing that minimum standards of noise abatement have been met. The Civil Aviation Act of 1982 permits the Secretary of State for Transport to require measures for limiting the effects of

Table 10.8 *Carbon dioxide emissions from transport, 1988*

Transport mode	CO_2 emissions
Passenger mode (CO_2 emissions per million passenger kms (tonnes))	
Car	35.74
Rail	19.51
Freight mode (CO_2 emissions per million tonne kms)	
Road	220
Rail	50

Source: Transnet, (1990) *Energy, Transport and the Environment*

aircraft taking off or landing at designated aerodromes. An efficient policy to tackle the problem of night flights would try to limit total aircraft noise whilst preserving some flexibility in how this target could be met. For example airline companies might be allowed to increase the flight of quieter aircraft if the number of noisy ones are reduced as well as being allowed to sell the rights to create noise to other companies. In this way airline operators are given the appropriate incentives to switch to quieter jet engines or reschedule their services either to a different time or even a different airport where the problem of night flights is not felt so acutely. Alternatively, airline companies could be made to face charges for aircraft noise. Such a scheme already exists at Luton airport where the authorities have a variable scale of charges related to 'excess' noise.

Charging for the cost of accidents

In this chapter, we have argued that the evidence linking the rate of motor vehicle accidents to traffic volumes was ambiguous. However, motorists must at least be 'charged' for the injuries caused to cyclists and pedestrians. In one sense motorists are already charged for the cost of the injuries to cyclists and pedestrians by being required to carry insurance against the risk of being sued in court for injuries caused. However this only happens when fault can be apportioned to the motorist and in any case courts typically fail to fine the motorist or his insurers an amount commensurate with the injuries caused (eg in our analysis £2m per life). One possibility is to restrain car use in built up areas via road pricing. However, what is more important is to encourage motorists to take more care. In this respect road pricing affords the opportunity to detect motorists whose average speed between the tolling beacons exceeds the prescribed limit and to issue an on-the-spot fine.

Subsidising public transport

Whilst it is preferable that each mode of transport is charged according to its full costs it is commonly heard from environmental bodies that public transport should be subsidised. This view has some merit – if for political or technological reasons it proves impossible to charge the full costs to road users then it may be advisable to dispense with the full cost rule for other modes too. Contrary to the political philosophy of some, subsidising public transport is not wrong in principle whilst governments fail to tax motorists for the external costs of their journeys. Charging private road users the full marginal costs of their journeys will increase the demand for mass transportation systems thus increasing the financial viability of these systems.

CONCLUSIONS

Having a sustainable road transport system means making each road user pay at least the full cost of his or her journey. At the moment users of the road network in particular pay only a fraction of the costs of their journeys and then these costs are not properly allocated between the different road users and different journeys. Continuing with current policies is likely to see mounting congestion, misguided investment decisions, too much pollution and increased costs to British industry.

The solution to the road transport problem lies in taxing each motorist in accordance with the external cost of their journey. In order to achieve this the government must develop the capability to monitor the movement of different vehicles because the government can only tax what it observes. Charging road users to prevent over excessive use of limited road space requires electronic road pricing whilst the fitting of odometers to HGVs is necessary to apportion road damage costs and noise costs. A fuel tax is inadequate to capture these effects since they are not related to fuel consumption and VED is a charge completely unrelated to use. The government will however need to retain command and control measures to deal with air pollution and noise pollution generally since these are things which it is currently impossible to monitor.

PART III

The political dimension

———— ◆ ————

Chapter 11

The UK and the global environment

INTRODUCTION

This chapter examines the UK Government's response to the two Conventions signed at the Earth Summit at Rio: on climate change and biological diversity. It is argued here that compliance with the two Conventions is not enough to ensure the sustainable use of the global climate system nor the conservation of the world's biological diversity. The Conventions are thus a necessary but not sufficient step towards sustainable management of these 'global commons'.

As of September 1993, neither the Climate Change or Biodiversity Convention has entered into force. The Conference of the Parties to both conventions will not meet until a given number of signatories – 50 for climate change, 30 for biodiversity – have ratified. Neither convention has yet been ratified by the UK Government, despite pledges to do so before the end of 1993.

THE CONVENTION ON CLIMATE CHANGE

Since its creation in 1988, the Intergovernmental Panel on Climate Change (IPCC) has succeeded in providing governments with a detailed analysis of the potential problem of climate change (IPCC 1990, 1992). Climate change could be triggered by increasing concentrations of so called greenhouse gases (GHGs) in the atmosphere. By far the most important GHG is carbon dioxide (CO_2) which arises predominantly from the burning of fossil fuels. Other GHGs include methane, nitrous oxides and CFCs and these are emitted from anthropogenic sources, such as fuel burning and industrial processes, and natural sources such as wetlands (see Brown and Adger, 1993a).

The current expectation among scientists is that a doubling of the concentration of carbon dioxide in the atmosphere is likely to lead to a 2.5°C rise in average global temperature and a change in patterns of precipitation (IPCC, 1992). This could adversely affect agricultural production as many crops are extremely sensitive to temperature and water availability, and cause rapid changes in ecosystems to which many species may not adapt. Losses of biological diversity could therefore accelerate, and a rise in sea level could threaten to inundate coastlines. The availability of water resources could change unpredictably and episodes of low level ozone pollution increase. The nature, scale and timing of possible climate change remain uncertain; and the impact of such changes on human populations adds further uncertainty. Yet the international community had, even before the start of the Rio conference, accepted the need for some control to be exercised over anthropogenic emissions of GHGs.

The highly preliminary nature of the impact assessments was not seen as an excuse for inaction. A better idea of the true response of the climate to increasing atmospheric concentrations of GHGs may not be available for several decades and continuing with 'business as usual' until a resolution of the uncertainty might commit the planet to dangerously high levels of warming. Nevertheless, considerable disagreement remained regarding the degree of control required and how the cost burden should be distributed. The Climate Change Convention represents a first attempt to address some of these issues.

The ultimate aim of the Climate Change Convention, which has been signed by 168 countries, is:

> the stabilisation of GHG concentrations in the atmosphere at a level which will prevent dangerous anthropogenic interference with the climate. Such a level should be achieved within a time frame sufficient to allow ecosystems to adapt naturally to climate change, to ensure that food production is not threatened and to enable economic development to proceed in a sustainable manner.

All nations are to prepare national inventories of GHG emissions and sinks. The Convention states that the climate system is to be protected with regard to the differentiated capabilities of states and that accordingly developed countries must be prepared to take a leading role. Developed countries are required to provide to the Conference of the Parties details of measures to individually or jointly reduce GHG emissions back to 1990 levels by the year 2000 (GHGs covered by the Montreal Protocol, primarily CFCs, were made an exception) within six months of the date of the Convention coming into force.

What happens beyond that date is not specified by the Convention. A certain degree of flexibility, however, was given to the economies in transition in respect of meeting this target. Developed country parties (excluding the transition economies) are further required to provide financial resources to meet the 'agreed full incremental costs' of implementing a range of measures in the developing country parties. However, the meaning of the term agreed full incremental costs is not defined and is open to differing interpretations (it is extensively analysed in *Blueprint 4: Capturing Global Value* which will be published by Earthscan in 1994).

The Convention must be ratified by at least 50 countries before it comes into effect. Up to September 1993 the Climate Change Convention had been ratified by 31 countries including the United States, China and many low lying island states, but none of the European Community countries. Ratification by the EC countries is anticipated by the end of 1993 but may be further delayed by disagreements regarding how the articles of the Convention should be implemented, and in particular over the desirability of a community wide carbon-energy tax.

There is still uncertainty over the scale of likely environmental damage, and the costs of reducing GHG emissions, which make assessment of the most cost effective reduction strategies difficult. The IPCC projects that under a 'business as usual' scenario emissions will rise from six to seven billion tonnes of carbon annually by the year 2000, so stabilising emissions at 1990 levels implies a 14 per cent reduction.

Recent analysis however (Nordhaus, 1993) suggests that a reduction of up to 30 per cent would be more desirable with increasing cutbacks over time. Certainly the measures advocated by the Climate Change Convention (even if they are perfectly adhered to) will not prevent climate change but merely slow its onset, as shown in Box 11.1.

The United Kingdom's responsibilities

In anticipation of its obligations to the Climate Change Convention the United Kingdom has produced forecasts of future carbon emissions and has initiated a consultation process to prepare a submission to the Conference of the Parties. In addition, the government has announced measures which it hopes will assist in returning emissions of carbon back to their 1990 levels. Official figures shown in Table 11.1 suggest that the emission of carbon attributable to the UK in 1990 was 160 million tonnes of carbon (mtC). However, Brown and Adger (1993a), provide a comprehensive analysis of emissions of other GHGs in the UK which shows that CO_2 accounts for about 67 per cent of aggregate GHG emissions, when the radiative forcing of the other gases is taken into account. The other major sources are industrial and agricultural emissions of methane and nitrous oxides. Table 11.1 provides government forecasts for the emissions of CO_2 in the absence

Box 11.1
CLIMATE CHANGE EVEN WITH GREENHOUSE GAS EMISSION REDUCTION

The targets agreed in the Climate Change Convention contradict the stated objective of 'avoiding dangerous anthropogenic interference with the climate system', as a) present concentrations mean that some global warming is already committed to; b) that meeting the targets set in the Convention will lead to further warming; and c) that even with aggressive emission reduction policies, global warming is certain and the impacts are uncertain. This has been shown in climate models which take different greenhouse gas emission scenarios as inputs into the system, translate these to atmospheric CO_2 concentrations and forecast the global mean temperature impact. The results presented here are reported in Warrick (1993), based on the climate model of Wigley and Raper (1992). Climate change impacts in the UK are described in detail in Hulme *et al* (1993).

- If all countries continued with a 'business as usual' growth in greenhouse gas emissions, the best projected results at present show an increase in global mean temperature in the order of 2.7°C and mean sea level rise of 58cm by 2100.
- If the OECD, primarily high energy-using industrialised countries, including the UK, reduced their emissions drastically with a long term aim of making fossil-fuel technologies virtually redundant, the global mean temperature would still rise by 2.2°C and mean sea level by 52cm by 2100 (Figure a)
- If all countries including the high energy using industrialised countries cooperated in a strategy much more radical than proposed under the Climate Change and reduced the growth rate of their emissions by half, the resulting temperature and sea level change would be reduced from 2.7C to 1.7C and from 58cm to 44cm by 2100 (Figure 11.1b).

Overall the results show that compliance with the Climate Change Convention does not lead to avoiding global warming. Global mean temperature and mean sea level rise do not show where or on whom the impacts are likely to occur, but it is clear that those with least resources, who are vulnerable to the physical impact of climate change (on agriculture for example) or of increased frequency of flooding, will suffer the greatest impact in the future. This intuitively fails to meet the criteria for sustainability set out in this volume.

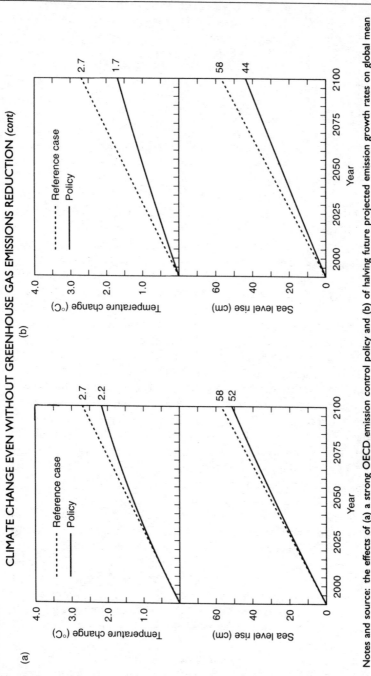

CLIMATE CHANGE EVEN WITHOUT GREENHOUSE GAS EMISSIONS REDUCTION (cont)

Notes and source: the effects of (a) a strong OECD emission control policy and (b) of halving future projected emission growth rates on global mean temperature (upper panel) and sea level rise (lower panel) (following Warrick, 1993)

Table 11.1   *UK carbon emissions projections by final energy consumer (millions of tonnes)*

Source	1990	1995	2000	2005
Households	41	39	41	42
Industry/agriculture	56	56	58	61
Commercial/public	24	23	26	30
Transport	38	41	45	49
Total	160	159	170	183

Source: Department of Energy, 1991

of any policy change and indicates that if the United Kingdom is to abide by the articles of the Convention, then savings amounting to 10mtC must be achieved by the year 2000. Due to uncertainty regarding the rate of economic growth and the future path of fuel prices a range of emissions for 2000 from 157 to 179mtC is possible.

A variety of measures have been announced to help reduce carbon emissions. Foremost among these is the planned introduction of VAT on domestic fuel and power at eight per cent from April 1994 and then at the full rate (currently 17.5 per cent) from April 1995. According to the government this could save 1.5mtC annually by 2000 (DoE, 1993a). The ending of VAT exemption for domestic energy caused a political furore because of its adverse distributional implications. Poorer families tend to spend a greater proportion of their income on domestic energy so VAT on domestic fuel and power represents a highly regressive tax. The average increase in VAT payable by households in the lowest 10 per cent of income under the new arrangements is likely to be £108 per year from April 1995 whilst for the top 10 per cent of households it is £135 (Giles and Ridge, 1993). In *theory* energy taxes may not be inherently unfair to the poor. The regressiveness of the tax depends upon the manner in which the additional government revenue is spent. Increasing the benefit payments to vulnerable groups would eliminate this undesirable aspect of the tax. However, such a step would conflict with the government's desire to raise revenue and cut the Public Sector Borrowing Requirement which was forecast to rise to £50.1 billion in the year 1993–94. Imposing VAT on fuel would alleviate this by raising £2.3bn in revenue in the financial year 1995–96, and is highly unlikely to be redistributed.

Studies into the past effect of price changes on the demand for domestic energy point to an elasticity of demand for energy equal to

–0.4. (The elasticity of demand for a commodity is equal to the percentage change in quantity demanded divided by the percentage change in price. Thus an increase in the price of energy by one per cent eventually leads to a reduction in demand of 0.4 per cent). Hence the imposition of VAT at 17.5 per cent might be expected to reduce domestic energy demand by seven per cent. Given that in the base case domestic energy consumption accounts for 41mtC this translates into a reduction of 2.9mtC – rather more than the Government's own projection. On the other hand the full response to price changes tends to be sluggish so the full effects might not be felt even by the year 2000.

The Chancellor also increased the duty on road fuel in his March 1993 budget with a commitment to raise duties further in future budgets. This too is expected to produce savings of 1.5mtC by the year 2000 (HM Government, 1993a) and to raise £1.02bn additional revenue in 1995–96. Prior to the Budget the average price of a gallon of unleaded four star petrol was 216.4p including duty of 107.5p. The Chancellor raised this duty by 10 per cent immediately to 117p and promised to raise it by an average of three per cent in real terms annually. This would imply an increase of the duty to 144.3p by the year 2000. Assuming no underlying change in the producer price of fuel the consumer price will increase to 253.2p (or by 17 per cent). With an elasticity of demand for fuel of –0.4 the change in demand is –6.8 per cent. On the government's own projections for transport emissions this might lead to a fall in carbon emissions of three mtC, again in excess of the government forecasts.

A variety of other initiatives have also been announced. The Energy Saving Trust (a body set up with the intention of encouraging households and small businesses to utilise energy efficient technologies) has adopted the goal of achieving reductions of 2.5mtC. The government has also set out proposals for the strengthening of Building Regulations which if enacted are projected to reduce CO_2 emissions by 0.25mtC. The Energy Management Assistance Scheme (set up to advise on the design and implementation of energy efficiency projects) could stimulate savings from small businesses of between 0.25 to 0.5mtC.

The government has also announced in its white paper on coal its acceptance of a report by the renewable energy Advisory Group that the contribution of renewable energy to electricity generation should rise to 1500MW by the year 2000 rather than the previously accepted objective of 1000MW. This might save a further 0.5mtC (see HM Government, 1993a, for further details).

Altogether these measures should save between 6.5 and 6.75mtC (see Table 11.2) taking the government two thirds of the way towards

Table 11.2 *Sources of saving on carbon emissions in the UK*

Measure	Carbon saved (mtC)	
	Government estimate	Authors' estimate
VAT on domestic energy use	1.5	2.9
Increased duty on road fuel	1.5	3.0
Energy saving trust	2.5	(2.5)
Improved building regulations	0.25	(0.25)
Energy management assistance scheme	0.25–0.5	(0.25–0.5)
Non-fossil fuel obligations	0.5	(0.5)
Total	6.5–6.75	9.4–9.65

Note: $C = CO_2$ as C; $1tC = 3.67t\ CO_2$

Source: See text

the 10mtC target. Using our own preferred estimates suggests that up to 9.65mtC are available. If economic growth proves stronger than expected or energy prices turn out lower than expected however, then more strenuous efforts than those outlined will be required.

In order to eliminate any remaining emissions in excess of the 160mtC limit, the government must concentrate on measures which, although justifiable in their own right, incidentally reduce carbon emissions. Indeed, the problem of global warming is intimately linked to existing environmental problems of air pollution and traffic congestion. Policies reducing the total environmental impacts in other sectors such as transport and industry – for example, a move towards road pricing (see Chapter 10) – may be sufficient to reduce emissions of GHGs from the UK to a level compatible with its international commitments. After exhausting the scope for negative cost emissions reductions one moves into the terrain of more conventional measures. Here there are strong reasons for supporting a carbon tax – a tax levied on fuels in direct proportion to their carbon content. A carbon tax provides exactly the right incentives for research and development and, by equating the marginal costs of carbon emissions abatement across all sectors of the economy, will reduce emissions at the least possible cost. It is important to distinguish between a carbon tax and an *ad valorem* tax like VAT. The measures announced by the Chancellor involve taxing fuel in proportion to its value not its carbon content. This is a more expensive way of reducing carbon emissions because it provides no incentive for consumers to switch from high carbon fuels such as coal to low carbon fuels such as gas.

By contrast the EC has proposed a Community-wide carbon-energy tax. Half of the tax is levied on the carbon content of different fuels whilst half is levied upon the energy content. Compared with a pure carbon tax the carbon-energy tax is a more expensive way of reducing emissions. Furthermore it is not clear that a carbon-energy tax is not superfluous from the perspective of the UK given the measures already announced and the scope for negative cost reductions in carbon emissions as outlined above.

The government might also wish to fund emission reductions or sink enhancements overseas as part of a 'joint implementation' strategy. Joint implementation refers to the ability of countries to reduce their emissions jointly by returning the sum of their emissions to 1990 levels: by agreement, one country could reduce emissions in another country and count the reduction as part of its own emissions reduction achievement. If joint implementation were taken up by many countries, this feature of the Climate Change Convention could, in theory, result in large cost savings due to the fact that the marginal costs of abatement might differ between countries.

A rational policy would attempt to balance the marginal costs of carbon abatement in the domestic economy with the marginal costs of purchasing those reductions overseas. However, uncertainties over the monitoring and enforcement of offsets, and high transaction costs may limit the application of joint implementation (see Brown and Adger, 1993b). Several European countries and the US, have, for a number of reasons which include public relations and in anticipation of domestic legislation, undertaken carbon offsets in foreign countries.

Norway, for example, is funding carbon cutting projects in Mexico and Poland. Such projects may also be undertaken through multi-lateral funds such as the Global Environment Facility, of which the UK is a donor/participant (see below). Examples of international carbon offsets projects are shown in Table 11.3.

Will the UK meet its obligations?

There seems little doubt that the UK Government will succeed in discharging its international obligations towards the Climate Change Convention at least in so far as cutting its own carbon emissions is concerned. However, the Convention will not succeed in preventing a significant increase in the atmospheric concentration of GHGs not least because: a) there remains substantial difficulty in securing the involvement of all countries; and b) because the terms of the Climate Change Convention already commit the world to significant impacts

Table 11.3 *Private and publicly financed international carbon offsets*

Donor	Recipient	Funding	Carbon offset	Description
GEF	Ecuador	$2.0m	355,500 tC $5.6 per tC	Reforestation of 5000 ha of degraded land with indigenous hardwood. Commercial forestry as well as expected land reclamation and wildlife habitat benefits.
Norway	Mexico Poland	$4.5m	Offsets not yet estimated	Extra funding (co-financing) for two GEF projects with objective of joint implementation. In Mexico, this is for a high efficiency lighting project and in Poland for a coal-to-gas conversion programme. The Norwegian funding originated as revenue from a carbon tax introduced in 1990. Government of Norway to receive a 'carbon offset certificate' to simulate accreditation of offset investments.
Tenaska	Russia	$0.5m	0.5 mtC $1–2 per tC	Reforestation project involving Russian Forest Service, with aims of soil and water conservation additional to carbon sequestration.
Applied Energy Services	Paraguay	$2m	13 mtC <$1.5 per tC	Agroforestry project undertaken with the US Nature Conservancy and others with aims to secure biodiversity and other benefits through forest conservation as well as sequestration.
Applied Energy Services	Guatemala	$2m (AES) $14m USAID	16.3 mtC $1.16 per tC	Agroforestry project supported by USAID and CARE. Offset calculated as active sequestration and displacement of use of standing forest for fuelwood supplies. Favoured because of availability of other funds and high chance of success as this was an ongoing project.

Source: Brown and Adger, 1993b

(Box 11.1). Disagreements regarding the 'full agreed incremental costs' of schemes may prevent developing countries from adopting measures to any meaningful extent. Yet their cooperation is axiomatic to the success of the Convention because it is in precisely these countries that the bulk of the growth in emissions is expected to occur.

THE CONVENTION ON BIOLOGICAL DIVERSITY

While developing countries in tropical regions contain much of the world's remaining biological diversity, the developed countries are dependent on these sources of genetic material, because of the links to their agricultural and other productive systems. Global biodiversity is therefore of common concern to all countries, and has come to be regarded by many countries in the North as a 'global common' (see Brown *et al*, 1993; *The Ecologist*, 1993: 170). The fundamental goal of biodiversity conservation is to support sustainable development by protecting and using biological resources in ways which do not diminish the world's variety of genes and species, and do not destroy habitats or ecosystems. There is an emphasis on not only protecting species *per se*, but also communities and habitats, which may provide a range of benefits, including pollutant filtration, nutrient cycling and climate control, as well as non-consumptive recreational, scientific and aesthetic values. The Biodiversity Convention puts primary emphasis on conservation *in situ*, although it recognises that in some circumstances *ex situ* conservation, for example, seed banks, may be necessary and desirable. Nevertheless these banks should wherever possible be based in and under the control of countries where the genetic material originates. Because the countries with richest biodiversity are in the tropics, these are likely to be developing countries.

The Convention commits signatories to develop national plans for conservation and sustainable use of biological diversity; to identify and monitor resources, especially those at risk, and to establish a system of protected areas where necessary. The Convention also requires that developed countries make funding available to developing countries to fulfil their obligations under the agreement, and also facilitate the transfer of technology. These commitments are discussed below.

Biodiversity in the UK: the UK Biodiversity Action Plan

Each Party ratifying the Convention is required to develop national strategies, plans or programmes for the conservation and sustainable use of biological diversity, or adapt existing plans to this purpose. Another requirement 'as far as possible and as appropriate' is the integration of conservation and sustainable use of biodiversity into relevant cross-sectoral plans and policies (Article 6). In addition, in Article 7, each Party is required (as far as possible and as appropriate) to identify important components of biodiversity, and monitor them, particularly those parts requiring urgent conservation action, or which offer the greatest potential for sustainable use. Article 7 also requires the identification and monitoring of those activities which have or are likely to have significant adverse impacts on the conservation and sustainable use of biodiversity.

Chapter 7 reviewed UK domestic policy on biodiversity, and highlighted the lack of intersectoral policy integration, standard method of monitoring and evaluation, or even a complete inventory of species found in the UK. UK conservation policy has been targeted on a limited number of protected areas, and has been criticised for producing 'islands of conservation in a sea of laissez faire' (Cowell, 1992: 28)

A major thrust of the UK Government's response to the Biodiversity Convention is the UK National Action Plan on Biodiversity. The Government has pledged to finalise this by the end of 1993. The objective is to bring together the Government's policies and programmes for wildlife. This was identified in Chapter 7 as a major factor affecting present policy failures. In addition, the Prime Minister, John Major announced the establishment of the 'Darwin Initiative for the Survival of Species' at the Earth Summit, and this fund, consisting of £6 million over three years starting in 1993, will fund projects by British institutions in collaboration with other countries, and training and assistance to overseas scholars.

The UK and global biodiversity: The Global Environment Facility

The Biodiversity Convention provides for funding by developed countries to developing countries in Article 20.2:

> The developed country Parties shall provide new and additional financial resources to enable developing country Parties to meet the agreed full incremental costs to them of implementing measures which fulfil the obligations of this convention and to benefit from its provisions and which costs are agreed between a developing country Party and the institutional structure referred to in Article 21.

'The institutional structure has been designated as the Global Environment Facility. This is not a new institution. It was established as an experimental pilot project in March 1991 and designed to provide developing countries with the means to address 'global' environmental problems (see Jordan, 1993a). The pilot phase runs until June 1994. The Global Environment Facility is a corporate venture between donors, who are mainly developed countries, but also include some developing countries, and three implementing agencies, the United Nations Environment Programme, the United Nations Development Programme, and the World Bank. Donations to the Global Environment Facility are made on a wholly voluntary basis. The UK has pledged some $60.1 million to the core fund as of 31 March 1993 (Global Environment Facility, 1993: 17).

The remit of the Global Environment Facility is to finance the agreed incremental costs of projects in developing nations that have the potential to benefit the global environment in terms of one or more of the generic impacts: reduction in greenhouse gas emissions; protection of biodiversity; protection of international waters; and reduction in ozone layer depletion. Table 11.4 shows the number and funding pledged to biodiversity projects by the Global Environment Facility up to April 1993. The first four tranches of the Global Environment Facility Pilot Phase work programme comprise 100 projects, costing $693 million.

Although biodiversity projects represented a relatively large proportion of the funding in the first four tranches, in the fifth tranche only $8.7 million (26 per cent of available funds) has been allotted to biodiversity projects in Africa and Asia only. Box 11.2 shows some examples of projects funded in the earlier tranches.

Private agreements and biodiversity prospecting

Perhaps the most controversial issue in the Biodiversity Convention – and that which it is assumed prevented the US from signing at Rio

Table 11.4 *Biodiversity projects funded by the Global Environment Facility, tranches I–V*

	Number of projects	$US million
Africa	17	76.2
Asia	11	75.1
Arab States & Europe	8	31.6
Latin America & Caribbean	14	107.8
Global	4	12.8
Total	54	303.5
% of Biodiversity	48	42.0

Source: Global Environment Facility, 1993

Box 11.2

SOME BIODIVERSITY PROJECTS FUNDED BY THE GLOBAL ENVIRONMENT FACILITY

Conservation of biodiversity in the Choco biogeographical region in Colombia

This is one of the most biologically rich areas of the world, with, for example, over 100 endemic bird species. Nine million dollars has been allocated to help the assessment of biodiversity in the region, support and train national scientists, and assess environmental protection in order to facilitate the definition of appropriate areas for conservation measures.

Trust Fund for Environmental Conservation in Bhutan

The Eastern Himalayas have been identified as one of ten global 'hotspots' with very high levels of endemism, and Bhutan's fauna and flora include over 500 bird species, and at least 5000 vascular plants. Ten million dollars will be used to support the trust fund, which provides institutional and legal support to the government's conservation efforts.

Forest biodiversity protection in Poland

The government of Poland will receive $4 million to protect the biodiversity of two forests, one in the Karkonosze National Park in the Southwestern Sudety Mountains, and the other in the Bialowieza area in Eastern Poland. The project will fund monitoring of environmental conditions, support a forest genebank, and aid management via a Geographical Information System.

Source: Global Environment Facility, 1992

(although of course the US has now signed under the new Clinton administration) – concerns intellectual property rights and access to genetic resources. The Convention recognises the sovereign rights of states over their natural resources and that authority to determine access to genetic resources rests with the national governments and is subject to national legislation. Furthermore, Article 15.7 of the Convention stipulates that the results of research and development and the 'benefits arising from the commercial and other utilisation of genetic resources must be shared in a fair and equitable way' with the Contracting Party providing such resources. The Convention can therefore be seen as an opportunity for the developing countries rich in biodiversity to capture some of the value of biodiversity which has in the past been exploited and treated as a free good by the industrialised countries. A prevalent view is that while the South may have the diversity, the North has the biotechnology. The Convention provides a framework for negotiating a fairer exchange between these two aspects, and to facilitate more equitable sharing of the benefits of exploitation between countries. Hence, Reid *et al* (1993) describe the Biodiversity Convention as setting the stage for a 'grand bargain'.

Although few grand bargains exist to date, the agreement between US-based pharmaceutical company Merck, and Costa Rica's National Institute for Biodiversity, INBio, a private non-profit-making organisation, is a much-cited example, and appears to benefit both organisations, and the Costa Rican Government and national parks system (see Reid *et al*, 1993). More agreements of this type are likely, and already in the UK private companies such as the Body Shop, and NGOs such as Royal Botanical Gardens, and WWF, are making contracts with organisations in developing countries for commercial exploitation of biodiversity which, it is hoped, will benefit local communities and be able to invest some share of profits from products developed into conservation efforts.

The likely effectiveness of the Convention

Attempting to stem biodiversity loss with a 'top down' international legal instrument presents enormous practical as well as theoretical constraints. Environmental phenomena such as depletion of the ozone layer, where cause and effect relationships are relatively discrete, and the number of actions finite, may in fact be inherently better suited to resolution through the international treaty process. In recognition of these limitations, the Biodiversity Convention does not impose targets but instead seeks to catalyse 'bottom up' processes aimed at protecting species through national-level actions.

Chapter 7 has defined biological diversity and highlighted difficulties in obtaining simple measurements which can be used in decision-making and monitoring and evaluating the effect of policies aimed at conservation policy. The lack of easily measured, quantifiable indicators of biodiversity makes policy formulation and target-setting difficult. Species indicators, and particularly species richness are often used as sole indicators of biodiversity, and this has often led to prioritising policy aimed at 'charismatic' species rather than most scientifically valuable habitats. The Biodiversity Convention stresses the need for an integrated, multisectoral approach to biodiversity conservation, and this is clearly lacking from UK conservation policy.

Chapter 7 also noted that the depletion of global biodiversity occurs as a result of a number of different causes, and that some may be described as proximate and others as fundamental. Proximate causes may be relatively easily identified; for example, land use conversion, the destruction or degradation of forests, or the destruction of coral reefs as a result of marine pollution. Policies can therefore be formulated to directly regulate and control such actions. However the fundamental causes – the forces which drive the destructive processes – may be much more difficult to remedy, as they often involve structural factors originating in political, institutional and economic systems at both national and international levels. Remedies which attack these root causes of biodiversity loss and which are necessary to make long term changes necessary for 'strong sustainability' will thus warrant intersectoral restructuring and changes in the economic development paths of nations involved and in the international economic system which links them. It seems unlikely that the current response to the treaty will do much to remedy these fundamental problems.

CONCLUSIONS

The Conventions on Climate Change and Biological Diversity represent attempts to secure international cooperation to solve two of the most pressing environmental problems. Without compliance with the terms of these Conventions sustainable development will not be possible. Meeting the targets of the Climate Change Convention – returning to 1990 CO_2 emissions by 2000 – will not stop global warming, and only takes us a little closer to achieving the ultimate objective of the Convention. We still do not know what level of concentration this is, and have little idea of the adaptability of different ecosystems to climate change. Likewise, measures undertaken in compliance with the Convention of Biological Diversity attempt to remedy some of the proximate causes of biodiversity losses, but are unlikely to redress more fundamental causes driving the global loss of biodiversity.

The UK is set to fulfil its obligations to the Conventions, and has pledged money to the Global Environment Facility to support developing countries attempting to comply. However, compliance with the Conventions alone is not enough to secure sustainable development either in the UK or globally.

Chapter 12

Sustainable development: the political and institutional challenge

INTRODUCTION

In its report *Our Common Future* (WCED, 1987), the Brundtland Commission drew attention to the monumental political and institutional changes that would need to be made if the principle of sustainable development was to be implemented at all scales, from the local to the international. This chapter summarises some of the political and institutional changes which would have to be made to implement sustainable development in the UK. The stronger versions of sustainable development are politically contentious, and moves to a strongly sustainable society will be resisted by many powerful groups. We introduce the concept of 'institution' and explain why institutional change is believed to be a necessary, but not a sufficient, condition for sustainable development. This is followed by an attempt to explain why the institutions of government in the UK fail to coordinate public policies in ways which are compatible with all but the very weakest forms of sustainable development. Some of the moves that have been made by the UK Government to address these problems are described; namely, the attempt to 'green' the machinery of government and to prepare a national sustainable development strategy.

These moves are assessed in the light of a 'map' which charts the shift towards sustainability. Completely sustainable development can only be an idea: an objective which nations and individuals seek to achieve. In this sense it is on a par with liberty, justice, freedom of expression, and rights to know – never completely attainable, but always worth fighting for.

SUSTAINABLE DEVELOPMENT: THE POLITICAL CHALLENGE

The phrase 'sustainable development' has staying power because most people want to believe in it. It survives because it appears to build bridges between the demands of environmentalists and developers. It sounds comforting – human well-being and economic security for ever, not brought to heel by ecological collapse or social distress. It is an article of faith, and in that sense almost a religious idea, similar to justice, equality and freedom. Indeed, when it reaches a par with these grand goals, it will have arrived at the first stage in its long journey of transition.

The notion of a 'sustainable' society is radical. Sustainable development confronts modern society at the heart of its purpose, because the human race is, and always has been a colonising species without an intellectual or institutional capacity for equilibrium (O'Riordan, 1993). Existing patterns of production, distribution and consumption thrive on creating environmental externalities in the form of pollution, habitat loss and ubiquitous waste disposal. Yet, it must be said that the present society is supported by a democracy that is led to believe that its best interests are served by minor adjustments to the status quo. This is buttressed by a general feeling of satisfaction amongst Western society's 'Contented Majority' – the economically fortunate and politically dominant sections of society – with this state of affairs (Galbraith,1992).

According to the Brundtland Report, the 'modern' development process fails to meet human needs and often destroys or degrades the resource base. A pattern of human development that favours the rich and those of the current generation at the expense of the poor and those yet to be born is, by definition, unsustainable in the sense of the Brundtland Report, though potentially sustainable in the conventional sense of being able to last. However, it is still doubtful whether even the very basic needs of at least one billion of the world's poorest people can really be met without an enormous convulsion in the denial of expectations over future consumption of materials and energy amongst the very wealthy. Moreover, existing experience provides little support for the hope that it is technically possible to bring the existing global population up to the living standards of, say, France, without environmental disruption on an enormous scale. At the very least, there would need to be a serious and prolonged commitment to technology transfer, to scientific and managerial capacity building in the South and fundamental adjustments to the international systems of trade, debt and aid. All these points were raked over in the run-up to the Rio Conference, and for the most part, appear as part of the 'wish list' in Agenda 21.

Part I outlined some of the fundamental principles of sustainable development. From a political perspective, one of the most important of these is *fairness*. This does not just apply to the rights of future generations to be able, realistically, to adjust to what this generation bequeaths them. It also applies to rights of all present generations to enjoy fundamental democratic rights and access to sustained livelihoods. The social dimension states simply, but powerfully, that a sustained society is also a truly democratic society with rights of expression, dissent, participation, self-reliance and equality of opportunity. Political and economic structures have to deliver social as well as environmental sustainability. This is the message that has still to be grasped by the politicians, and, indeed, most citizens.

The transition to sustainable development will be an intensely political process because it will create a new set of gainers and losers in society. This is hardly surprising, since all patterns of development generate gainers and losers and a change to sustainable development will be no exception. That transition will also require active government intervention in markets through the provision of price and quantity incentives, especially through the introduction of environmental taxes and charges for using environmental assets.

The current political incentives are such that politicians have to be more concerned with generating policies that secure the short term goal of re-election, rather than tackling the inevitably fraught transition towards more sustainable development. Ironically, it is probably democracy itself that is the greatest political barrier to a truly sustainable future. Without democracy, nothing can be achieved without losers, and losers can readily block some of the changes that are required for sustainable development. This potential conflict between what people want now and the interests of future generations is, of course, familiar in any democratic process. The conflict can be reduced only through persuasion of the majority that sustainable development is the right development path. Moreover, where there remains a conflict between the means of achieving sustainability and democratic wishes, the balance must lie with the perpetuation of democracy.

Any shift towards sustainability will inevitably be slow, taking generations, not years. Full sustainable development involves a cultural shift, not just economic and political tinkering. The goal is elusive, so we must learn to experiment and adjust towards sustainability, shedding failure and misunderstanding and capitalising on success and support for well-intentioned trials. As Lee (1993) has put it, we need both a compass and a gyroscope: a 'scientific' compass to chart our way, and a gyroscope to retain political and democratic stability as we move from one stage to the next. Table 12.1 outlines a possible compass and gyroscope.

Table 12.1 *A possible map of the sustainable transition*

	Policy	Economy	Society	Discourse
Stage 1 Ultra weak sustainability	Lip service to policy integration	Minor tinkering with economic instruments	Dim awareness and little media coverage	Corporatist discussion groups; consultation exercises
Stage 2 Weak sustainability	Formal policy integration and deliverable targets	Substantial restructuring of microeconomic incentives	Wider public education for future visions	Round tables; stakeholder groups; Parliamentary surveillance
Stage 3 Strong sustainability	Binding policy integration and strong international agreements	Full economic valuation; green accounts at business and national level; green taxes; offsets	Curriculum integration; local initiatives as part of community growth	Community involvement; twinning of initiatives in the developed and developing world

Inevitably, the early stages of the transition are the most difficult: vision is very dim and resistance very strong. Much depends on building structures of support, understanding and learning capability rather than radical new policy measures that will be fought by an unprepared policy. There are three stages, the first two perhaps taking up to 20 years to complete, the third even longer. The stages can be characterised in four distinct dimensions: policy; economy; society and participatory structure. Arguably, the UK is not even fully at Stage 1. Even party political doctrine barely puts the parties on the road to Stage 2. Stage 3 does not appear to be in party strategists' minds.

SUSTAINABLE DEVELOPMENT: THE INSTITUTIONAL CHALLENGE

Sustainable development is a process that must encompass every section of society and every role that we play: citizens and parents, children and students, civil servants and teachers, business leaders and employees. Sustainability will not simply 'happen'; neither can it be imposed 'top down' by authoritarian governments. Nevertheless, the transition to sustainable development will still need to be managed, planned and administered. It also needs a sense of purpose – at least a hazy 'vision' of where society is heading. Only governments can provide these things by taking the lead in the transition to sustainable development. Inevitably, this will require institutional change.

The term 'institution' is a broad one. It applies to organisations such as government departments that have a defined structure and resources, but also to less tangible customs, decision making procedures, laws and codes of practice. The 'market' is an institution as is the network of international law. Institutions play a critical role because they influence human interaction, aid the resolution of disputes and help to determine what is, or is not, socially acceptable.

Governments can make many institutional changes to ensure that individuals act in ways that are more sustainable. They can enact new legislation which prescribes what people should or should not do, or they can introduce more economic incentives (such as pollution taxes) to persuade and cajole them. The chapters in Part II of this book are replete with examples of institutional failure and how these can be addressed: regulations to safeguard wildlife habitats (Chapter 7); alterations to artificial subsidies which encourage agricultural over-production (Chapter 8); packaging taxes to reduce waste arisings (Chapter 6). Institutional change is a vital prerequisite for sustainable development. One of the most important institutional changes that governments can make is to alter the institutions of public administration. In the next section we concentrate on why the *institutions of government* in the UK have so far failed to act in ways which might be considered sustainable.

WHY UK GOVERNMENTS FAIL

In the UK, as in most other post-industrial democracies, the institutional structure and procedures of government are ill-prepared for the challenge of implementing sustainability. There are three interlinked reasons for this.

Unsustainable development and the structure of government

First, unsustainable development is built into the very fabric of government in the UK. The bulk of the staff at the Department of Transport (DoT) for example, deal with planning and building roads rather than developing public transport or even cleaner car technology (Joseph, 1992: 3). Likewise, the Ministry of Agriculture Fisheries and Food (MAFF) has consistently favoured agricultural intensification and biotechnological wizardry over wildlife conservation. Any transition to sustainable development will require changes in the structure of these institutions, but also the working practices and political allegiances of those who work in them. In many respects, departmental 'culture' and structure become self reinforcing.

Second, it is not only the structure of government which would hinder a swift transition to strong sustainable development, but also the way in which government policies are developed. Many political analysts have sought to show that politics and policy making in the UK are more usually characterised by continuity than radical change (Jordan and Richardson, 1987: 1a). Most policy is not made by the Prime Minister and the Cabinet, simply handed down to civil servants to be implemented. Policy tends to arise from a complex process of consultation and bargaining in 'policy communities of interested groups and government departments', rather than animated and publicly visible debate in the Houses of Parliament (Jordan and Richardson, 1987). Policy ideas also require the support of these groups and agencies to be properly implemented. The importance of 'behind the scenes' consultation and bureaucratic accommodation ensures that most policy change is gradual and incremental, rather than innovative and radical. On this analysis, all governments, be they left or right wing, would find it difficult to implement radical policies such as strong sustainable development.

Finally, the composition of the relevant 'policy community' can have an important influence on the type of policies adopted and the extent to which they are implemented. Two of the most stable and cohesive policy communities are those for agriculture and transport. The former is dominated by the Ministry of Agriculture Fisheries and Food (MAFF) and farmers, and it has consistently advocated agricultural support as a means to increase agricultural production (Cox *et al*,1986). Chapter 8 analyses some of the environmental impacts of the resulting policy. Transport is dominated, *inter alia*, by the motoring organisations, the Society of Motor Manufacturers and Traders, hauliers associations and business leaders – groups which have a vested interest in the building of new roads rather than railways, and which will not take kindly to congestion taxes or carbon taxation (Kay, 1992).

Many of these characteristics of public administration and policy making help to safeguard the non-sustainable status quo. They ensure that 'economic progress' often, though not always, triumphs over conservation and long term regard for the environment. They also conflict with Brundtland's emphasis on rights to openness and meaningful public participation in decision making (WCED, 1987: 65).

Policy coordination and integration

The second deficiency is the failure to integrate and coordinate policies. Many analysts have sought to show that policy making is rarely strategic or properly coordinated (Greenaway *et al*, 1992: 56). On this view, the government resembles a 'polo mint': policy is largely determined by the great departments of state (industry, transport, defence), with only minimal coordination from the centre (the Cabinet and Treasury) (Dunleavy and Rhodes, 1990). Whitehall functions not as a single monolithic unit, but a 'federation of departments, each of which jealously guards its own political and administrative autonomy' (Dunleavy, 1990: 106). Rather than policy proceeding in rational steps towards defined objectives, it tends to be born out of a jumbled conflict between individual departments for resources and political power. Again, this is not the ideal climate in which a purposeful and structured policy for implementing sustainable development might develop, or indeed, a context where well-meaning experimentation may be encouraged.

In the UK, the lead agency on environmental issues is the Department of the Environment (DoE), but this agency also has responsibility for various other 'non-environment' issues such as council taxation, housing and local government. The DoE does not have control over all the levers of environmental policy, because many environmental problems have their roots in 'non-environment' sectors of the economy, such as transport, energy and agriculture, and fiscal measures. Each of these sectors of the economy has a corresponding government department. Hence, responsibility for overall environmental policy is splintered across a number of departments (including the Departments of Environment, Trade and Industry, Health, Transport, the MAFF and the Scottish and Welsh Offices). The result can sometimes be a chaotic jumble of policies: institutions are mismatched with problems; some issues are dealt with by two or three departments, some by none; policies pursued by one agency or department inadvertently undo policies in another sphere. Examples of policy failure are described in Boxes 12.1 and 12.2.

The case studies in Boxes 12.1 and 12.2 illustrate some of the difficulties of balancing the need to protect the environment with the public demand for economic growth and material comfort. The car is regarded as an important component of modern society. Its production rate is seen as an indicator of economic health and it is closely associated with the notion of personal freedom; aggregates are required to build roads on which cars travel. However, both activities also have enormous environmental effects. When it has been necessary

---

Box 12.1
A MICRO-CASE STUDY OF POLICY FAILURE: AGGREGATES

Aggregates (ie sand, gravel and crushed rock) are required for building and road construction. What would a sustainable strategy for aggregates look like? At present about 15 per cent are re-used in road beds or building foundations; the rest is disposed of. The demand for aggregates is projected in terms of economic growth rates; indeed it is almost assumed that the need for fresh aggregates is a sign of a healthy economy, rather as energy growth was visualised in the 1970s. In 1991, the DoE estimated that demand for construction aggregates would rise from 300 million tonnes (1989) to 505 million tonnes (2011); a rise of 2.5 per cent per annum (Adams, 1991). This raises two very important questions.

First, where would all this material come from? As the scope for winning aggregates in Southern England or off the coast is reduced due to local protest and the need to nourish beaches, fresh aggregates are being sought from the hard rock 'peripheries', notably the outer Scottish islands. If Scottish 'super-quarries' create jobs and provide a restoration bond (which will not compensate for the loss of regional amenity and wildlife), is this socially and environmentally acceptable? The answer may be yes on very weak sustainability grounds, but less clear cut on strong sustainability grounds.

Second, which department would put in place a sustainable policy for aggregates? The DoE really only handles planning and it comes in at a relatively late stage in the policy proceess. The demand-led modelling is rooted in the Departments of Transport and Trade & Industry. Any attempt at amenity policy would have to pass through these two departments as well as the Treasury, which would be very unwilling to see any earmarking of funds for compensation or restoration. Any coherent policy on aggregates would have to connect demand reduction, recycling, planning betterment and pricing in a highly sophisticated manner: not easy.

---

to impose environmental (sustainability) constraints on these and other areas of policy (more often as a means to safeguard human health rather than critical natural capital), they have normally been articulated at either the back end of the decision making cycle or not at all. In the main, environmental quality is treated as a luxury or an adjunct to sectoral policymaking – something which can be bolted on or off existing sectoral policies. For sustainable development to flourish, 'environment' needs to act as a constant and transforming factor at the heart of all policy making.

Environmental policy and a strategy for sustainable development

The third failing is that the UK has never really had a structured policy

Box 12.2

A MICRO-CASE STUDY OF POLICY FAILURE: TRANSPORT AND THE ENVIRONMENT

In 1989, the Department of Transport (DoT) announced a £2.3bn road building programme. Implementing this programme will require enormous quantities of aggregates. It will also produce a new source of noise and air pollution, and alter large parts of the countryside. There are serious doubts as to whether the objectives of the programme can be reconciled with the UK's national policies for reducing air pollution and the government's own 'long standing policy of keeping roads away from protected areas such as Areas of Outstanding Natural Beauty (AONBs) or Sites of Special Scientific Interest (SSSIs)' (HM Government, 1990: 102). In fact, the government's erstwhile advisory body on nature conservation, the Nature Conservancy Council (NCC), claimed that the proposals may affect *inter alia* 161 SSSIs, 1 National Nature Reserve and 3 local nature reserves (NCC cited by Hopkinson, *et al*, 1990: 2.4). Parts of the 1989 road programme are now being implemented: two SSSIs, part of an AONB and an historic monument at Twyford Down have already been damaged by an extension of the M3 motorway around Winchester.

The tension between environment and transport policy objectives was revealed by the contents of several government statements issued during July 1993. First, the Secretary of State for Transport unveiled plans for the widening of the M25 up to 14 lanes, the day after the Secretary of State for the Environment had conceded that current estimates of traffic increases were not compatible with the government's aim of sustainability (*The Guardian*, 22 July, 1993). The DoE's opposition to the scheme had apparently been pushed aside during a Cabinet battle (Anonymous, 1993). In another statement a few days later, the Secretary of State for the Environment revealed the contradictions between the government's transport policy and its international obligations to cut emissions of carbon dioxide (*The Guardian*, 27 July, 1993). The transport sector is the fastest growing source of CO_2 emissions in the UK (HM Government, 1992b), and the DoE has confirmed that 'the objectives for a sustainable transport policy ... will need to be consistent with national policies for carbon dioxide ...' (HM Government, 1993c: 35). In the same month, a transport Minister confirmed that 'road traffic is largely linked to economic growth. It would be unrealistic to set a ceiling on this' (Caithness, 1993).

for the environment or sustainable development and is very much a result of the other two. In terms of the environment:

government structures and law relating to the environmental protection have been ... an accretion of common law, statutes, agencies, procedures and policies. There is no overall environmental policy other than the sum of these individual elements.

(Lowe and Flynn, 1989: 256)

Below central government, there are also various tiers of local government. Local authorities play an important role in planning, waste disposal and environmental health protection. The net result is a sectorised and tangled pattern of agencies and departments; a pattern which ill-suits the holistic and connected operation of environmental systems. Furthermore, as all the chapters in Part II show, sectoral policies are rarely made within sustainability constraints or with sustainable development as their overall goal. Rather, the institutional bias has tended towards the satisfaction of some *predicted* level of future demand (be it transport, electricity, tourism, aggregates etc) – with the environment trimmed to fit – rather than working within the limits set according to what the environment (and society) can really bear (Owens and Owens, 1991: 18). These tentative predictions can then be used to justify the provision of extra capacity (a new quarry, a new power station) on the basis of 'national need'.

GREENING GOVERNMENT: PRINCIPLES AND PRACTICE

The need for institutional change

Institutional change as a precondition for sustainable development lies at the heart of the Brundtland challenge:

> Governments' general response to the speed and scale of global [environmental] changes has been a reluctance to recognize sufficiently the need to change themselves ... [t]he real world of interlocked economic and ecological systems will not change; the policies and institutions concerned must.
>
> (WCED, 1987)

As recently as 1989, the UK Government was still asserting that it would not be necessary to create new institutional machinery to translate the concept of sustainable development into reality (DoE,1989: 13). Yet, a year later, the Government produced a White Paper (*This Common Inheritance*) outlining Britain's 'environmental strategy' (HM Government, 1990). It was the first comprehensive statement of environmental policy made by a UK Government and it included a whole section on institutional and consultative reform. In the Paper, the Government expressed its support for the principle of sustainable development (HM Government, 1990: 47) and under-lined the importance of ensuring that:

> policies fit together in every sector; that we are not undoing in one area what we are trying to do in another; and that policies are

based on a harmonious set of principles rather than on a clutter of expedients.

(HM Government, 1990: 8)

In 1992, the UK Government announced that it would prepare a detailed strategy for sustainable development and submit it to the nascent UN Commission on Sustainable Development (DoE,1993c). The strategy will outline the actions being taken to implement Agenda 21.

Conventional wisdom suggests that there are several interlinked principles which should guide the process of institutional overhaul. These are the *integration of policy*, the *enforcement of public rights to information* and *appropriate mechanisms for ensuring public accountability through transparent targeting and reporting*. As such they fit into the 'Policy' column of Table 12.1, as necessary introductory ingredients in institutional change. In the following sections of this chapter we discuss these principles and compare them to some of the UK Government's current practices.

Policy integration: the principles

In principle, integration can act in a variety of dimensions: it can be achieved by *concentrating* environmental responsibilities in one distinct ministry, or *extending* them across all government departments; it can involve creating new (or reorganising old) *institutional structures* or adapting the *processes and procedures* by which they operate. In practice most countries prefer to choose a mix of these, in which case it is the balance between them which is most important.

Arguably, most governments have tended to rely on concentrating the responsibility for ensuring high environmental standards within one large environment ministry – the BMU in Germany is the most notable example; the US Environmental Protection Agency (EPA) another. The BMU combines environmental protection with nature conservation and, in the aftermath of Chernobyl, nuclear reactor safety. This is a labyrinthine body with 458 employees and 413 administrative civil servants. So large is the total policy arena that segmentation automatically takes place even within environmental policy sectors. And of course, however large the environmental ministry it simply cannot cover, or have any semblance of control over, key policy areas such as finance, trade and aid. The story is much the same with the US EPA (Davies, 1990).

In the UK, the DoE was also born out of a process of 'integration by concentration'. In 1991, the UK Government announced that it would also create an integrated pollution control agency with a responsibility to regulate emissions from all classes of industry, regardless of whether they discharge to air, water, land or all three. After intense inter-departmental wrangles over the structure and function of the agency, the whole plan has been delayed, and the agency may not now appear until 1995 or 1996. Both Labour and the Liberal Democrats have expressed their firm support for building new regulatory and policy integrating institutions. These include a strengthened DoE and an Environmental Protection Agency (Liberal Democratic Party, 1991: 15); an Environmental Protection Executive (Labour Party, 1991: 17).

Building new ministries and agencies is publicly visible and politically attractive, but it does not always address unsustainable development at root or deal with situations where sectoral policies are clearly running in opposition to each other. In the two case studies outlined in Boxes 12.1 and 12.2, we find the DoE, reputedly sixteenth in the Cabinet pecking order (Hughes,1991), fighting far stronger departments in the battle to impose environmental (sustainability) constraints on development. Certainly an environment secretary would be in no position to overrule the Treasury, the Department of Trade and Industry, the Foreign and Commonwealth Office or even the Department of Health. But, until 'environment' figures in every department, there can be no meaningful transition to sustainable development. As such, governments should begin to identify the ways and means of ensuring that environmental factors are integrated into policy making in every sector. This may require new institutional machinery (inter-departmental committees and environmentally-biased cabinet groups) to share ideas, resolve conflicts, and ensure that sectoral policies pull in the same direction. This would accord with the principle of horizontal (or extended) integration.

Strategic Environmental Assessment (SEA) is one way of helping with this. In essence, SEA builds on the process of environmental impact assessment (EIA) required by the EC and now incorporated in to UK legislation. The introduction of EIA means that plans for many types of new project (eg a new road or power station) must be accompanied by an environmental impact statement (EIS), which predicts the likely impacts of the proposed project and provides suggestions as to how these might be mitigated (Fortlage,1990). In the UK, the EIS must be made available to the public. Although EIA ensures that local planning authorities are more systematically informed of the likely environmental impacts of a proposed project, it does not usually address the root cause of such impacts – causes which are often located much further back in the decision-making chain. Each individual project is often just one small part of a wider programme, which in turn is guided by a broader policy. In the case of transport for example, the planning and design of a more 'environmentally sensitive' road project is constrained by the form of the overall road building programme and, ultimately, the strategic policy decision to build more roads rather than railways as the means to meet the nation's transport 'needs'. Proponents of SEA argue that the quality of decision making can be improved if EIA is extended vertically up the decision making ladder to cover plans, programmes and overall policies. They argue that SEA should be viewed as 'an integral step in the attainment of sustainability' (Therivel *et al*, 1992: 126). It could also help to 'green' all sectors of Whitehall from within; contribute to a more integrated approach to land use planning; and provide the public with an opportunity to participate in the process of policy making. But even SEA cannot do the trick of creating sustainable development if the right accounting systems are not in place. SEA is a tool in the hands of a particular decision making climate. It can be no better or worse than the political and economic conditions that are set for it.

Policy integration: UK practice

In terms of greening central government, the UK has already made some headway, at least in rhetoric. However, this is still 'pre-Stage 1', as outlined in Table 12.1. In its 1990 White Paper, the government made a tacit admission of failure when it proposed a number of institutional changes 'which will integrate environmental concerns *more effectively* into all policy areas' (HM Government, 1990: 230) (authors' emphasis). These included, *inter alia*, two new standing committees of Cabinet Ministers (one to consider overall strategy, the other to oversee the implementation of the White Paper agenda); an energy efficiency committee to monitor how well the government's estate is improving energy efficiency; a nominated 'Green Minister' in each department, to be responsible for considering the environmental implications of that Department's policies and spending programmes; a requirement that all departments publish annual reports on their 'environmental stewardship and objectives' (HM Government, 1991: 5). A guide on policy appraisal has been prepared to assist civil service administrators deal with environmental issues in policy making and analysis (DoE, 1991b), as has a 'Green Action Guide'. The latter is designed to help Civil Service managers prepare 'strategies' (by the end of 1992) to improve each department's environmental 'housekeeping' (HM Government, 1991: 87). The government has also made a commitment to appoint more environmental experts onto public bodies and advisory committees (HM Government, 1991: 87), and to ensure that papers for Cabinet and Ministerial committees cover, where appropriate, any significant costs or benefits to the environment (HM Government, 1992: 29).

These institutional initiatives were arguably the single most important reforms announced in the 1990 White Paper. In May 1991, the then Secretary of State for the Environment (Michael Heseltine), claimed that the government had put in place 'some of the most sophisticated machinery to be found anywhere in the world for integrating environment and other policies' (quoted in Green Alliance, 1991: 3). Many would not dispute this assertion and indeed in comparison to many other states, the UK is still in the vanguard (the EC for example, is still failing to integrate its own internal policies a decade after policy integration was identified as a political priority and seven years after it became a legal obligation (Baldock *et al*, 1992: 1)). Tom Burke, currently political adviser to the environment secretary, felt the White Paper's institutional reforms would 'quietly move the environment closer to the heart of decision making' (*The Times*, 26 September 1990). Whether this is borne out in practice remains a moot point.

Clearly the reforms have not resulted in the overnight greening of 'key' departments like energy and transport, which are, for the most part, still pursuing policies which are patently unsustainable. Moreover, Whitehall's resistance to change should not be underestimated: several departments are believed to have told DoE officials 'that their policies have no environmental impacts' (ENDS, 200: 3). A year after the 1990 White Paper, the DoE revealed that two of the 'green' Cabinet committees had met on just one and two occasions respectively (*The Observer*, 11 September 1991). By means of a justification, the environment secretary argued that Cabinet Committees only meet in the event of 'a failure or major clash', and that 'most of the work is done by bilateral negotiations with other departments or by correspondence' (quoted in ENDS, 200: 16). In response to a Parliamentary question, the Prime Minister revealed that the Green Ministers had met only once as a group in the year 1992–3 (Major, 1993). Following the 1992 General Election, the Ministerial committee on energy efficiency and one of the other two cabinet committees were disbanded (ENDS, 200:3), and a new Ministerial Committee on the Environment (EDE) created in its place (HM Government, 1992: 29). The White Paper set all government departments a target of reducing their energy consumption by 15 per cent in the period 1990–1996. In its first report, the Committee announced that half of the government departments surveyed had actually increased their energy consumption in the months to 1991–2

(ENDS, 209, 4). The DoE is reported to have described this increase as 'disappointing' (*The Observer*, 15 August 1993).

A report by Environmental Data Services Ltd (ENDS), indicates that the government is also failing to fulfil many of the other promises it made in the 1990 White Paper (ENDS, 223: 3). This is not even Stage 1 action: yet the Dutch are moving in the direction of Stage 2 with their national sustainability strategy ('green plan') (Bennett, 1991).

In reality, it is very difficult to assess the real impact of these institutional initiatives because so much potential evidence is simply not made public. Individual departments are not obliged to accompany new policies or programmes with a public statement of their environmental implications, and since Cabinet and Ministerial Committee papers are not released immediately, the public has no way of knowing if environmental costs and benefits have actually been 'taken properly into account' (DoE, 1991: 1) or whether 'business as usual' predominates.

The two guides on policy appraisal and good housekeeping could be a potent vehicle for driving sustainability principles into the heart of government, but they are non-mandatory, rely on self-policing, and are largely silent on the need for consultation and public participation (Therivel *et al*, 1992: 64). The use of the guide on policy appraisal is to be monitored by an inter-departmental group of officials, although it is not clear whether the results of this exercise (or indeed any of the appraisals themselves) will be made public. The Prime Minister needs to give the monitoring process a strong push by linking it to meaningful and accountable departmental performance assessments.

In a useful analysis of the annual departmental reporting system, the Green Alliance found that almost all departments failed even to mention all their White Paper commitments, and many give only scant information on their environmental impacts (Green Alliance, 1991: 4). In a second year update, improvements were noted, but most departments seemed unable to offer a 'systematic, comprehensive and integrated' report on their environmental initiatives and policies (Green Alliance, 1992: 22). Others claim to have found no 'convincing evidence inside departments that giving Ministers ... specific 'green' responsibilities had made any real difference to their perceptions or policies' (Gordon and Fraser, 1991: 19). In its report on progress up to 1991, the normally well-informed ENDS report acknowledged that the government had put in place important institutional mechanisms, but had failed to make them work effectively (ENDS, 200: 17). In 1992, the Council for the Protection of Rural England (CPRE) maintained that the new machinery was still lodged in 'bottom gear' (CPRE, 1992).

As for the environmental assessment of policies, programmes and plans, the DoE's planning policy guidance note, PPG 12, enjoins local planning authorities to subject their local plans to an environmental assessment (DoE,1992c), but the government remains opposed to a formal system of SEA. For instance, the government has rejected the EC's proposal for a Directive on SEA as 'half baked' (House of Commons,1991), even though it simply requires one government department to audit another, and has little to say on arrangements for public consultation.

Targets and reporting mechanisms: the principles

Targets and reporting mechanisms have been mentioned several times in the foregoing discussion. These should be viewed as indicators of the all-important transition to Stage 2 as outlined in Table 12.1. Targets and regular mechanisms of performance review provide two important disciplines to the process of institutional 'greening': *direction* and *dynamism*.

First, institutional changes should be directed towards delivering sustainable development, but this is too vague as an operational principle, so it should be broken down into sectoral targets. For example, policies should be formulated to achieve a suite of targets (such as water quality objectives, recycling targets, maximum fossil fuel or mineral abstraction rates), or to maintain particular features of the environment which are so critical as to be deemed 'inviolable' (DoE, 1993c: 10). The important thing about these targets is that they should be made explicit and based on what is socially desirable, rather than on meeting some predicted future demand for resources without proper regard for the environment. In the longer run, precautionary principle type policies will be necessary for strong sustainability. The UK Government has begun to adopt the principle of critical loads – the amount of pollution an ecosystem can tolerate in the long term without suffering damage – to determine the extent to which emissions of acid gases should be reduced (see Chapter 4). In other countries, there is a growing recognition that targets should be the framework around which a sustainable development strategy is built. For example, the European Community's Fifth Action Plan (*Towards Sustainability*) includes 'indicative targets' for seven priority areas of policy, and the Dutch 'green plan' includes a host of quantified objectives, including firm limits on traffic growth to meet pre-defined CO_2 emission reduction targets.

Second, target-setting can also play an important role in ensuring that the institutional machinery, once in place, is actually dynamised and is not left simply to whither on the vine. The setting of a target, with an appropriate and realistic date by which it should be met, can have an important catalysing effect. Progress in meeting these targets should be reported both internally within Whitehall and externally to pressure groups and the public. The discipline of internal and external review, coupled with Parliamentary scrutiny, should amount to a far more potent force for 'greening' than self-regulation and voluntaristic intent.

Targets and reporting mechanisms: UK practice

The UK has a number of environmental targets enshrined within legislation, but there is a need for many more. Since the 1990 White Paper, the government has produced two updates which report the progress made against the original 350 commitments. The two updates also contain further pledges, and report the progress in achieving these. This rolling programme of target setting and reporting now looks set to become an annual process. However, many of the targets contained in these documents are vague and unambitious, or they simply require actions that should have been done anyway – implementing EC Directives for example. The reports themselves are largely self-serving and lack self-criticism. The parallel annual departmental reports are also difficult to assess, for they also contain few explicit objectives such as that for improving energy efficiency. Targets need to be set consistently across all departments for a number of key parameters such as waste recycling, waste emissions and air pollution. Without these, it is very difficult to differentiate short term, incremental measures from purposeful and deliberate long term progress towards sustainability (ENDS, 205: 3).

Information and public accountability: the principles

Without adequate and formal mechanisms of scrutiny and review, 'taking account of the environment' carries no weight in relation to the powerful forces that support the unsustainable status quo. Rather, sustainability should be incorporated in the terms of reference of cabinet and governmental committees, and a duty of environmental care should be laid against all departments, overriding all existing statutory duties and subject to judicial review (O'Riordan and Weale, 1990: 18). This is the minimal requirement for the crucial transition to Stage 3 as outlined in Table 12.1. The duty should be examinable through the publication of annual departmental statements of practice, observance and intent, and the publication of documents which explain how sustainability is being implemented in sectoral policies and programmes. These reports would force departments to reflect upon and then justify their environmental performance. They would need to be more comprehensive than the annual departmental reports prepared as part of the White Paper exercise and would have to be made available to the public and Parliament for scrutiny. Parliamentary scrutiny of the government's environmental record could operate in much the same way as the Public Accounts Committee supervises the government's financial expenditure. To ensure that Parliament has the capacity to scrutinise the performance of the Executive, improvements should be made to the Select Committees – more research staff, greater powers and perhaps even arrangements for joint committee reports on the government's record in implementing sustainable development.

If individuals are to make informed choices about the future, they must be fully aware about the impact of their activities on the environment. Citizens must also be able to scrutinise the activities of governments in order to ensure that the proposals for institutional change are properly implemented. Therefore, all these organisational reforms should be accompanied by a widening of guarantees of open information in government such as the extension of public access to information and the facilitation of the use of the courts to ensure public access and rights of participation, through public hearings, in standard setting and performance review. This will necessitate a Freedom of Information Bill, more publicly intelligible registers of information on industrial discharges, a comprehensive and independently produced annual state of the environment report, regular reports on the national 'green' account, a comprehensive inventory of industrial releases and relevant statistical reports on environmental damage and human health. Openness and accountability are vital if the process of greening is to be purposeful and meaningful, rather than a cloak to mask practices that fail to conform with all but the weakest forms of sustainable development.

Information and public accountability: UK practice

The UK Government has so far shown little inclination to adopt a statutory duty of environmental care, although public access to environmental information is definitely improving, driven, in part, by John Major's desire for more open government. In 1993, the Government prepared a White Paper on open government, which canvassed a voluntary code of practice but fell short of proposing a formal and accountable Freedom of Information Act. On this occasion, the government argued that an Act would be expensive and give more power to judges rather than Parliament (*The Guardian*, 16 July 1993). Campaigners have given the move a cautious welcome, but are worried that the final decision about what to publish will still be made by civil servants (*The Independent*, 10 May 1993). Critics claim that the document represents a victory for the 'culture of secrecy' in Whitehall (*The Guardian*, 24 August 1993).

Two of the most recent pieces of environmental legislation (The Water Act (1989), the Environmental Protection Act (1990)) provide for public access to registers of information on discharges and pollution consents and no restrictions on private enforcement action, but commentators have claimed that the registers still fail to reveal how different factors are weighed up in the process of preparing an emission permit (Jordan, 1993b). A recent EC Directive on public access to environmental information may open up the process even further, although Friends of the Earth has already lodged a formal complaint with the European Commission alleging that the UK Government has failed to comply with the Directive in full (ENDS).

CONCLUSIONS

In this chapter we have discussed some of the political and institutional changes thought necessary to implement weak sustainable development in the UK. Many of the institutional initiatives announced in the 1990 White Paper reveal that the government understands many of the principles of sustainable development – integration, coordination, openness, target setting and strategic reporting. However, this readiness to speak the language of sustainable development has, as yet, not been translated into a comprehensive set of real and meaningful political outcomes. In many respects, the White Paper was a calculated but only half-hearted attempt to respond to the wave of green enthusiasm which swept through western democracies in the late 1980s; although conceptually powerful, it has not yet been followed up with the necessary political will and commitment.

Table 12.1 indicates that a much more fundamental revolution still awaits the UK. Some straws are, however, in the wind. The national sustainable development strategy exercise aimed at the UN Commission on Sustainable Development will be an annual event that must surely impinge on the annual White Paper process. The sustainability exercise has activated industry into thinking more seriously about Stage 2 targets and eco-oriented economic accounting, a process that must develop. About six local authorities have developed their own versions of Agenda 21 initiatives, and this appears to be snowballing, notably in the light of authority-wide eco-auditing. The recently created Forum for Education and Sustainability has already begun work on greening the whole national curriculum so that environmental values become infused in the long process of learning. Its ambitious aim is to get the UK to Stage 3 (Table 12.1), coupled to local authority audits and community initiatives.

Ideally the transition from very weak to weak to strong sustainability should take place across all aspects of policy, economy and society. This book suggests why we are still at the very weak (pre-Stage 1) stage and how we can evolve at least to Stage 2 within the foreseeable future. Hopefully, strong international obligation, encouragement for adventurous schemes abroad and citizen power will combine to launch the UK into Stages 1 and 2 via its all-important sustainability strategy. Just as the first hundred metres of training are the most stressful for the ultra-unfit, so the modest achievement even of Stage 1 will be a vital breakthrough. We are now on this path.

References

Adams, J. (1991), 'Determined To Dig, the Demand of Aggregate Demand Forecasting', *National Minerals Planning Guidance*, Council For the Protection of Rural England, London.

Adger, W.N. and Whitby, M. (1993) 'Natural Resources Accounting in The Land-Use Sector: Theory and Practice', *European Review of Agricultural Economics*, 20, 77–97

Adger, W.N., Brown, K., Shiel, R.S., and Whitby, M.C. (1992), 'Carbon Dynamics of Land Use In Great Britain', *Journal of Environmental Management*, 36, 117–133.

Advisory Committee on Business and the Environment (1991), *First Progress Report To the Secretaries of State for the Environment and for the Department of Trade and Industry*, HM Government, London.

Ahmad, Y.J., El Serafy, S. and Lutz, E. (eds.) (1989) *Environmental Accounting for Sustainable Development*, The World Bank, Washington DC.

Alter, H. (1991). 'The Future Course of Solid Waste Management In the US', *Waste Management and Research* 9, 3–20.

Amann, M., Bertok, I., Cofala, J., Klaasen, G., and Schoepp, W. (1992), *Strategies for Reducing Sulphur Dioxide Emissions in Europe*, paper presented at the UNECE Task Force Meeting on Integrated Assessment Modelling, June 1992, Bilthoven, The Netherlands.

Anderson, K. (1992), 'Effects On the Environment And Welfare of Liberalising World Trade, the Cases of Coal And Food', in Anderson, K., and Blackhurst, R. (eds), *The Greening of World Trade Issues*, Harvester Wheatsheaf, Chichester, 145–172.

Anonymous (1993), 'Wheels Steer Green Policies', *New Scientist*, 31 July, 3.

Baldock, D. *et al* (1992), *The Integration of Environmental Protection Requirements Into The Definition And Implementation of Other EC Policies*, Institute for European Environmental Policy, London.

Barbier, E.B., Markandya, A. and Pearce, D.W. (1990), 'Environmental Sustainability and Cost-benefit Analysis', *Environment and Planning* 22, 1259–1266.

Bartelmus, P., Stahmer, C. and van Tongeren, J. (1991) 'Integrated Environmental and Economic Accounting: Framework for a SNA Satellite System', *The Review of Income and Wealth*, 37(2), 111–148.

Bennett, G. (1991), 'The History of the Dutch National Environmental Policy Plan', *Environment*, 33(7), 6–9 and 31–33.

Benson, J.F. and Willis, K.G. (1992), 'Valuing Informal Recreation On the Forestry Commission Estate', *Forestry Commission Bulletin* 104, Forestry Commission, Edinburgh.

Bergstrom, J.C. (1990), 'Concepts and Measures of the Economic Value of Environmental Quality, A Review', *Journal of Environmental Management* 31, 215–228.

Bishop, R.C. (1993), 'Economic Efficiency, Sustainability, and Biodiversity', *Ambio* 22, 2–3, 69–73.

Bojo, J., Mäler, K-G., and Unemo, L. (1990) *Environment and Development: An Economic Approach*, Kluwer, Dordrecht.

Brisson, I. (1993), 'Packaging Waste and the Environment, Economics and Policy', *Resource, Conservation and Recycling* 8, 183–292.

Bromley, D.W., and Hodge, I.D. (1990), 'Private Property Rights And Presumptive Policy Entitlements, Reconsidering the Premises of Rural Policy', *European Review of Agricultural Economics*, 17, 197–214.

Brookshire, D.S., and Coursey, D.L. (1987), 'Measuring the Value of a Public Good, an Empirical Comparison of Elicitation Procedures', *American Economic Review* 77, 554–565.

Brookshire, D.S., Ives, B.C. and Schulze, W.D. (1976), 'The Valuation of Aesthetic Preferences', *Journal of Environmental Economics and Management* 3, 325–346.

Broome, J. (1992), *Counting the Cost of Global Warming*, White Horse Press, Cambridge.

Brown, K. and Adger, N. (1993a), 'Estimating National Greenhouse Gas Emissions under the Climate Change Convention', *Global Environmental Change*, 3, 149–158.

Brown, K., and Adger, N. (1993b), *Forests for International Offsets, Economic and Political Issues of Carbon Sequestration*, Centre For Social And Economic Research On the Global Environment, *Working Paper GEC 93–15, CSERGE*, *University of East Anglia and University College London*.

Brown, K., Adger, N., and Turner, R.K. (1993), 'Global Environmental Change and Mechanisms For North South Resource Transfers', *Journal of International Development*, 5, 571–589.

Bryant, C. and Cook, P. (1992), 'Environmental Issues and the National Accounts', *Economic Trends*, 496, 99–122.

Buckwell, A.E. (1992), 'Should We Set Aside Set-Aside?', in Clarke, J., *Set-Aside*, Monograph 50, British Crop Protection Council, Farnham, 275–283.

Bunce, R.G.H. (1993), 'Terrestrial Vegetation, Composition, Distribution and Change', *Countryside Survey 1990, A Preview*, Institute for Terrestrial Ecology, Merlewood, Cumbria, *mimeo*.

Button, K. (1990), 'Environmental Externalities And Transport Policy', *Oxford Review of Economic Policy*, 6(2).

Caithness, the Earl of (1993), *House of Lords Hansard, Written Answers*, 22 July 1993.

Centre for Agricultural Strategy (1978), *Phosphorus, a Resource for UK Agriculture*, Centre for Agricultural Strategy, Reading.

Central Statistical Office (1992), *The Blue Book: United Kingdom National Accounts*, HMSO, London.

Coase, R. (1960), 'The Problem of Social Cost', *Journal of Law and Economics*, 3, 1–44.

Colman, D.R. (1989), 'Economic Issues from The Broads Grazing Marshes Conservation Scheme', *Journal of Agricultural Economics*, 40(3), 336–344.

Colman, D.R. (1991), 'Land Purchase as a Means of Providing External Benefits from Agriculture', Hanley, N. (ed), *Farming and the Countryside*, CAB, Wallingford.

Common, M. and Perrings, C. (1992), 'Towards An Ecological Economics and Sustainability', *Ecological Economics* 6, 7–34.

Conway, G.R. and Pretty, J.N. (1991), *Unwelcome Harvest, Agriculture and Pollution*, Earthscan, London.

Coopers and Lybrand (1993), *Landfill Costs and Prices, Correcting Possible Market Distortions*, HMSO, London.

Council for the Protection of Rural England (1992), *How Green Is Our Government?* Council for the Protection of Rural England, London.

Countryside Commission (1989), *A New National Forest in the Midlands, A Consultation Document*, Cheltenham.

Countryside Commission (1993), 'Protect Forest Access', *Countryside – the Newspaper of the Countryside Commission*, August.

Countryside Recreation Network (1993), *Countryside Recreation Network News*.

Cowell, R. (1992), 'Environmental Compensation, A Legitimate Niche For the Quid Pro Quo?', *ECOS* 13(4), 27–33.

Cox, G., Lowe, P. and Winter, M. (1986), 'Agriculture And Conservation In Britain, A Policy Community Under Siege', in Cox, G. *et al*, *Agriculture, People and Politics*, Allen and Unwin, London.

Crichton, M. (1991), *Jurassic Park*, Arrow, London.

Crocker, T.D. (1985), 'On the Condition of the Forest Stock', *Land Economics* 3(6), 244–254.

Croft and Campbell (1990), 'Characteristics of 100 UK Landfill Sites', *Harwell Waste Management Proceedings*, Harwell, Oxford.

Cunningham, I. (1991), 'Introduction Summary and Conclusions, Forestry Expansion – a Study of Technical, Economic and Ecological Factors', *Forestry Commission Occasional Paper 33*, Forestry Commission, Edinburgh.

Daly, H.E. (1989) 'Toward a Measure of Sustainable Social Net National Product', in Ahmad *et al, op cit.*

Daly, H.E. (1991), 'Towards An Environmental Macroeconomics', *Land Economics* 67, 255–259.

Daly, H.E. (1992), 'The Steady-State Economy, Alternative to Growthmania', reprinted in Daly, H.E. (ed), *Steady-State Economics*, second edition, Earthscan, London.

Daly, H.E. and Cobb, J. (1990), *For the Common Good*, Greenprint Press, London.

Davies, T. (1990), 'The United States, Experimentation and Fragmentation', in Haigh, N. and Irwin, F. (eds), *Integrated Pollution Control in the UK, Europe And North America*, Conservation Foundation, Washington DC.

de Gorter, H. and Tsur, Y. (1991), 'Explaining Price Policy Bias In Agriculture, the Calculus of Support Maximising Politicians', *American Journal of Agricultural Economics*, 73, 1244–1254.

Department of Energy (1991), *Energy Paper 59, Energy Related Carbon Emissions in Possible Future Scenarios in the United Kingdom*, HMSO, London.

Department of Transport (1992a), *Transport Statistics Great Britain 1992*, Department of Transport, London.

Department of Transport (1992b), *Road Accidents Great Britain 1992, the Casualty Report*, Department of Transport, London.

Department of Transport (1993), *Paying For Better Motorways*, Department of Transport, London.

Dubourg, W.R. (1992) *The Sustainable Management of The Water Cycle: A Framework for Analysis*, GSERGE Working Paper WM92.07, Centre for Social and Economic Research on The Global Environment, University College London and University of East Anglia.

Dubourg, W.R. (1993) *Sustainable Management of The Water Cycle in The United Kingdom*, CSERGE Working Paper WM93.02, Centre for Social and Economic Research on The Global Environment, University College London and University of East Anglia.

Dunleavy, P. (1990), 'Government At the Centre', in Dunleavy, P., Gamble, A. and Peele, G. (eds) *Developments In British Politics*, 3, Macmillan, London.

Dunleavy, P. and Rhodes, R. (1990, 'Core Executive Studies In Britain', *Public Administration*, 68, 3–28.

The Ecologist (1993), *Whose Common Future? Reclaiming the Commons*, Earthscan, London.

Economic Commission for Europe and the European Community (1993), *Forest Condition in Europe – Results of the 1992 Survey*, UN/ECE, Geneva.

ECOTEC (1993) *A Review of UK Environmental Expenditure*, HMSO, London.

English Nature (1993), *Strategy for the 1990s, Natural Areas, Consultation Paper*, English Nature, Peterborough.

Environmental Data Services (ENDS) Report (1993), 'Environmentalists Worry About Guide To Greening Of Whitehall', *Environmental Data Services Report*, 200,3.

Environmental Data Services (ENDS) Report (1993), 'Government's Line on SO_2 Leaves Many Wildlife Sites at Risk', *Environmental Data Services Report*, 222, 6.

Environmental Data Services (ENDS) Report, 'Turning The Environment Into Whitehall's Common Inheritance', *Environmental Data Services Report*, London, 200, pp 3, 16–17.

Environmental Data Services (ENDS) Report (1993), 'Latest Whitehall Reports Lack Environmental Targets – UK Environmental Policy', *Environmental Data Services Report*, London, 205, 3.

Environmental Data Services (ENDS) Report, 'Greening Of Whitehall Fails to Convince', *Environmental Data Services Report*, London, 209, 4.

Environmental Resources Limited (1992), *Natural Resource Accounts for the U.K.*, HMSO, London.

Faber, M. and Proops, J.L.R. (1993) 'Natural Resource Rents, Economic Dynamics and Structural Change: A Capital Theoretic Approach', *Ecological Economics*, 8(2), 17–44.

Fankhauser, S. (1993), *Evaluating the Social Costs of Greenhouse Gas Emissions*, CSERGE, University College London and University of East Anglia.

Forestry Commission (1987), *Bulletin 63, Census of Woodlands and Trees 1979–82*, Edinburgh.

Forestry Commission, various years, *Annual Report and Accounts*, Edinburgh.

Forestry Industry Committee of Great Britain (1993), *The Forestry Industry Yearbook 1992–1993*, London.

Forsyth, P.J. (1986) 'Booming Sectors and Structural Change in Australia and Britain: A Comparison', in *Natural Resources and The Natural Economy*, Neary, J.P. and Van Wijnbergen, S. (eds), Basil Blackwell, Oxford.

Fortlage, C.A. (1990), *Environmental Assessment, a Practical Guide*, Gower, Aldershot.

Freeman, A.M. (1990) 'Air and Water Pollution Control: A Benefit–Cost Assessment', in Portney, P. (ed) *Public Policies for Environmental Protection*, Resources for The Future, Washington DC.

Friends of the Earth (1992), 'Environmental Protection Act 1990, Section 49, Recycling Plans – A Preliminary Analysis', summarised in *ENDS Report* 211, August 1992.

Galbraith, J.K. (1992), *The Culture of Contentment*, Sinclair Stevenson, London.

Garrod, G. and Willis, K. (1991), 'The Environmental Impact of Woodland, A Two Stage Hedonic Price Model of the Amenity value of Forestry in Britain', *Working Paper 19, Countryside Change Unit, University of Newcastle Upon Tyne*.

Giles, C. and Ridge, M. (1993), 'The Impact on Households of the 1993 Budget and the Council Tax', *Fiscal Studies* 14, 1–20.

Global Environment Facility (1992), *A Selection of Projects From the First Three Tranches*, GEF Working Paper, Series Number II, June 1992, Global Environment Facility, Washington DC.

Global Environment Facility (1993), *Report by the Chairman to the May 1993 Participants Meeting*, April 1993, Global Environment Facility, Washington DC.

Glomsrod, S., Vennemo, H. and Johnsen, T. (1992), 'Stabilization of Emissions of CO_2, A Computable General Equilibrium Assessment', *Scandinavian Journal of Economics*.

Gordon, J. and Fraser, C. (1992), *Institutions And Sustainable Development, Meeting the Challenge*, Global Environmental Research Centre, London.

Green Alliance (1991), *Greening Government, the Failure of the Departmental Annual Reports To Reflect Integrated Policy Making*, The Green Alliance, London.

Green Alliance (1992), *Greening Government 2 (Update To the 1991 Report), the Failure of the Departmental Annual Reports To Reflect Integrated Policy Making*, The Green Alliance, London.

Greenaway, J., Smith, S. and Street, ZJ. (1992), *Deciding Factors In British Politics, A Case Studies Approach*, Routledge, London.

Gregg, P. and Machin, S. (1993) British Labour Statistics 1889–1990, personal communication.

Guardian (1993), 'Rural England Lost in Concrete', *The Guardian*, 29 July 1993, 2.

Hamilton, K. (1989), 'Natural Resources and National Wealth, National Accounts and Environment Division', Discussion Paper No 1, *Statistics Canada*, Ottawa.

Hamilton, K. (1992), 'Proposed Treatments of The Environment and Natural Resources in The National Accounts: A Critical Assessment', *Statistics Canada*, Ottawa, *mimeo*.

Hamilton, K. (1993) Resource Depletion, Discoveries and Net National Product, Centre for Social and Economic Research on The Global Environment, UCL and UEA, University College London, *mimeo*.

Hamilton, K., Pearce, D.W., Atkinson, G., Gomez-Lobo, A. and Young, C. (1993) *The Policy Implications of Environmental and Resource Accounting*, Report to The World Bank, Washington DC.

Hanley, N. (1991), The Economics of Nitrate Pollution Control In the UK, in N. Hanley (eds), *Farming And the Countryside, An Economic Analysis of External Costs And Benefits*, CAB International, Wallingford, 91–116.

Hanley, N. and Ruffell, R.J. (1993), 'The Contingent Valuation of Forest Characteristics, Two Experiments', *Journal of Agricultural Economics* 44(2), 218–229.

Harrison, A. (1989), 'Introducing Natural Capital into The SNA', in Ahmad *et al, op cit*.

Harrison, A. (1993), 'Natural Assets and National Accounting', in Lutz, *op cit*.

Hartwick, J.M. (1978), 'Investing Returns From Depleting Renewable Resource Stocks and Intergenerational Equity', *Economic Letters*, 1, 85–88.

Hartwick, J.M. (1990), 'Natural Resources, National Accounting and Economic Depreciation', *Journal of Public Economics*, 43, 291–304.

Hartwick, J.M. (1993), 'Forestry Economics, Deforestation and National Accounting', in Lutz, *op cit*.

Hartwick, J.M. and Hageman, A.P. (1993), 'Economic Depreciation of Mineral Stocks and The Contribution of El Serafy', in Lutz, E. *op cit*.

Hau, T., 'Electronic Road Pricing Developments In Hong Kong 1983–1989', *Journal of Transport Economics*, May 1990.

Henderson, N. (1992), 'Wilderness and the Nature Conservation Ideal, Britain, Canada and the United States Contrasted', *Ambio* 21(6), 394–399.

Herrington, P. (1990 *Notes on Sustainable Development and Resource Pricing for Water*, OECD Workshop on Resource Pricing.)

Heuth, D., Voorhees, S. and Cosagrande, R. (1982), 'Estimating the Benefits from Controlling Nuisance Pests, An application of the Interactive Bidding Technique', Contributed paper, annual meeting of the American Agricultural Economics Association, Clemson, South Carolina.

Hicks, J.R. (1946) *Value and Capital*, 2nd edition, Oxford University Press, Oxford.

HM Government (1989), *Sustaining Our Common Future, A Progress Report By The UK Government On Implementing Sustainable Development*, HM Government, London.

HM Government (1990), *Environmental Protection Act 1990*, HMSO, London.

HM Government (1990), *This Common Inheritance: Britain's Environmental Strategy*, Cmnd 1200, HMSO, London.

HM Government (1991), *The Potential Effects of Climate Change in The United Kingdom: First Report of The United Kingdom Climate Change Impacts Review Group*, HMSO, London.

HM Government (1991), *This Common Inheritance: Britain's Environmental Strategy – The First Year Report*, Cmnd 1655, HMSO, London.

HM Government (1991a), *Recycling*, Waste Management Paper no 28, HMSO, London.

HM Government (1991b), *Policy Appraisal And The Environment, A Guide For Government Departments*, HMSO, London.

HM Government (1992) *The UK Environment*, HMSO, London.

HM Government (1992), *This Common Inheritance: Britain's Environmental Strategy – The Second Year Report*, Cmnd 2068, HMSO, London.

HM Government (1992a), *Digest of Environmental Protection and Water Statistics*, HMSO, London.

HM Government (1992b), *Climate Change, Our National Programme For CO_2 Emissions, A Discussion Document*, HM Government, London.

HM Government (1992c), *Policy Guidance Note 12, Development Plans and Regional Planning Guidance*, HM Government, London.

HM Government (1993a), *Climate Change, Our National Programme for CO_2 Emissions, Addendum To The Discussion Document*, HMSO, London.

HM Government (1993b), *Digest of Environmental Protection and Water Statistics*, HMSO, London.

HM Government (1993c), *UK Strategy for Sustainable Development, Consultative Paper*, HM Government, July 1993.

HM Treasury (1972), *Forestry in Great Britain, An Interdepartmental Cost-benefit Study,* HM Treasury, London.

Hodge, I. and Dunn, J. (1992), *Rural Change and Sustainability, a Review of Research,* Economic and Social Research Council, Swindon.

Hohl, A. and Tisdell, C.A. (1993), 'How Useful are Environmental Safety Standards in Economics? The Examples of Safe Minimum Standards for the Protection of Species', *Biodiversity and Conservation,* 2, 168–181.

Holmes, J.R. (1992), *The United Kingdom Waste Management Industry,* Institute of Waste Management, Northampton, UK.

Hopkinson, P.G., Bowers, J. and Nash, N.A. (1990), *The Treatment of Nature Conservation in the Appraisal of Trunk Roads, Submission to the Standing Advisory Committee on Trunk Road Assessment (SACTRA),* NCC, Peterborough.

House of Commons (1991), *House of Commons Parliamentary Debates, Official Reports (Hansard),* 190 (1557), 8 May 1991, HMSO, London.

House of Lords (1989), *Select Committee on Science and Technology, Hazardous Waste Disposal [Fourth Report],* HMSO, London.

Hughes, S. (1991), 'The Liberal Democrat Response', in Gordon, J. and Fraser, C. (1991).

Hulme, M., Hossell, J.E. and Parry, M.L. (1993), 'Future Climate Change and Land Use in the United Kingdom', *Geographical Journal,* 159, 131–147.

Innes, J.L. (1992), 'Forest Condition and Air Pollution in the United Kingdom', *Forest Ecology and Management* 51, 17–27.

Intergovernmental Panel on Climate Change (1990), *Climate Change, the Scientific Assessment,* Cambridge University Press, Cambridge.

Intergovernmental Panel on Climate Change (1992), *Climate Change 1992, the Supplementary Report to the IPCC Scientific Assessment,* Cambridge University Press, Cambridge.

Jenkins, R.R. (1993), *The Economics of Solid Waste Reduction,* Edward Elgar, Aldershot.

Jordan, A.G. and Richardson, J.J. (1987), *British Politics and the Policy Process,* Allen and Unwin, London.

Jordan, A.J. (1993a), 'Financing the UNCED Agenda, the Vexed Question of Additionality', *mimeo,* Centre for Social and Economic Research on the Global Environment, University of East Anglia and University College London.

Jordan, A.J. (1993b), 'Integrated Pollution Control and the Evolving Style and Structure of Pollution Control in the UK', *Environmental Politics,* 2(3), 405–427.

Jordan, A.J. (1993c), *The International Organizational Machinery For Sustain-*

able Development, Rio And the Road Beyond, Centre for Social and Economic Research on the Global Environment, Working Paper GEC 93–11, CSERGE, University of East Anglia and University College London.

Joseph, S. (1992), 'The Politics of Transport and the Environment', *ECOS,* 13(4), 2–6.

Kay, P. (1992), *Where Motor Car Is Master, How the Department of Transport Became Bewitched By Roads,* Council For the Protection of Rural England, London.

HM Treasury (1972), *Forestry in Great Britain, An Interdepartmental Cost–Benefit Study,* HM Treasury, London.

Kindler, J. and Russell, C.S. (eds) (1984) *Modeling Water Demands,* Academic Press, London.

Korotkov, A.V. and Peck, T.J. (1993), 'Forest Resources of the Industrialized Countries, an ECE/FAO Assessment', *Unasylva* 44 (174), 20–30.

Labour Party (1991), *An Earthly Chance,* Labour Party, London.

Lee, K.N. (1993), *Compass and Gyroscope, Integrating Science and Politics for the Environment,* Island Press, Washington DC.

Leipert, C. (1989), 'National Income and Economic Growth, the Conceptual Side of Defensive Expenditures', *Journal of Economic Issues* 23, 843–856.

Liberal Democratic Party (1991), *Costing the Earth,* Liberal Democratic Party, London.

Liesner, T. (1989), *One Hundred Years of Economic Statistics,* Economist Publications, London.

Lind, R. (1982), *Discounting for Time and Risk in Energy Policy,* Baltimore, Johns Hopkins University Press.

Litterick, G. (1991), 'Charging for Discharging to Controlled Waters', *Integrated Environmental Management,* December.

Lowe, P. and Flynn, A. (1989), 'Environmental Politics and Policy In the 1980s', in Mohan, J. (ed), *The Political Geography of Contemporary Britain,* Macmillan, London.

Lutz, E. (1993), *Toward Improved Accounting for The Environment,* World Bank, Washington DC.

MacGarvin, M. (1993), 'The Implications of the Precautionary Principle for Biological Monitoring', *The Broad Challenge of the Precautionary Principle,* Green College Centre for Environmental Policy and Understanding, Oxford, and Centre for Social and Economic Research on the Global Environment, University of East Anglia, 31 March–1 April 1993.

MacMillan, D.C. (1993a), 'Indicative Forestry Strategies – an Investment Perspective in the Borders Region of Scotland', *Scottish Forestry* 47(3), 83–89.

MacMillan, D.C. (1993b), 'Measuring Passive-Use Values for the Natural Environment, a Case Study of Acid Rain in Scotland', Conference Proceedings of *Land Use Science*, edited by J. Milne, Macaulay Land Use Research Institute, Aberdeen.

Major, J. (1993), *House of Commons Hansard, Written Answers*, 14 April 1993, HMSO, London.

Mäler, K-G. (1991), 'National Accounts and Environmental Resources', *Environmental and Resource Economics*, 1 1–15.

Mäler, K-G. (1986) Comment on R M Solow, 'On The Intergenerational Allocation of Natural Resources', *Scandinavian Journal of Economics*, 88.

Mann, C.C. and Plummer, M.L. (1993), 'The High Cost of Biodiversity', *Science* 260, 25 June, 1868–1871.

Marsh, D. and Rhodes, R. (eds) (1992), *Implementing Thatcherite Policies*, Open University Press, Milton Keynes.

Mather, A. (1993), 'Afforestation in Britain', in Mather, A. (ed), *Afforestation, Policies, Planning and Progress*, Belhaven, London.

Matthews, R.C.O., Feinstein, C. and Odling-Smee, J. (1982) *British Economic Growth 1856–1973*, Clarendon Press, Oxford.

Ministry of Agriculture Fisheries and Food (1974), *Annual Review of Agriculture 1974*, HMSO Office, London.

Ministry of Agriculture Fisheries and Food (1993), *Agriculture in the United Kingdom 1992*, HMSO, London.

Mitchell, B. (1988), *British Historical Statistics*, Cambridge University Press, Cambridge.

National Audit Office (1986), 'Review of the Forestry Commission's Objectives and Achievements', *Report by the Comptroller and Auditor General*, London.

National Rivers Authority (1991a), *Demands and Resources of Water Undertakers in England and Wales: Preliminary Report Under Section 143(2)(a) Water Act 1989*, National Rivers Authority, Bristol.

National Rivers Authority (1991b), *NRA Facts 1990*, National Rivers Authority, Bristol.

National Rivers Authority (1991c), *The Quality of Rivers, Canals and Estuaries in England and Wales*, National Rivers Authority, Bristol.

National Rivers Authority (1991d), *Water Resource Planning – Strategic Options*, R&D Note 35, National Rivers Authority, Bristol.

National Rivers Authority (1992), *Water Resources Development Strategy: A Discussion Document*, National Rivers Authority, Bristol.

Navrud, S. (1992), *Pricing the European Environment*, Scandinavian University Press.

Newbery, D. (1990), 'Acid Rain', *Economic Policy* 5, 297–346.

Newbery, D. (1990), 'Pricing and Congestion, Economic Principles Relevant to Pricing Roads', *Oxford Review of Economic Policy*, 6(2).

Nordhaus, W. (1993), 'Optimal Greenhouse Gas Reductions and Tax Policy in the DICE Model', *American Economic Review*, 83(2), 313–317.

Norton, B.G. and Ulanowicz, R.E. (1992), Scale and Biodiversity Policy, A Hierarchical Approach, *Ambio* 21, 244–249.

Noss, R.F., Cline, S.P., Csuti, B. and Scott, J.M. (1992), 'Monitoring and Assessing Biodiversity', in Lykke, E., *Achieving Environmental Goals, the Concept and Practice of Environmental Performance Review*, Belhaven, London, 67–85.

O'Carroll, L.A. (1993), *Public Land Purchase and Conservation*, unpublished PhD thesis, University of Manchester, Department of Agricultural Economics.

Offerström, T. (1992), *Evaluating the Environmental Impact of Road Traffic Emissions in Monetary Terms Using Indirect Valuation Methods*, Swedish School of Economics, Helsinki, *mimeo*.

O'Riordan, T. and Weale, A. (1990), *Greening the Machinery of Government*, Discussion Paper No. 3, Friends of the Earth, London.

O'Riordan, T. (1993), 'The Politics of Sustainability', in Turner, R.K. (ed), *Sustainable Environmental Economics and Management*, Belhaven, London.

O'Riordan, T., Wood, C. and Shadrake, A. (1993), 'Landscapes For Tomorrow', *Journal of Environmental Planning and Management* 36(2), 123–148.

Olson, M. (1985), 'Space, Agriculture and Organisation', *American Journal of Agricultural Economics*, 67, 928–937.

Organisation for Economic Cooperation and Development (1987), *Pricing of Water Services*, OECD, Paris.

Organisation for Economic Cooperation and Development (1990), *Natural Resource Accounts, Report on the Pilot Study Concerning Forest Resources*, OECD, Paris.

Organisation for Economic Cooperation and Development (1991), *State of the Environment*, OECD, Paris.

Organisation for Economic Cooperation and Development (1992), *Environment and Economics, a Survey of OECD Work*, OECD, Paris.

Overseas Development Administration (1992), *British Aid Statistics*, Overseas Development Administration, London.

Owens, S.E. and Owens, P. (1991), *Environment, Resources And Conservation*, Cambridge University Press, Cambridge.

Parfitt, J.P., Powell, J.C., Grey, P.C.R., Brainard, J.S., Lovett, A.A. and Roberts, L.E.J. (1993), *The Risk Management of Hazardous Wastes, Their Transport and Disposal*, Environmental Risk Assessment Unit, University of East Anglia.

Pearce, D.W. (1988), 'Optimal Prices for Sustainable Development' in Collard, D., Pearce, D. and Ulph, D. (eds), *Economics, Growth and Sustainable Environments: Essays in Memory of Richard Lecomber*, Macmillan, London.

Pearce, D.W. (1991), 'Assessing the Returns to the Economy and Society from Investments in Forestry', *Forestry Expansion – a Study of Technical, Economic and Ecological Factors*, Forestry Commission Occasional Paper 14, Forestry Commission, Edinburgh.

Pearce, D.W. (ed) (1991), *Blueprint 2: Greening the Global Economy*, Earthscan, London.

Pearce, D.W. (1993a), *Economic Values and the Natural World*, Earthscan, London.

Pearce, D.W. (1993b), 'Sustainable Development and Developing Country Economics, in Turner, R.K. (ed), *Sustainable Environmental Economics and Management*, Belhaven, London.

Pearce, D.W., Brown, K., Swanson, T. and Perrings, C. (1993), *Economics and the Conservation of Global Biological Diversity*, Global Environment Facility, Washington DC.

Pearce, D.W. and Turner, R.K. (1990), *Economics of Natural Resources and the Environment*, Harvester Wheatsheaf, Hemel Hempstead.

Pearce, D.W. and Turner, R.K. (1992), 'Packaging Waste and the Polluter Pays Principle', *Journal of Environmental Planning and Management* 35, 5–15.

Pearce, D.W. and Turner, R.K. (1993), 'Market-based Approaches to Solid Waste Management', *Resources, Conservation and Recycling* 8, 63–90.

Pearce, D.W. and Warford, J. (1993), *World Without End: Economics, Environment and Sustainable Development*, Oxford University Press, Oxford.

Pearce, D.W., Markandya, A. and Barbier, E.B. (1989), *Blueprint for a Green Economy ('Blueprint 1')*, Earthscan, London.

Pearce, D.W., Turner, R.K. *et al* (1991), *The Development of Environmental*

Indicators, A Report to the Department of the Environment, University College London and University of East Anglia.

Pearce, D.W., Barbier, E. and Markandya, A. (1990), *Sustainable Development*, Earthscan, London.

Pearce, D.W., Bann, C. and Georgiou, S. (1992), *The Social Costs Of Fuel Cycles*, Report to The UK Department Of Trade And Industry, CSERGE, London.

Pearce, D.W. (1993c), *The Economic Value of Externalities from Electricity Sources*, paper to Green College, Oxford, seminar on Environment and British Energy Policy, April 1993.

Pearce, D.W. and Atkinson, G. (1993), 'Capital Theory and The Measurement of Weak Sustainability: A Comment', *Ecological Economics*, 8, 103–108.

Peskin, H.M. (1989), 'Accounting for Natural Resource Depreciation in Developing Countries', Environment Department Working Paper 13, World Bank, Washington DC.

Petts, J. (1992), 'Incineration Risk Perceptions and Public Concern, Experience in the UK Improving Risk Communication', *Waste Management and Research* 10, 169–182.

Pezzey, J. (1992), 'Sustainability', *Environmental Values*, 4, 321–362.

Prendergast, H.D.V. (1992), 'Kew at Home not Abroad', *British Wildlife*, 4(2), 109–11.

Proops, J.L.R. (1991), 'National Accounting and The Environment: A Review for The World Bank', University of Keele, *mimeo*.

Proops, J.L.R. and Atkinson, G.D. (1993), 'A Practical Criterion For Sustainability When There Is International Trade', CSERGE GEC Working Paper, CSERGE UCL and UEA, forthcoming.

Quinet, E. (1989), 'Evaluations du cout Social des Transports', in *Proceedings of the Fifth World Conference on Transport Research*, WCTR, Yokohama.

Rae, J.R. (1991), 'Environment and Agriculture, an OECD Perspective', in Miller, F.A. (ed), *Agricultural Policy and Environment*, Centre for Agricultural Strategy Paper 24, Reading, 27–41.

Redclift, M. (1984), *Development and the Environmental Crisis, Red or Green Alternatives*, Methuen, London.

Redfern, D., Boswell, R. and Proudfoot, J. (1993), 'Forest Condition 1992', *Research Information Note 236*, Alice Holt Lodge, the Forestry Authority.

Reed, D. (ed) (1992), *Structural Adjustment and the Environment*, Westview, Boulder.

Reid, W.V. (1992), 'How Many Species will there be?' in Whitmore, T.C. and

Sayer, J.A., *Tropical Deforestation and Species Extinction*, Chapman and Hall, London, 55–74.

Reid, W.V., Laird, S.A., Gamez, R., Sittenfield, A., Janzen, D., Gollin, M. and Juma, C. (1993), *Biodiversity Prospecting, Strategies for Sharing Benefits*, World Resources Institute, Washington DC.

Reid, W.V., McNeely, J.A., Tunstall, D.B., Bryant, D.A. and Wonograd, M. (1992), *Developing Indicators of Biodiversity Conservation*, draft, World Resources Institute, Washington DC.

Repetto, R., Magrath, W., Wells, M., Beer, C. and Rossini, F. (1989), *Wasting Assets, Natural Resources in The National Accounts*, World Resources Institute, Washington DC.

Royal Commission on Environmental Pollution (1992), *Sixteenth Report: Freshwater Quality*, HMSO, London.

Royal Commission on Environmental Pollution (1993), *Seventeenth Report, Incineration of Waste*, HMSO, London.

Royal Society (1983), *The Nitrogen Cycle of the United Kingdom*, Royal Society, London.

Royal Society for the Protection of Birds (1993), *Energy and Biodiversity*, Discussion Paper, RSPB.

Sandnes, H. (1992), *Country to Country Deposition Budget Matrices for the Years 1985, 1987, 1988, 1989, 1990, and 1991*, EMEP/MSC-W Report 1/92.

Scott, A. (1956), 'National Wealth and Natural Wealth', *Canadian Journal of Economics and Political Science*, 22(3), 373–378.

Solow, R.M. (1993), 'Sustainability: An Economist's Perspective', in Dorfman, R. and Dorfman, N.S., *Economics of The Environment: Selected Readings*.

Solow, R.M. (1986), 'On The Intergenerational Allocation of Natural Resources', *Scandinavian Journal of Economics*, 88(1), 141–149.

Swanson, T. (1992), *The Global Conversion Process, the Fundamental Forces Underlying Losses of Biological Diversity*, Global Environmental Change Working Paper, GEC 92-41, CSERGE, University of East Anglia and University College London.

Thayer, M. (1981), Contingent Valuation Techniques For Assessing Environmental Impacts: Further Evidence', *Journal of Environmental Economics And Management*, 27–44.

Therivel, R. *et al* (1992), *Strategic Environmental Assessment*, Earthscan, London.

Touche Ross Management Consultants and Gibb Environmental Services (1991), *Waste Recycling Credits – Systems and Mechanisms*, Report prepared for the Department of the Environment, Touche Ross, London.

Townsend, P. (1985), 'A Sociological Approach to The Measurement of Poverty', *Oxford Economic Papers*, 37.

Turner, R.K. (1992), 'Municipal Solid Waste Management, an Economic Perspective', in Bradshaw, A.D., Southwood, R., and Warner, F. (eds), *The Treatment and Handling of Wastes*, Chapman and Hall, London.

Turner, R.K. (1993), 'Sustainability, Principles and Practice', in Turner, R.K. (ed), *Sustainable Environmental Economics and Management, Principles and Practice*, Belhaven, London.

Turner, R.K. (ed) (1993), *Sustainable Environmental Economics and Management, Principles and Practice*, Belhaven, London.

Turner, R.K., Pearce, D.W. and Bateman, I.J. (1993), *Environmental Economics, an Elementary Introduction*, Harvester Wheatsheaf, Hemel Hempstead.

Tyers, R. and Anderson, K. (1988), 'Liberalising OECD Agricultural Policies in the Uruguay Round, Effects on Trade and Welfare', *Journal of Agricultural Economics*, 39, 197–216.

United Nations Development Programme (1992), *Human Development Report*, Oxford University Press, New York.

United Nations Statistical Office (1990), *SNA Handbook on Integrated Environmental and Economic Accounting*, preliminary draft of Part 1, general concepts., New York.

Uno, K. (1991), 'Economic Growth and Environmental Change in Japan: Net National Welfare and Beyond', in *Ecology and Economics: Towards Sustainable Development*, eds. Archibugi and Nijkamp, P., Kluwer Academic Press, Dordrecht.

Usher, M. (1992), 'Land Use Change and the Environment', in Whitby, M.C. (ed), *Land Use Change, the Causes and Consequences*, ITE Symposium no. 27, HMSO, London.

Vitousek, P.M., Ehrlich, P.R., Ehrlich, A.H. and Matson, P.A. (1986), 'Human Appropriation of the Products of Photosynthesis', *Bio Science* 36, 369–373.

Walker, B. (1992), 'Biodiversity and Ecological Redundancy', *Conservation Biology* 6, 18–23.

Walsh, R.G. (1986), *Recreation Economic Decisions, Comparing Benefits and Costs*, Venture Publishing.

Warrick, R.A. (1993), 'Slowing Global Warming and Sea-level Rise, the Rough Road From Rio', *Transactions of the Institute of British Geographers*, 18, 140–148.

Whitby, M.C. (ed) (1994), *Economic Incentives for Countryside Management, the Case of Environmentally Sensitive Areas*, CAB International, Wallingford.

Wigley, T.M.L. and Raper, S.C.B. (1992), 'Implications for Climate and Sea Level Rise of Revised IPCC Emission Scenarios', *Nature*, 357, 293–300.

Willis, K.G. and Garrod, G.D. (1991), 'An Individual Travel Cost Method of Evaluating Forest Recreation', *Journal of Agricultural Economics*, 42, 33–42.

Willis, K.G. and Garrod, G.D. (1993) 'Valuing Landscape, a Contingent Valuation Approach', *Journal of Environmental Management* 37(1), 1–22.

Willis, K.G. and Garrod, G.D. (1994), 'The Ultimate Test, the Benefits of ESAs', in Whitby, M.C. (ed), *Economic Incentives for Countryside Management, the Case of Environmentally Sensitive Areas*, CAB International, Wallingford.

Wilson, E.O. (1988), *Biodiversity*, National Academy Press, Washington DC.

Wilson, J. and Fuller, R. (1992), 'Set-Aside, Potential and Management for Wildlife Conservation', *ECOS* 13(3), 24–29.

World Bank (1991), *World Tables*, World Bank, Washington DC.

World Commission on Environment and Development (WCED) (1987), *Our Common Future*, Oxford University Press, Oxford.

World Conservation Monitoring Centre (1992), *Global Biodiversity, Status of the Earth's Living Resources*, Chapman and Hall, London.

Young, M.D. (1992), *Sustainable Investment and Resource Use*, Parthenon, Carnforth.

Young, M.D. (1993), 'Natural Resource Accounting: Some Australian Experiences and Observations', in Lutz, *op cit.*

Index

Other titles in the series

Blueprint for a Green Economy

'a political event of the first importance'   *The Guardian*

The most influential account available of the policies needed to achieve sustainability in a national economy. Widely referred to by policy-makers around the world, it has been adopted as a student text on a number of courses.

£10.95   paperback   ISBN 1 85383 066 6   192pp

Blueprint 2: Greening the World Economy

'admirably clear-headed in an area where muddle is often king'
The Financial Times

Follows *Blueprint for a Green Economy* by extending the application of environmental economics to management of the global environment, providing an agenda for international and governmental action.

£10.95   paperback   ISBN 1 85383 076 3   224pp

Blueprint 4: Sustaining the Earth

'a massively important text'   *Preview*

Examines the opportunities for using market forces for environmental ends, and assesses a range of possible 'global bargains' which give all parties an incentive to improve the global environment. Also includes a review of the principal global issues to be addressed, an explanation of the mechanics of resource degradation, and descriptions of the operation of trade on the environment and the effects of population growth and consumption patterns. Shows how environmental value may be captured, and describes the basis, means and institutions for doing so.

£10.95   paperback   ISBN 1 85383 184 0   224pp

Blueprint 5: The True Costs of Road Transport

The Government's road-building programme and other transport policies have provoked outrage across the country, and new evidence continues to surface concerning the impact of benzene emissions and particulate matter on human health. Blueprint 5 explains in detail why previous policies have resulted in too much pollution and congestion and too little investment in public transport, and attempts to quantify the external costs of road transport while suggesting new paths to a sustainable transport policy.

£10.95   paperback   ISBN 1 85383 268 5   176pp